# BURN FARM

When it came to Kenny's death, she had fabricated two stories. First she told her attorneys that she beat him to death with a sledgehammer. In the other story they were enjoying sadomasochistic sex. She had beaten him with a belt before sexual intercourse and they had fallen asleep naked. She woke up with his hands around her neck—or, in another version, she woke up and he was going through her purse. Either way when she woke up he ran upstairs to the bathroom, where she said $2,000 was hidden in the wall. They fought, he slipped in the tub and fell and hit his head. She claimed she administered CPR, cut a hole in his neck and tried to insert a straw through it in an effort to save him. Later, in a dream, she claimed she heard Kenny's voice telling her that he didn't want his mother to touch his body again. She said she never meant for Kenny to die. It was all an accident. Of course, her account is inconsistent with the physical evidence found at the house. Days earlier Kenny had been seen so weak, so ill, that he couldn't run up a flight of stairs and fight her.

# THE BURN FARM

## MICHAEL BENSON

**PINNACLE BOOKS**
Kensington Publishing Corp.
http://www.kensingtonbooks.com

Some names have been changed to protect the privacy of individuals connected to this story.

PINNACLE BOOKS are published by

Kensington Publishing Corp.
119 West 40th Street
New York, NY 10018

All Kensington Titles, Imprints, and Distributed Lines are available at special quantity discounts for bulk purchases for sales promotions, premiums, fund-raising, and educational or institutional use. Special book excerpts or customized printings can also be created to fit specific needs. For details, write or phone the office of the Kensington special sales manager: Kensington Publishing Corp., 119 West 40th Street, New York, NY 10018, attn: Special Sales Department, Phone: 1-800-221-2647.

Pinnacle and the P logo Reg. U.S. Pat. & TM Off.

ISBN-13: 978-0-7860-2030-0
ISBN-10: 0-7860-2030-X

First Printing: September 2009

10 9 8 7 6 5 4 3 2

Printed in the United States of America

*To all of the victims,
still here and gone,
known and unknown.*

# ACKNOWLEDGMENTS

The author wishes to thank the following individuals and organizations, without whose assistance the writing of this book would have been impossible: Tekla Benson; Catherine "Kay" Casavant; Jim Cole; Detective Richard B. Cote; the Cross Roads House in Portsmouth; my keen eyes and ears in New Hampshire, Suzanne Danforth; director of transportation and dirt-road adventurer for the project, Anne Darrigan; Joy Deloge; Dr. Albert Drukteinis; my agent, Jake Elwell; editor Gary Goldstein; my hot wife, Lisa Grasso; Judith S. Greenstein; Erin Mainey; Steven Martello; Bonnie Meroth; the New Hampshire State Police; Pamela Paquin; Cindy Perrault; Marcie Vaughan; Nathan A. Versace.

# Foreword

This story takes place in a nightmarish world that New England tourists don't get to see, a hardscrabble world of harsh climate, poverty, low-level crime, and desperation—a world populated by outlanders, bikers, and the dispossessed. The savings and loan scandal hit New Hampshire hard, and foreclosures started there many years before they caused a national tragedy.

Although this is a true story, some names will be changed to protect the privacy of the innocent. Pseudonyms will be noted upon their first usage. When possible, the spoken word has been quoted verbatim. However, when that is not possible, conversations have been reconstructed as closely as possible to reality, based on the recollections of those that spoke and heard the words. In places there has been slight editing of spoken words, but only to improve readability. The denotations and connotations of the words remain unaltered.

A special note should be made about Sheila LaBarre's relentless accusations toward her lovers and their families of criminal behavior, homosexuality, incest, pedophilia, and other sexual deviance. She has been diagnosed as acutely delusional and sadistic. Her accusations are lies designed to hurt. Whether or not LaBarre herself believed them to be true, her accusations should not be construed in any way as evidence of fact.

# Sheila LaBarre

It was like an X-rated retelling of "Hansel and Gretel." The witch—a black widow dominatrix witch—liked to push boys into the oven. She burned her victims while quoting Daniel 3, a biblical chapter that depicted *punishment by incineration*.

This wicked witch lived in an idyllic setting, a farmhouse in the woods. The house had an old-fashioned New England chimney on its roof and wide-board pine paneling inside. As you approached the bucolic scene from the road, there were tall pine trees and a barn behind, several vehicles parked here and there to the left, a wishing well to the right, and fenced-in fields all around. Slats were falling off the shutters. Winters were hard on everything in New Hampshire, especially shutters. Along the sides of the house, a few rabbits nibbled at grass.

The nearest neighbors were a long ways away. A man being flogged here could scream and scream, and no one would hear.

The horse barn was well-tended, but the farmhouse

was trashed. The place had run down since the old man died. It used to be a beautiful farmhouse, but not anymore. Now that the witch was living there alone—there was chaos and decay. The dormer was rotted and open to the elements. The porch screen was ripped out. Inside, wallpaper was peeling. Farm animals had been given the run of the place, and the air was heavy with the scent of rabbit shit and putrefaction. The floors were covered with piles of clothes and garbage. In the kitchen the linoleum was ripped up near the stove. The wide pine board floor in the hallway was warped. Crucifixes everywhere. The oven was filled with charred matter. There was a rotting steak in the sink. Here and there was old blood spatter—hard to see now that it had grown brown and covered with dust.

No one slept in the master bedroom anymore. In that room there was just an empty bed frame and a dresser. Above the head of the bed was a painting of a leopard reclining on a jungle branch. Sitting on the dresser was a photo of the woman with the witchy hair, nude. *Power, baby. Don't ever let them forget you got tits and ass.*

The bathroom window had been nailed shut. Hefty bags covered the windows. By the sink was toothpaste and men's deodorant. In the upstairs bathroom there was just a large hole in the wall behind the bathtub, a hole that went all the way through to the eaves.

And there were rabbits. Rabbits everywhere.

"My babies, my beautiful children," she said.

The only scenario we have for the witch's final grisly murder is a construction of her faulty mind, so take it with a grain of salt. We do know for a fact, because she made audiotapes, that her known murders tended to follow the same pattern. She would recruit her men from the ranks of the lost—men who were slight of

stature, dim of wit, and far from home. She liked them
mentally slow, and horny. She ran the same routine on
them, made them dependent on her sexually—*oh, the
power of the pussy*—and did things to hurt them, to make
them sick, to make them bleed, to change the color of
their skin to that of an olive-stained parchment. And she
grilled them. Her need to dominate men took the form
of religious zealotry. She knew what it was like to be
dead. She'd been there, and the men in the white beards
told her in Hebrew that they were going to send her
back to earth on a mission. She was an angel—a mean
bitch angel—an angel of vengeance! She was to rid the
world of pedophiles. It was as if the mission had been
handpicked for her. She had come from a home in Alabama where, when she was just a little girl, so little, she
had to play bad games with Daddy and the men she was
told to call "Uncle."

"Sheeeeeeeelaaaaaa. That's a Spanish name," one
uncle would say as he reached up under her skirt, so
high, so deep. She had been hurt by pedophiles. And
now she was to rid the world of them.

Sometime at a tender age, Sheila decided that life
equaled war. As would any expatriate of the coven, she
used both violence and her feminine charms to fight.
When she lost a battle one night—to a man!—she took
her own life and went to Heaven. They sent her back.
Her time on earth wasn't through. She still had too much
fight in her, fight that could be used to send perverts—
whose unnatural touching made her shiver and squeeze
herself—to Hell, where they belonged. She "got chills
just thinking about it."

Her love affairs ran hot at first, although she let them
know up front that she wasn't "fond o' fellatio." Not
fond of oral in general, pitching or catching, so it was

fair. She liked men who could get it up twice a night, but it was okay if they couldn't. Her vagina was tiny. Infantile. Some men were too big for her. When she was young, she thought she would stretch, but she never did.

Bad things happened when the sex cooled off. Her men did very, very bad things, horrible things. She lubricated herself as she thought about how horrible—and they needed to be punished. That was when the hate started, the need to humiliate and torture. She physically hurt her men, beating them with a stick. Or a belt. Or whatever was handy.

The abuse was also verbal. She debased her lovers. With the humiliation came brainwashing. She told them that they had raped children. That they'd had sex of every imaginable sort with their own mothers. Oh, the horror! Oh, the sweet, unholy viciousness. It needed to be wiped from the face of the earth. And she made them confess: "Yes, I raped children." "Yes, I had sex with my mother."

After a while, after they started looking sick, like a thick layer of putty-colored death had been smeared over their faces and bodies, they would vanish. If anyone asked, and sometimes they didn't, she'd say they'd run off. Police wouldn't think twice. Until the last one . . . the one she called Adam.

Just a few days before, things had gotten switched. She lost *control*. He had the power. Sheila had called her sister and in a cold whispery voice told her she was naked and all balled up and sitting under the kitchen table. She couldn't look at Adam. She was afraid. He was staring at her with those evil, pedophile, incestuous eyes, freaking her out. She thought about the places his Vaseline fingers had been and she hugged her knees and rocked back and forth. Chills!

But she got that control back. As she told it, she and Adam had been enjoying sadomasochistic sex. That was why the windows were covered with black plastic. So snoopers couldn't see their fun. She beat him with a belt. They'd fallen asleep naked. She said she woke and caught him rummaging through the house, looking for stuff to steal. That was the last straw. She could feel his hands on her throat. Or perhaps they were the hands of Captain Shaw, the ghost who haunted her house. Whatever, they were choking her. It had to end. Adam was a horrible, horrible person. It was time for the angel to avenge—time to send the pervert to hell. He was a large rabbit that needed to be put down. She chased him up the stairs and they fought. He fell and cracked his head open on the tub. Maybe she helped with the bashing in of his skull. The first time she told the story she included mention of taking a sledgehammer to him.

Either way, his head was bashed. For a time she was calm. The violence, like sex, had peaked, and now she was in a nurturing peace. The avenging angel in her had been appeased. Maybe she could save the dying man. She plunged a knife in the front of his neck, a knife with a small blade, one she usually used to cut baling twine. She unsuccessfully tried to jam a straw in the hole she had made. But it didn't matter. He was dead. She put his naked body entirely in the tub and went to get her tools—the hedge clippers, the pruning shears, the big-bladed knives—and she took care of the necessary labor. She sawed and smashed and snipped the bones. Carrying Adam to the fire, she cremated him—just as she had the others.

# Dreams Squandered

Sheila Kaye Bailey was born on the Fourth of July, 1958, and raised in Fort Payne, Alabama, a mill town with a population of about thirteen thousand. Sheila was the youngest of six children, the baby of the family. Daddy worked for the state of Alabama in the highway road division. He used to like to take the family driving down the roads that he had built. He was also drunk, and mean, and he dripped of sick lust. Mama worked in environmental services at the hospital. She was too weary to do anything about Daddy. She'd married him for life, and that's the way it was, no matter how twisted he was.

"Sheila was very smart and never much trouble," her mother, Ruby Bailey, said, eighty-eight-years old in 2006 and still living in Fort Payne. "Some people are kind of slow learners to read and things. She always was real easy to learn things. But she never did nothing bad that I know of when she grew up."

Sheila didn't remember having friends as a child. It wasn't until puberty hit—and it hit her hard—that she had friends. Mama wouldn't let her be a majorette because majorettes went off with the boys. Mama didn't want Sheila getting pregnant. Mama had gotten pregnant, and life had been hell ever since.

"I didn't travel in the circle of the popular girls," Sheila later recalled. "I didn't drink and I didn't do pot then. Boys would call me. I started seeing a Cherokee Indian boy and my family hated him. We never had penetrating sex. That never occurred. He said he didn't want to do that to me. I don't know how to say this. It's kind of graphic. I'm very tight, I'm very small, I think I have an introverted uterus. Might even need a C-section. My mother used to always say to me, 'Sheila, something just tells me you should never have children.'"

After the Native American came the black guy. Robert. "This was in the seventies, the Barry White music, the incense, the African-American guys, they tend to be very romantic," Sheila recalled. Again, the family wasn't thrilled. This was Alabama. White folks still used the N word. Robert never completely penetrated her either.

"Like he would get over me and put it in me just that much." She gestured with her thumb and forefinger. "He had a long, tapered penis. 'No,' he said, 'you are the tightest girl I'd ever met. I wouldn't because I would split you!' Still, it felt good."

One Fort Payne resident who had vivid memories of Sheila was Anthony McAnelly. "We were best friends since grade school," McAnelly recounted. "We had a little deeper relationship. We rode bicycles, dated a little. We were figuring what we wanted out of life. Sheila really blossomed in high school. She entered a junior miss pageant and her talent was reading a poem she wrote. She was a knockout. She really was a knockout."

She liked to sing, hated math, and often functioned

on too little sleep, awake listening to her drunken father rant, or, worse, waiting for him to come home. Nobody slept when Daddy came home.

Sheila graduated from Fort Payne High School in 1976 with dreams of becoming a fashion model. Friends recalled that her dreams were squandered by a series of bad relationships with men. After high school Sheila worked at a motel, as did Lynn, her older sister. After that, she worked as an assistant administrator at a nursing home. She liked that job until her female boss hit on her. At least she felt like she was being seduced. Sheila liked to wear boots. The boss urged her to dress more feminine. "You look like you're goin' riding. Go home and put on a dress, Miss Bailey," the boss said. Sheila went home, all right. She went home and never came back. She was eager to get the hell out of Alabama, but when a boyfriend asked her to move to Texas with him, she thought it was too big a change. She had her own apartment for a while, but her landlord, she said, jammed his tongue down her throat, so she moved back home. Depressed, she stood on bridges and thought about jumping. She was forging prescriptions for painkillers.

Several of Sheila's bad relationships with men turned into bad marriages. One of those bad marriages was to Ronnie Jennings, of Fort Payne. Ronnie flipped burgers at a restaurant. Jennings later said, "She didn't care about anyone. She just wanted everything her way."

They were married by a judge in Georgia sometime during the 1980s, and the marriage became downright peculiar within minutes of the wedding ceremony. According to Jennings, "As soon as we got out back to the car, she turned to me and said we shouldn't have got married. She had really wild mood swings. Pretty soon I was thinking it wasn't that great of an idea either."

The relationship became violent. Sometimes—a lot, actually—she was the one dishing out the pain. According to Jennings, Sheila was beautiful but unbalanced. He said, "She was just crazy, to put it bluntly."

According to Sheila, one problem was that she had extremely tight genitalia and he was hung like a horse. They had to use Vaseline. She thought her vagina needed to be stretched. She thought it would get better with time. Finally she realized she just couldn't handle him.

Jennings told how Sheila had threatened him: "If you're fooling around, I'll . . ."

He said, "I'll bang whoever I want."

She countered, "I want a divorce."

He said, "I ain't never givin' you a divorce."

"I want out. I'll show you how bad I want out," she replied. And so she knocked back a bottle of pills with Wild Turkey right in his face. She grabbed his keys and took off in his car, driving until she lost consciousness at the wheel.

"Last I remember, everything was turning gold and I felt like I was entering a new dimension," Sheila later recalled. She got a helicopter ride to the University of Alabama at Birmingham Medical Center, where they pumped her stomach. She was in a coma for eight days.

Jennings was asked what were some of the marriage's other low points. He recalled the one night near the end of their relationship when, during an argument, Sheila threatened to stab him to death with a pair of scissors while he was asleep. He stayed awake all night, afraid to go to sleep for fear that Sheila would make good on her threat.

The pair eventually moved to Chattanooga, Tennessee, where their relationship continued to deteriorate. They divorced—after four long, long years of marriage—and Ronnie Jennings lost track of her.

In Tennessee, the newly single Sheila, living in a YMCA, an "adult trying to make it on my own," tried to get some spiritual help. She went to her local clergy and bared her demons. The clergyman tried to get Sheila to sit on his lap. She tried a shrink—an attractive guy, too, with dark hair—but he asked questions like: "Did Ronnie penetrate your rectum with his penis?" And he called her at home to ask, "What are you doing right now? Are you touching yourself?"

Although many men found Sheila to be attractive, she preferred after her first marriage to find her boyfriends using personal ads in newspapers and in magazines. Maybe it was because Sheila had unusual tastes when it came to the mating process, and she didn't want to hook up with any men who might get the wrong idea. Sheila wanted to be dominant. She wanted to be in charge, both in bed and in life. Perhaps she fantasized about becoming a dominatrix. By using personal ads to find sex partners, perhaps she could more efficiently weed out the men who were not willing to be submissive to her. She eventually met Bill LaBarre in 1987 through a personal ad in what Sheila referred to as a "dating magazine." He placed the ad and she answered it. They hit it off right away.

# The Gentleman Farmer

Widower Dr. Wilfred "Bill" J. LaBarre was a chiropractor who owned a horse farm in New Hampshire. He was born in Norwich, Connecticut, in 1926, graduated from the Norwich Free Academy, and attended Aviation Technical School in Putnam, Connecticut. He was an aerial gunner specialist in the navy during World War II, and after the war he attended chiropractic school. He was licensed to practice in 1953. Since the early sixties he'd been living in Epping, New Hampshire. He served as Epping's health officer and established the successful Straight Chiropractic Clinic in nearby Hampton, where—it was said—he had a perfect attendance record. His partner in the practice was also his first cousin, Dr. Edward G. Charron, known as Ed. Wilfred's father and Ed's mother were siblings. Ed brought a little flavor to the practice. In addition to adjusting spines, he taught drums, played in jazz bands, and was a former New England gymnastics champ who had once run away with the Siebrand Circus.

During the 1960s and 1970s, Wilfred served as president

of several chiropractic societies, and in 1983 he was named "Chiropractor of the Year" by Sherman College of Straight Chiropractic. His first wife, Edwina, died in 1983. He quickly remarried a woman named Leone, but she left him after a couple of years. From his first marriage he had a daughter, Laura, and a son, Gregory. After that, he had a vassectomy.

In 1987 he was a lonely sixty-year-old man, once widowed and once divorced, visiting Tennessee. Sheila was twenty-nine and had plenty of curves. She was into photography and dreamt of becoming a country-music singer.

Sheila and Wilfred visited Fort Payne a few times during their relationship, and Sheila's mother recalled, "He was a real good guy. She actually seemed to like him. I never heard her say anything about not liking him."

Within months of their meeting, Bill brought Sheila to his 115-acre farm, on Red Oak Hill Lane, just north of Epping, where they lived together for a time. The farm was one of several working farms in the area, interspersed with old farmhouses, and newer custom-made homes. To get there, you had to turn off the main road onto a narrow paved country road, and turn off again onto a rutted dirt road, which worked its way into a woods. After a while the dirt road was straddled by New England–style stone walls. Beyond those walls were hay fields. The farmhouse was small and well covered by trees. It had been painted white some years back, but had weathered to a light gray.

Sheila was blissed out by life on the farm. "I'd never heard a June bug before," she recalled. The remoteness made her feel peaceful, a previously unknown peace.

Dr. LaBarre was a highly-respected and well-liked chiropractor and a beloved member of the community. "He is a *master* chiropractor," Sheila liked to brag. He was a horse lover and gentleman farmer. Neighbors remembered him as a man who enjoyed harnessing his favorite Standardbred and driving into town on weekends in his carriage. He would often ride around town on his horse and buggy, offering rides to small children. When a dying neighbor asked that Bill ride his horse and buggy in his funeral procession, Bill was proud to oblige. He was not only loved by his patients, but by the whole town. There was quite a buzz along the grapevine when news got out that Dr. LaBarre was back from Tennessee—and he was traveling with a woman! And what a woman.

Sheila didn't have to live in tiny Epping (population seven thousand) for very long before the locals noticed her. She was flashy and loud and she liked attention. Opposites attract, some said, but others shrugged and said aloud, "I sure hope Bill didn't make a mistake."

As soon as Sheila moved in, she decided that the horse farm needed a distinctive name. Up until Sheila's arrival, the farm had been known as the Old Harvey Farm, since it used to be owned by the Harvey family—who were still around and were neighbors. The hill upon which the farm sat was informally known as Harvey Hill—although its official name was Red Oak Hill.

Sheila convinced Bill to change the name of the farm. She wanted something bold and sassy, just like her. She chose the Silver Leopard Farm, and the country chiropractor was powerless to disagree. A sign was made up and placed at the entrance. She liked the name, unaware that it made some of the locals snicker, while others simply raised an eyebrow.

Sheila gained notoriety in the community in other ways too. Driving around the New England town in her sleek silver Mercedes, well, you couldn't miss her. Not long after arriving in Epping, she strode onto a local airstrip while wearing a leopard print flying outfit. She announced that she wanted flying lessons. The pilots nicknamed her "Sheiler the Peeler" in hopes that her provocative stride might culminate in her peeling off her clothes.

It didn't take long before Sheila acquired the worst kind of reputation in Epping. In most of the nearby towns as well. She was an easy lay. Promiscuous. Those fellows weren't psychologists, of course, but the word "nympho" came to mind.

At first, Bill was smitten. Sheila had lots of everything. Lots of *these* and lots of *those*. Lots of body, lots of reddish brown hair, lots of smarts, and lots of libido. She quickly became the talk of the town. But what had initially appeared to be flirtatious eccentricity fast developed into something far more menacing. It was a peaceful place, and she had an incendiary temper that often caused her to threaten violence. She often reminded people with whom she disagreed that she owned guns, and wasn't afraid to use them. Sheila had a piercing voice, and when the wind was blowing in the right direction, neighbors could hear it, filled with anger, barking orders, in charge and dominating, echoing off the hills that surrounded the LaBarre farm.

Neighbor Bruce Allen recalled that the honeymoon period between Wilfred and Sheila had been short-lived. Not long after she moved onto the Epping farm, she could be heard screaming at the man.

Wilfred's daughter, Laura Melisi, heard Sheila screaming at her father, "I'm gonna kill the horses and I'm going to kill you too."

Laura later recalled, "My father was not a fearful person at all, but after Sheila came, his whole personality changed."

Sheila tried to take over every portion of Dr. LaBarre's life, including the professional side. Before Sheila's arrival, LaBarre's office in Hampton was a family affair. His patients paid what they could, there was often bartering involved, and daughter Laura was the office manager. It was a relaxed place, suitable for treating people with sore backs and other ailments. In 1990 Sheila decided to assume control of Bill's chiropractic business. It wasn't making enough money. She was going to do something about it. Instead of patients paying according to their budget or the doctor's whims, Sheila made up a fee chart and pasted it on the wall. In the past Dr. LaBarre and Dr. Charron had often lingered with patients who needed treatment, sometimes healing their stress as much with friendly conversation as with hands-on manipulation. Sheila put a stop to that. If a session was running long, she would angrily interrupt it, bursting right in on the doctor and his patient, saying, "Come on, hurry it up. Why is this taking so long?"

"He had a mountain of work to do," Sheila later explained. "I was the one who changed all that for him. That didn't happen until a few years after I was up here, but he asked me—he asked me to simplify." When someone who owed Bill money would skip town, Sheila played private eye and tracked him down. She was very happy. She filed numerous small claims in Hampton District Court. A clerk there, John Clark, called her the most organized plaintiff he'd ever encountered. Always polite, Sheila was a joy to have around the courthouse.

She did lots of little things to make Bill happy, Sheila believed. At first, she was a hero to his family.

Sheila and Bill had a sexual relationship for a while. They talked of marriage, but never seriously. Things were good. *If it ain't broke, don't fix it.* "He encouraged me to take his name and said we had a common-law marriage," she later claimed.

Even though the dirt road to the LaBarre property was a town road, Sheila considered it a private driveway and had been known to threaten with a gun pedestrians who dared walk past the house. Neighbors and the townspeople came to fear Sheila. They would talk about "Sheila sightings," and conversations about her always took the form of ridicule. That was what she brought out in people when she wasn't terrorizing them. Wilfred's first cousin Ed decided to retire rather than continue in the practice. Sheila had raised Ed's rent in the apartment above the chiropractic office, and he suspected she had killed his dog.

According to Sheila, Bill condoned her affairs. Bill called himself an old fart and told Sheila that he worried about her, so far from home in case something happened to him. She should find a younger man, she claimed Bill said. She didn't like to think about Bill aging, but it was a fact. "His heart would stop beating sometimes," she later said.

# Wayne Ennis

One of these lovers was a Jamaican immigrant named Wayne Ennis. She'd known Ennis for years, even before she met Bill. She'd gone to Jamaica on vacation and Ennis was a guy who drove tourists around. When she returned to Jamaica with Bill, she made sure they crossed paths with Ennis. The Jamaican had recently been hit by a bicycle and Bill examined his spine. Sheila decided to work on getting Ennis a visa so she could take him back to New Hampshire with her. She would later say that she was never in love with Ennis. Bill had stopped having sex with her and she had needs. Simple as that. She didn't completely ignore Bill. Dr. LaBarre was well-equipped for sex and she still, as she later put it, "satisfied him with her hand."

Sheila's relationship with Ennis was as volatile as her others. Sheila explained: "Oh, he was wonderful in the beginning, but then he showed his true colors." On January 15, 1995, Sheila drove to the Epping police station and filed a report complaining that Ennis had assaulted her the day before. "He tried to force my car off the road, he punched me in the head and kicked me. He threatened to cut off my fingers and shoot me in the face," Sheila claimed. Sheila sought and received an order of protection.

Despite the fact that she was still in ever-increasing control of Bill's life, and police had to get involved at least once more with her relationship with Ennis, Sheila decided that it was a good idea for her to become a bride. According to Sheila, Wayne Ennis begged her to marry him and she finally said okay. Bill gave them his blessing. She could tell by the look in his eye that he was disappointed, but he mostly wanted her to be happy. Ennis moved into the farmhouse at first; Bill slept in one bedroom alone. When the brawls started, Ennis and Sheila moved to the apartment over the chiropractic office, the same space recently occupied by cousin Ed and his ill-fated dog.

Sheila retained her dreams of being an actress and country singer. A prenuptial agreement written by Sheila, and signed by Sheila and Ennis, read: *Sheila will forever be the only owner of any songs she wrote, sold and/or recorded prior to or after marriage. Any proceeds from Sheila's singing, songwriting, or acting remain hers alone.* The prenup stated that if the marriage produced any children, Sheila would get full custody. *Any property acquired after the marriage will be sold and the proceeds split. The property is to be sold by Sheila and Sheila will give full disclosure of any amounts paid to Wayne.*

Sheila and Wayne were married on August 22, 1995, in York, Maine. Not long after the wedding, Sheila claimed, Ennis began drinking Red Stripe beer, and he didn't stop.

On December 28, 1996, almost two years after the first complaint involving Sheila and Ennis, Epping police received a 911 call from the LaBarre farm, followed by a disconnect. By this time Sheila and Ennis were married, but they had already decided to get a divorce. Using caller ID, police were able to determine the source of the call, and a car was sent out to the farm to see what, if anything, was the trouble. As it turned out, trouble started when Ennis caught Sheila in bed with another man. When police arrived, Ennis claimed that Sheila had struck him four times in the head with the phone as the other man held him down. Sheila told the other man, Ennis claimed, to go out to her car and get her gun.

In March 1997 Ennis and Sheila completed a court-ordered alternative dispute resolution program. The program didn't take. On April 2, 1997, Sheila was granted a restraining order against Ennis. In her divorce papers Sheila wrote about Ennis, *The defendant has been arrested many times for assaulting me, but there are no children.* Her implication seemed to be that "assault" led to "children." According to Sheila, Ennis went to Brooklyn to deal drugs on Flatbush Avenue. He had family there. Sheila refused to follow.

Sheila and Ennis were divorced in 1996. They had been married only sixteen months. Despite her marriage and divorce to another man, Sheila never left Bill alone. She chased Bill with a gun and twice asked Ennis to kill Bill for her. When Ennis told Wilfred's daughter, Laura, about this, Laura wrote a request for a restraining order, which would prevent Sheila from going near her dad. The restraining order was granted for a period of one year. Sheila continued to use the last name LaBarre. "Of course," Bill's daughter said. Bill LaBarre was where the money was. Sheila would have had children with Bill, except he'd had a vasectomy.

# James Brackett

After Wayne Ennis, Sheila took up with a guy she claimed to have copped pot from, James "Jimmy" Brackett. "We loved each other," Sheila later recalled. "I was very gentle and very patient, and I cured him of his premature-ejaculation problem." Despite the love, and all of those *mature* ejaculations, this relationship was just as explosive as the others.

On September 25, 1998, Sheila and Brackett had a fight at the apartment that got out of hand. According to Sheila's statement to police, the violence started when she decided to call the cops. To stop her, Brackett grabbed a knife and tried to cut the phone line. As he was doing this, he cut Sheila's finger, drawing blood. This infuriated the woman, who armed herself with a pair of cuticle scissors. (Apparently, scissors were a favorite weapon of hers, dating back to her first marriage when she threatened to stab her husband with a pair as he slept.) She later claimed that she tried to just "poke him a little bit" with the scissors but "accidentally" opened up what Officer William Bourque, of the Hampton Police

Department (HPD), described as a "significant cut" across Brackett's forehead, just above the hairline. The cut required several stitches. Both Brackett and Sheila were arrested and charged with felony counts of second-degree assault. According to the formal complaint, Sheila *did recklessly cause bodily injury to another by means of a deadly weapon, to wit: did stab James Brackett in the head with a pair of scissors.* The police report characterized the incident as a *lover's quarrel.*

At Sheila's arraignment, also on September 25, she was defended by attorney Phil Desfosses, of Portsmouth. The arraignment hearing was held before Hampton District Court judge Francis Frazier, who ordered that Sheila would be eligible for release on $1,000 cash bail, if the court received a psychological evaluation finding Sheila "is not a danger to herself or others if bailed."

During the court hearing Officer Bourque tried to testify about the incident, but Sheila went nuts, yelling, "This is the cop who refused to come to my aid, even though I was bleeding from the vagina!" She screamed it repeatedly until Judge Frazier asked Officer Bourque to leave the courtroom. She worked herself into a state and grabbed her chest. They took her downstairs and paramedics came, but she declined medical assistance.

One witness to Sheila's demonstration was court clerk John Clark, the same fellow who had called Sheila "a joy" when she was filing small claims on behalf of Bill's chiropractic practice. Shouting about bleeding from the vagina was totally uncharacteristic, Clark thought. It was like two different women.

On September 28, three days after the fight, Judge Frasier wrote on Sheila's complaint that the court had received a written evaluation and, as a result, she *was eligible for bail.* The judge also ordered Sheila not to come within five hundred feet of Brackett. Sheila wrote a personal check to the court for $1,000 and was released.

As evidence that Sheila was a master at manipulating the system, despite the order of protection, she managed to gain power of attorney over Brackett. Acting as his legal representative, she submitted a motion to dismiss regarding the scissors incident. The motion was granted by a judge, and since the case had been dismissed, Sheila got her $1,000 back.

The scissors incident was not the only time Sheila injured or frightened Jimmy Brackett. She frequently scratched his face, twice fired a gun at him, three times threatened to kill him, and once struck him in the face with a large grill-type basting brush, causing extreme dental trauma.

# The Death of
# Bill LaBarre

Wilfred made repeated attempts to get Sheila out of his life. According to his daughter, Laura, he went as far as to buy Sheila a house in Tennessee, but Sheila still refused to go.

"He would just live in denial," Laura Melisi said of her father. "He didn't think there was anybody—including an attorney—who was smarter than her."

And so Sheila was still in charge of Bill's possessions and business when he suddenly died at the age of seventy-four, in December 2000. The coroner determined the cause of death to be a massive heart attack, hypertension, and arteriosclerosis. Bill's estate included the 115-acre horse farm, his chiropractic practice in Hampton, two houses in Somersworth, and one house in Portsmouth. Following his death, Wilfred was taken to the Brewitt Funeral Service & Crematory. According to a court document, when filling out the death certificate, Sheila insisted that she was Wilfred's wife.

"Could I see your marriage certificate?" Tom Brewitt, the undertaker, asked.

According to Bill's son-in-law, John Melisi, who was present as the death certificate was being filled out, Sheila answered: "I don't have a license, but I have a pistol, and I know how to use it."

And so, Sheila's name went onto the death certificate as Bill's wife.

Despite the fact that Sheila had been married to another man while living at the LaBarre farmhouse, Sheila had successfully claimed at the time of Bill's death to have been the chiropractor's common-law wife. She immediately claimed control of Bill's property in Epping, and ordered that Bill's body be hurriedly cremated.

Miguel Brewitt, Tom's son and a director of the funeral home, said that neither he nor his father remembered the incident, and although there may have been a request to change the death certificate, he didn't believe that his father was threatened by Sheila over the matter.

Bill's will backed up Sheila's claims. The will stated that he was leaving the bulk of his cash, stocks, bonds, real estate, and personal property to *a very special lady known as Sheila Kaye Jennings LaBarre*. The will all but ignored Bill's children.

Sheila got not just the farm, but Bill's other properties as well. Bill's family was shocked by this and believed that Sheila had forced Bill to make the will. Sheila may have been able to push a mortician around with her handgun, and her ability to use it, but she had less luck intimidating New Hampshire tax officials—although she tried. Even though Sheila was willing to fight anyone who said she wasn't the rightful owner of Bill LaBarre's farm, she did not believe she needed to pay taxes on it. In 2001 she petitioned the court to have herself officially proclaimed the common-law wife of Wilfred LaBarre. If she was his wife, she wouldn't have to pay inheritance tax. When she received notice from the New Hampshire State Department of Revenue Administration that she owed taxes on the farm, Sheila decided—as she usually did—that the best defense was a good offense. Sheila got the home phone number of the revenue administration's assistant counselor at the time, a woman named Kathleen J. Sher, and made a phone call.

"Are you afraid?" Sheila asked.

Sher later recalled, "Her tone and words were very confrontational and threatening. I reported the call to the police and my employer. It was really pretty creepy."

This only ticked Sheila off more. Sheila decided that she was going to "get" Kathleen Sher.

Sheila applied for a pistol permit during 2001. The request was originally denied because of her history of violence, but it was later granted when she said she had a legitimate need for protection. She explained that she had been threatened and harassed and that her car window had been smashed.


Sheila was forced in 2002 to drop her case claiming to be Mrs. LaBarre when she learned that the state had multiple witnesses willing to testify that she did not live with Wilfred during the final three years of his life, but rather had lived in an apartment in Hampton with Jimmy Brackett. Sheila's case was also hurt when documents surfaced in which she told a psychologist that she and Bill had not been romantically involved since the 1980s.

Laura Melisi decided to get a restraining order preventing Sheila from coming near her. In her request she said Sheila ended up controlling everything her dad owned through extortion and threats on his life and property. Laura also noted that despite Sheila's claims to be her dad's common-law wife, the information Sheila had given to the psychologist was true: it had been more than a decade since Sheila and Bill had been romantically involved.

Sheila didn't care for people who stood up to her—like that taxwoman, for example. She'd show that bitch who was boss. Sheila filed a grievance in 2003 with the New Hampshire Professional Conduct Committee complaining about Kathleen Sher's "personal vendetta" against her. The grievance stated that Sheila was determined that Sher *be exposed for the trouble maker she actually is.*

Sher was investigated by the committee, but she had done nothing wrong. Sher was shaken up by the incident, though, and quit her job at the New Hampshire State Department of Revenue Administration. Sher later recalled, "Ms. LaBarre gives the impression that she can play the system much better than anyone else, but when people stand up to her, there is nothing to support her. Standing up to her makes a big difference." Sher's interpretation was that Sheila was a bully.

The courts moved slowly. Despite the civil suit from Bill's family and the tax board's decision that Sheila was not Bill's common-law wife, she continued to refer to herself as Sheila LaBarre, and she continued to live at the Silver Leopard Farm.

Ronald Levesque, a local horse owner, who was executive director of the Epping chapter of Equine Protection of North America (EPONA) horse rescue league, said he checked on Dr. LaBarre's five horses several times a year after the chiropractor had died.

"One time I called Sheila LaBarre to offer her a bag of grain that had been donated to the rescue league," Levesque said. "She said she could use it and agreed to have me meet her at the farm a few hours later. When I got there, she met me at the driveway with a shotgun. She never pointed it at me. She just made all these accusations about what my intentions were with the horses. That was the last time I set foot on the farm. But I've driven across the back fields to check on the horses, and I never saw anything unusual." Levesque said he'd last checked on the horses sometime in December 2005.

Sometimes Sheila lived alone, but most of the time she shared the farmhouse and her bed with men she hired to help out around the place. During this time she had—or, rather, continued to have—a series of tumultuous relationships.

# Michael Deloge

One of these relationships was with Michael "Mikey" Deloge, a man who lived on the LaBarre farm, off and on, for about two years. Deloge was a transient type—a diminutive and lonesome hobo. He grew up in West Haven, Connecticut, a blue-collar town, living with his father and his stepmother. "As a boy he dreamed of being a songwriter," his stepmother, Joy, later said. That would have been something that he and Sheila had in common, a penchant for creating music. In 1993 Michael married his girlfriend when she became pregnant with his son, Aaron.

His stepsister recalled, "He was really funny. He always had a lot of energy. Michael had a hard life, but it was still a life. Whatever happened to him, it needs to be found out."

Both women admitted that Deloge had a long history of trouble with drugs and alcohol—and his job skills were limited. His marriage ended in divorce, and Deloge's family quickly lost touch with his ex-wife and son. Deloge decided to get a fresh start in life in 2003 and moved north to New Hampshire, where he eventually ended up at the Cross Roads shelter for the homeless in Portsmouth. That was where he was living when Sheila came into his life.

On Lafayette Road (Route 1) in Portsmouth was a large green building right across from the Bowl-a-Rama called the Cross Roads House. Since 1982 the Cross Roads House had offered shelter to and helped homeless individuals and families. The facility was originally located in an old building that had formerly been Portsmouth's whorehouse, but after five or six years outgrew that locale, and moved to its current location. Twenty years later the facility had grown into the largest emergency and transitional shelter in New Hampshire, offering 24/7 housing for up to 107 people on any given night. It was usually full. Cross Roads offered food and shelter, as well as programs designed to help individuals find a place to live and acquire the skills necessary to find work. A GED tutor was on staff for those seeking to take the high-school diploma equivalency test. A mobile health-care van visited twice a week to provide free medical service. Mental-health counselors also visited regularly. AA meetings were held. And anyone with a housing crisis was eligible to stay there. The only people who were refused shelter were those with a history of arson and convicted child-sex offenders.

During Michael Deloge's residence there, as always, the residents had a wide range of problems. Some had substance abuse issues. Others had mental-health difficulties. The economy was bad in New Hampshire and some occupants were former middle-class families who had lost their jobs and homes. According to one Cross

Roads employee, there were not a lot of problems inside the facility. There was a mutual respect among residents, and folks tended to leave each other alone. "You can have a junkie sleeping in a room with a paranoid schizophrenic, with an alcoholic, with someone's who's down on their luck, and not have any problems," she said. "People tend to get along pretty well—which isn't to say that we don't have things getting stolen every now and again. Of course, there are some assholes, but most of the people are pretty respectful of each other.

"I remember Michael Deloge very well. He was very tiny. He was a tiny man. Not burly or intimidating in any way. When he stayed at Cross Roads, his time here was sporadic. He would be here for a couple days, and leave. A few days later he would return. I never sat down with him or did any one-on-one counseling with him or anything, but I do remember that he appeared to be slightly mentally retarded. He had definite developmental issues. People like Michael make up a particularly malleable population."

According to Donna Boston, her son Michael Deloge met Sheila at the Cross Roads House in early 2003 when Sheila came in and hired him to work on her horse farm.

According to employees at the facility, it was not the first time Sheila had come there to recruit men to work on her farm or, unbeknownst to them, share her bed.


In addition to his birth mother, Mikey's stepmother, Joy Deloge, recalled that Sheila, at first, seemed like a good thing.

"He was very happy," his stepmother recalled. "He said he had met this woman Sheila. He said he was in love with her. At first, it seemed normal. But during the summer of 2004, I got a phone call in the middle of the night. It was this crazy woman, quoting Scriptures from the Bible. I remember her saying that he was a child molester and how could I let him do that." During the phone call, she could also hear Michael Deloge in the background. He spoke slowly and his words were slurred. Sheila then said that Michael had sexually abused his younger siblings.

After that phone call the family never heard Deloge's voice again.

During July 2004 Michael Deloge's dad received a letter purportedly written by his son: *Dear Dad, Joy and I had intimate relations on the couch and in the kitchen right under your nose.* The letter went on—Michael admitted he was a child molester, that he lied to his father. He claimed also that Sheila rescued him from a homeless shelter and spent thousands on him.

As far as the stories of incest went, Michael Deloge's stepsister could not have been more clear in her denunciation. "Not true. Not true. Not true. Sheila said to my mother, how could she let this happen? And supposedly he molested us when we were younger, and it's just so untrue," the alleged victim said.

On February 8, 2005, Michael Deloge sent a letter to his mother. It read: *Ma, just to tell you, I do not want to send you a Valentines Day card. That was Sheila's idea, she was trying to be nice. The problem is you.* He said to never call the police to the farm again, that she was just trying to make trouble.

In March 2005 Sheila wrote up a suit for small-claims court that "Michael Todd Deloge" owed her $5,000.

Sheila and Deloge settled out of court days later, with him signing a "financial agreement." The document stated that Mikey Deloge admitted that he owed Sheila money and set out a payment plan. If he was late with his payments, he would owe Sheila an additional $500. It was signed by Michael Deloge.

Sheila took Deloge to the bank and made his checking account a joint account. That way, she said, she would be able to get to his money in case he had medical problems.

Sometime during the winter of 2004–5 Sheila's neighbor Bruce Allen spotted a man in bad shape walking down the road past his property on foot. It was not the first time Allen had seen young men who appeared to have been beaten and ill coming from the direction of Sheila's farm, but he would later tell the *Boston Globe* that this was the worst he had seen.

The slight man's face was cut so badly that he was dripping blood and his skin was extremely sallow—in fact, the color of green olives. He recognized the man as Michael Deloge, a man who had been living on the LaBarre farm for a couple of years.

"Mikey, what's the matter with you?" Bruce Allen asked.

"Sheila," Mikey said. "Sheila."

Jessica LaDuke, a resident at the Cross Roads House at the time Sheila met Mikey, described the man as a "friendly and caring" person. She later told the *Union Leader* that Deloge disappeared for several weeks and returned, telling stories of a "violent and frightening" woman named Sheila.

"He came back and said he was with this crazy lady in Epping," LaDuke said. "He said he had to walk to Portsmouth from Epping just to get away." That would have been a twenty-mile hike. "He was covered with bruises. He said, 'I left someone insane, controlling.' It was very weird. I didn't see him again."

Michael Deloge hadn't hiked far enough. Sheila just got in the car and came to get him. Not long after that, Sheila turned on her tape recorder and memorialized Mikey's "confession." He had molested a young girl, she forced him to say, a member of his family.

"Did you touch her on her pussy?"

"Yes."

"On her titties?"

"Yes."

"Did you obtain erections and ejaculations?"

"Yes."

"Where did you ejaculate?"

"In her pussy."

"And sometimes you shot off in your pants, didn't you?"

"Yes."

Then Sheila switched to a different victim, a different small girl, and he said yes when she asked if he "stuck his cock in her." She asked him whose house they were in when they did it. He admitted to babysitting and getting a hard-on when he gave the kids a bath. She had him admit that he punched holes in the wall and allowed rabbits to escape, that he had hurt rabbits by "fisting them," that he set fire to buildings, and that he had been locked in the chicken coop as punishment. He confessed to stealing vodka and weed from his mother. She forced him to admit to killing family pets when he was a kid, to worshipping the Devil while in Connecticut, to his mother being a prostitute when he was a kid, and that he had seen his mother's pussy "too many times to count." She made him admit that he choked his ex-wife after she became pregnant.

"Do you obtain an erection when you watch lesbians kiss?" she asked.

"Yes," Mikey replied.

Sheila then took the microphone and addressed whoever was someday listening to the tape: "He is not competent, he is not sane, he is not safe, he is very dangerous. Most pedophiles, before they kill, do many of the same things that Michael Deloge has done. I cite Jeffrey Dahmer as an example. Also, too, I have personally witnessed Michael Deloge fondling the area close to the female vagina of his mother, Donna Boston, in Somersworth. They were fondling, touching, and smacking each other's asses," Sheila said. "I have been told by many people at Cross Roads that he has been 'freaky' with his mother. His penis is small enough to be inserted into an underage girl possibly without detection afterward even by examination by a medical doctor. He continues to have what Michael calls 'blow job sessions.' Please do not give him money. Why should you give someone money who has molested your children? Slashed your tires? Stolen from you? I have made this tape for the sole purpose for the protection of children everywhere. Remember, there is no statute of limitations in regard to pressing charges for molestation. I pray that all of you will turn your back on this evil person, for he bears the mark. He is not treatable. He is never going to change. He is not safe for you to have around. Do not be taken in and do not feel sorry for him. Get some security cameras, people, in case he comes creeping around."

After that tape was made, nobody ever saw Michael Deloge again. Sheila sent out notes to the appropriate authorities. She wanted his name off their joint checking account. Deloge no longer worked for her. He'd gone to New Haven, she wrote. To the Connecticut Child Support Processing Center (CCSPC), which kept track of Michael Deloge, Sheila wrote, *Do not send any more mail to Red Oak Hill Lane. I do not live there anymore and the person that does live there doesn't [like] my mail coming to her house. I do not have an address right now. I have been living here and there.*

# Kenny

During the early months of 2006, when Sheila was working a job hauling trash in her pickup, she met a young man who was to profoundly change her life. His name was Kenny.

She'd just gone through a tough time, alone in the farmhouse during a bleak New Hampshire winter. During February she'd taken to writing letters to Chief Gregory Dodge, of the Epping police. She complained that someone had poisoned her cat six years before, that she still recalled spreading Wilfred LaBarre's ashes on the farm, that Wilfred's children were ungrateful, that Laura Melisi had made a scene, and that she had sung a cappella at Wilfred's funeral. She wrote that despite her struggles, she could still function *emotionally and financially.* The chief thought the letters were "nonsensical" but "typical of her." Eight days later she sent another letter in which she accused the chief of *oppressing her. That's not legal,* she reminded him. The issue was the snowplow. The road to her house was a town road. You could look it up on a map, she stressed. But the snowplow only plowed up to her gate, because he thought the rest was private driveway. She asked the chief not to allow his *hatred and intimidation of me to enter into your duties* and that he do the right thing. In one letter she asked: *Are you obsessed with me for some reason? If not why don't you treat me equally? Let's have [peace] in the valley. I will face you in court! Did you burn me at the stake in another life?*

The chief didn't overreact to the letters. He had a Sheila file, a thick one, and he just put them in there. There'd been close to one hundred calls regarding Sheila, some by her, some about her. But the letters were a sign of extreme loneliness. Sheila needed a man. And she knew how to get one. She'd call a sex chat line and talk to many men so that she'd be able to find the right one, the kind she liked.

Kenneth M. Countie, twenty-four years old—born July 18, 1981—of Wilmington, Massachusetts, moved out of his mother's home for the first time since his failed attempt to serve in the army. Kenneth, or Kenny, was described as "learning disabled, possibly mentally retarded." He had the mental capacity of a twelve-year-old. Even though he was living on his own, according to his mother, they remained best friends. Kenny and his mom saw each other or spoke on the phone every day. His employer at Shields Car Wash in Massachusetts later said that Kenneth was a simple, dedicated worker, but barely literate, struggling with even the most simple paperwork. Kenneth's roommate, Eric Ingram, later described him as "easygoing, responsible, and lonely."

In February 2006, a month after moving out, Kenneth's loneliness was getting the better of him, and he may have attempted suicide. In a desperate attempt to meet a woman, he registered with a phone-sex service called Tele-Mates, a dirty chat line for persons seeking sex partners. The service encouraged its clients with the slogan "Serve your passion." On the service's Web site there were categories for "female escorts, male escorts, transsexual, fantasy/fetish, massage, and adult phone."

Soon thereafter Kenneth and Sheila found each other through the service. They made a date to meet in person on Valentine's Day at the Ashworth by the Sea Hotel in Hampton Beach. They met in the bar. She thought he had pretty eyes and a pretty smile. She ordered a Cape Cod, but she didn't drink it. They went out to Sheila's Cadillac in the hotel parking garage and put back the front seat. Kenneth had some pot so they smoked. Must have been good stuff. She usually had a high tolerance for THC. According to Sheila, "He went to nuzzle me and I started kissing him on the neck. Things got more advanced. I didn't want to do something, but I did. I started getting excited. I felt myself beginning to lubricate. He started getting more and more aggressive, not in a dangerous way, but in a manly way. He felt my breasts. He said, 'I want some pussy.' That's exactly what he said: 'I want some pussy.' Turned me on." They had sex twice in the backseat. Missionary position. Kenny was in love. She let him follow her in his car, coming out of the Ashworth parking garage. Shouldn't have, she later explained, but she did. She was lonely, and scared. Her house was haunted and she preferred being there with a man.

"I'm not trying to be cute. This is not my imagination. The house is haunted," Sheila would say. "One day I heard ghost laughter. Upstairs. One time it felt like something pushed me—something went into the center of my back and pushed me. The stairs are very, very small. This was not long after I moved in." It was Captain Shaw—the ghost of Captain Shaw.

Anyway, Kenneth followed. For a while. On the way from Hampton Beach to Epping, Kenneth got lost. When she got home, Kenneth's car was no longer behind her, and she had to face the ghost of Captain Shaw alone. Still, it had been a good date, and she called Kenneth. A few times. She told him he should move in with her and he said okay.

On February 18, four days after his first date with Sheila, as Countie was leaving his home in Wilmington, he told his roommate, Eric, that Sheila was going to pick him up, that they were going to spend the night together, and that he would be back the next day. Sheila came to get him in her brand-new Nissan truck. Eric recalled that Kenny took "no personal belongings" with him. Kenny left in Sheila's truck, leaving his own van behind in Massachusetts. But when the next day came, Kenny did not return. In fact, Kenny never returned.

Sheila's version: "He asked me if he could come and stay with me. He was adamant about that, he said I can't take it anymore. My mother and father are pressuring me about money I owe them. He began divulging things. He was under medical care. Something to do with his penis, the little hole there that you urinate through. I thought, 'My God, what are these people, what are they doing to him?' He was upset. He started divulging things to me. I wasn't sure if I should believe him in the beginning. He talked about it and cried about it. His mother, he seemed so sincere about it. He didn't start immediately, this isn't all the same night. We smoked pot, we watched movies, we made love, we tried to stay warm, because of the broken furnace. We just bonded. We talked. He started telling me things. Something about divorcing your parents. I said, 'Well, I believe it is legally possible, but do you want to take a step like that!' It came out in bits and spurts. He would be okay and then he would put his hand up to his head. I would say, 'What are you thinking about?' Then he started coming out with his mother had been making him have sex with her as far back as he can remember. I said, 'Do you mean actual your penis-in-her-vagina sex?' To which he each and every time answered in the affirmative. And he said, 'I hate her, I hate her for doing it to me.' He said, 'I have told my dad, I have told him over and over and he does not believe me.' Mom was a nudist who beat her husband with a belt. She was an alcoholic. She gave him booze to keep him sedated. She tied him up with cords and stuck a carrot up his rectum. He was very young. It was sadism. Sexual torture. One thing we had to take care of right away was his name. Kenneth. That was the name of my brother who just died, so it was tearing me up. I called him Adam. He had gotten accustomed to sexual sadism and asked that I beat him with a belt."

On February 20 Kenny's concerned—and completely innocent—mother, Carolynn Lodge, of Billerica, Massachusetts, called Sheila and asked to talk to her son. She later recalled that when Kenny came on the line, he was crying.

"What's wrong?" she asked.

"Eric's brother called Sheila names," he replied. Before the mother could respond to that, her son added, "Sheila wants to talk to you."

Sheila grabbed the phone.

"Kenny is f***ing twenty-four years old, so leave him alone. We're happy," Sheila said.

Carolynn was about to inform Sheila that this wasn't just any woman she was talking to, but Kenneth Countie's mother, but she never got the chance. Sheila slammed down the phone.

The next day, February 21, Carolynn was feeling panicky. Something was wrong. Desperately wrong. She could feel it in her bones. Maybe Kenny had gone to work. She called Kenny's boss at the car wash. The boss told her that he was concerned about Kenny because he hadn't shown up for work or called in to say where he was. Sergeant Richard Mitchell, of the New Hampshire State Police, later got in touch with Kenny's boss at the car wash too.

By February 24 Carolynn had decided it was time to take legal action. She filed a missing persons report with the Epping police. She told police that she became concerned when he failed to show up that week for his job at a car wash. She told police that her son was mentally deficient and unable to take care of himself. He had only recently moved out of her home to attempt independence. His only previous attempt had been in the army when he had failed to complete boot camp. She said she was especially worried because her son had attempted suicide in February.

Epping police contacted the county sheriff's department, and one of the first things the sheriffs did in response to Carolynn's report was call the Cross Roads House homeless shelter in Portsmouth. People who ran away or were unable to cope had been known to seek refuge there in the past.

According to one Cross Roads employee, "Sometimes you get people with mental deficiencies shuffled off into the system, the family doesn't know where they are, and they get shipped off to the shelter."

The deputy gave the employee at the shelter a description of Kenneth. The employee said that Kenneth wasn't there, but they would be on the lookout for him and call back if someone matching his description arrived.

In the meantime, in response to the missing persons report, Sergeant Sean Gallagher and Detective Richard Cote, of the Epping police, went to visit Sheila at her farm. Gallagher parked the car and the men approached the house on foot.

Both men were familiar with Sheila. About twice a year they had to come to the farm to investigate a complaint by or about Sheila, and they always went in pairs, because if she got alone with a cop, she would expose herself. One time back in 2001, Sheila had tried to show Gallagher a series of nude photos of herself, photos that indicated that she was fairly limber for a big gal. When Gallagher told her to knock it off, she began rubbing one breast with one hand and the inside of her thigh with the other.

Now Gallagher heard a voice coming from the house.

"What do you want?" it asked sharply.

Gallagher looked up and saw Sheila sternly looking at him from a window. The policeman identified himself and told the woman he was responding to a missing persons report. "I'm looking for Kenneth Countie," he said.

"He ain't missing. He's here," Sheila barked back.

"Ma'am, could you come to the door, please?"

"No!"

"I'm going to need to speak with Mr. Countie, ma'am," Gallagher said.

"He can't talk to you right now. He's naked in the tub," Sheila replied.

"I'll wait," Gallagher said.

"I'm going to make a phone call," Sheila said. She hadn't been born yesterday. She was going to make sure this cop wasn't trying to pull the old wool over her eyes. She called the Wilmington Police Department in Massachusetts to make sure a missing persons report had actually been filed. The Wilmington police told Sheila that the report had indeed been filed.

Sheila got Kenny and brought him to the door. Well, almost to the door. Kenny never got closer than five feet to the door. He wore jeans and was naked from the waist up. Gallagher observed Kenny to be healthy and well.

"Mr. Countie, are you all right?" Gallagher asked.

"Yes," Kenny said.

"Are you being held here against your will?"

"No."

Gallagher took a good look at Kenny and noted that he appeared ambulatory and free of injury.

"You heard him," Sheila said. "Now get the f*** off my property!"

Sheila faxed a statement to Epping police on February 25 with Countie's signature on it. The statement read: *I am an adult, safe, sane, and very happy. I only TRUST Sheila LaBarre and do feel safe and secure in her presence.*

The statement added that Countie's mother had filed a false missing persons report: *I was never MISSING. I would like to be left completely alone.*

# Wal-Mart

In an incident that made little sense—no matter how you look at it—Kenny was next seen on March 11 at the Wal-Mart in Epping. He had visible cuts on his face, and Sheila led him to the customer service desk.

"My husband was just attacked," Sheila said.

"What happened?" the store's employee asked with concern.

"A woman customer just grabbed my husband by the arm and pushed him out of her way," Sheila said.

"Are you saying this woman caused the cuts on his face?" the store employee asked.

"Yes, well, no," Sheila said. "This is from a car accident. A really bad car accident. He was burned on his arm and all up here. He's in a lot of pain. Can't you see that he's in a lot of pain?" Sheila said, pulling up Kenny's shirt.

The employee could see that there were burns on the man's arm and upper torso. The employee later described the man's skin as being a "greenish yellow color."

Kenny's demeanor was described as "quiet, almost

timid." He kept his head down and never looked at anyone as Sheila showed his wounds to the store employee.

The employee described Sheila's demeanor as "angry, unreasonable, and very defensive." Sheila, witnesses said, repeatedly threatened to sue Wal-Mart because of what had happened to her "husband."

Eventually Sheila left, but the incident had been sufficiently bizarre that several store employees wrote incident reports documenting what had occurred.

Sheila and Kenny Countie returned to the Wal-Mart at about 8:00 P.M. on March 17. This time she was pushing the young man in a wheelchair. She again referred to him as her "husband" and as having been assaulted by another customer in the store on March 11.

Store employees, including Elaine Mainard and Wendy Peterson, became concerned with both Kenny's appearance and Sheila's behavior. Countie was still ashen, still had cuts on his face and hands, and appeared to be unable to move on his own. There was a particularly bad gash across his nose and his hands were swollen. The man was withdrawn and only spoke when Sheila spoke to him.

"Would you like to have us call the police for you?" a store employee asked.

"No, I don't need the police. I'm a lawyer," Sheila replied loudly. "I'm a multimillionaire. I don't need police. I own a horse farm." The woman was clearly trying to draw attention to herself.

"I think your husband needs medical care," Wendy Peterson offered.

"I have a medical background. I'll treat his wounds," Sheila countered.

When she sensed that the employees in the store were not taking her seriously, she made a production of buying a disposable camera in the electronics department and began taking photographs of the store's aisles and, most disturbingly, the locations of security cameras.

Those same security cameras, in turn, took video of Sheila and Kenneth and showed clearly what bad shape the young man was in. At one point Sheila could be seen touching his shoulder, causing him to jump as if in pain.

"I know my husband is telling the truth when he says he was assaulted in this store," Sheila said. "I paid seven hundred dollars for a polygraph examination and he passed with flying colors."

At that point one store employee became so concerned that he called the Epping police. He said there was a woman creating a disturbance in the store. He asked that they come to the Wal-Mart right away and get her off the property.

Responding to the call was Sergeant Sean Gallagher and Detective Richard Cote. When the policemen arrived, Sheila was in the frozen-foods section, still snapping photos with her disposable camera. Nobody was staring at her. She hadn't drawn a crowd, although she was speaking loudly and quickly.

"What are you doing, Sheila?" Gallagher asked.

She told him that the man in the Wal-Mart wheelchair had been assaulted during a previous visit to the store and she was photographing their security system in preparation for filing suit.

The cops got a look at Kenny. Gallagher could see that the man who had been ambulatory and devoid of injuries, when he went looking for him on Sheila's farm, now failed to meet either of those criteria.

Sheila left on her own volition, pushing Kenny in the

wheelchair. The cops followed them out. Gallagher wanted to make sure Kenneth was able to walk on his own, and Kenny, although his gait was slow and he was still hunched over at the shoulders, passed the test.

"Are you all right?" Detective Cote asked Kenny.

He didn't respond.

"Don't f***ing answer their question! Don't talk to them!" Sheila yelled.

With that, Sheila and Kenny were allowed to get into Sheila's car and leave.

Wendy Peterson later said, "Kenneth looked like he should have been in a hospital. His face was green and had multiple scrapes and bruises all in different stages of healing. He was humped over in a wheelchair and she kept asking him if he was going to faint."

Police later viewed the store's surveillance videotape. It showed Sheila buying a number of yellow diesel fuel containers and stacking them in Countie's lap in the wheelchair.

Gallagher wrote a report regarding the incident. He sent a copy both to Carolynn Lodge and to Sheila.


On Monday, March 20, Sheila paid a visit to her friend Michelle Bennett, who also lived in Epping. The two women had known each other for five years because several of Bennett's children had done odd jobs for Sheila on the farm. Sheila parked the car and went into Bennett's home. The two woman chatted for an hour and a half, then decided to get pizza. Bennett's dog was dying. Kidney failure. It would only eat pizza.

"I have a friend in my car," Sheila said.

"Goodness gracious, why didn't you invite him in?" Bennett exclaimed.

"Oh, Michelle, I would never bring a stranger into your home," Sheila said.

As Bennett got into the car, she could see that there was a young man in the backseat, wearing a hat and an oversized coat.

"This is Kenneth, but I call him Adam," Sheila said, gesturing toward the backseat.

The car was dark and Bennett did not get a good look at the young man. On the way to get pizza, there was some small talk in the car, but the young man didn't say much. After getting the pizzas, Sheila took the woman back home. Michelle Bennett was unaware that she would be the last person, other than his murderer, to see Kenneth Countie alive.

The next time Bennett visited, on about March 22, Sheila told her she'd given Kenneth the boot because he was a pedophile. Sheila was burning something on the lawn, something that smelled horrible. Sheila said it was just garbage. Sheila later pointed to a mattress on the living-room floor and said, "That's where I sleep."

# A Rabbit or
a Pedophile?

Sheila received her copy of the written report on the Wal-Mart incident from Sergeant Gallagher on March 23. She wasted no time calling him on the phone.

"I just want you to know he doesn't live with me anymore," Sheila said.

"Where is he now?" Gallagher asked.

"I have no f***ing idea," Sheila replied. "He said he was going back to Massachusetts."

"Why did he leave?"

"Don't know and don't care," she replied. "He didn't do anything around here anyway."

Sergeant Gallagher informed Carolynn Lodge of what Sheila had said, and Carolynn immediately filed a second missing persons report with the Epping police. The report was received by Sergeant Gallagher.

At 1:00 A.M. on March 24, 2006, Sheila again called the Epping police. She spoke to Sergeant Gallagher, who was working the 6:00 P.M. to 2:00 A.M. shift. As soon as he came on the line, she started, as he put it, to "cry hysterically."

"I don't know or care where Kenneth Countie is," she said. "I just woke up one morning and he was gone. Here—I want you to listen to a tape I made." *Click.*

She played for Gallagher over the phone a tape recording she had made. On the tape Sheila's voice could be heard interrogating "Adam," proclaiming herself a justice of the peace, and alleging that Adam had raped several young children. The attacks, she claimed, had taken place in Massachusetts. Her interrogation was rapid-fire, consisting of an accusation, each followed by the phrase "Isn't that true?"

In a voice so low that it was barely audible, Kenny could be heard replying yes to her accusations.

"Talk right!" she could be heard screaming.

Near the conclusion of the tape, Gallagher heard an urgent gurgling noise, a sound he recognized as the start of regurgitation. Kenny could be heard vomiting seconds later. Apparently speaking directly into the tape recorder's microphone, Sheila said that the vomiting wasn't real. Kenny, she said, was just faking throwing up. After the retching noises ceased, she could be heard saying, "You didn't faint, stop faking that you fainted."

When the tape ended, Sheila came back on the line in person and, once again, cried hysterically for Gallagher's benefit.

"Where's Kenneth Countie?" Gallagher asked.

"I don't know. I never want to see him again," she said.

Gallagher said he would get back in touch with her and they hung up. He called Carolynn Lodge and asked her if she had any other contact numbers for Sheila other than her landline. Carolynn said that she had a cell phone number and gave it to him. The number turned out to be a Nextel number associated with a pre-paid phone. Gallagher discovered that the minutes had expired, and Carolynn had no other number for Sheila.

At approximately 6:00 P.M., Gallagher and Detective Cote visited Sheila LaBarre's farm in person. It was dark. As they parked their vehicle and approached the house on foot, they noted that, despite the fact that all of Sheila's known vehicles were there, no one appeared to be home. They used the headlights on their car and flashlights to see where they were going.

About twenty feet from the entrance to the farm-house's front porch was a "burnt-through" mattress and box spring. There was wood piled on top of that. The fire, it appeared, had gone out.

The policemen observed a second fire about thirty-five feet away from the mattress and box spring, and in this fire they could see a fifty-five-gallon barrel and a pile of hay. In the fire was a knife with a partially melted blade, clippers, and a burnt chair.

Upon closer examination police could make out smaller objects in each burn pile as well. Sticking out of the hay was a bone, which looked to be about three and a half inches in length and one inch in diameter. Detective Cote reached into the fire, grabbed the bone, and picked it up for a moment to get a better look at it. It was moist. Greasy. He dropped it back into the ashes. The bone was "straight in appearance," and at one end was a ball joint that was thicker in diameter than the rest of the bone. The other end of the bone was jagged. On the ball end of the bone, the policemen observed, there was attached what Gallagher remembered as being "soft tissue." The meaty mass had been charred by the fire. Since they were responding to a missing persons report, and that bone could conceivably have belonged to a human being, the policemen returned to their car and placed a call to Patricia Conway, assistant Rockingham County attorney.

They explained the situation to her and she authorized a "well-being check" of the interior of the farmhouse. This allowed the police to enter the home legally to make sure Sheila and Kenny, or anyone else who might be around, were okay.

To make sure no one was home, they knocked on the farmhouse door, but no one answered. After jiggling the doorknob, Gallagher kicked the front door and it opened.

"Hello? Hello?" the police called into the house. Just as they were about to enter, a car pulled up to the house. Driving the car was a woman who identified herself as Michelle Bennett. Sitting in the passenger seat was Sheila. The driver told the police that she was a friend of Sheila's.

"Is the town gonna pay for that door?" Sheila asked.

"We would like your consent to search your home for Kenneth Countie," Gallagher replied to Sheila.

"Go ahead, but I can tell you right now, he left yesterday morning sometime," she answered.

Sheila led the men on a tour of the house. The police took their time searching the house. Upstairs, downstairs. They even looked in a room that could only be accessed by a ladder, a room they would not have known existed, unless Sheila pointed it out. Down in the cellar on the dirt floor, they found a pair of men's gray sneakers.

"Who do those belong to?" the police asked.

"Those belonged to Kenneth Countie. I purchased those for him at Wal-Mart," she said.

"We would like your permission to seize those sneakers," the police said.

"You may *not* have my permission," Sheila snapped.

"We request that you leave those sneakers right where they are," the police said.

Sheila was silent.

The policemen left the house and walked out onto the front lawn. Sheila followed them, keeping an eye on their every move. Sergeant Gallagher walked up to the burn pile with the bone in it.

"What's that bone?" he asked.

"I don't know," she said.

"No idea?"

"It's from a rabbit. I cremate my rabbits when they die," she explained.

"Where do you cremate them?"

"In the wood-burning stove."

"When was the last time you cremated a rabbit?" Detective Cote inquired.

"About a week ago," she said.

"That bone is too big to belong to a rabbit," Cote commented. "Come on. What is it?"

"It's a rabbit. It's a rabbit or a pedophile," Sheila blurted out.

"Why would you say it is a pedophile?" Cote asked.

"I didn't say that," Sheila replied.

"You did say it. I just heard you say it. Sergeant Gallagher heard you say it. There's a big difference between a rabbit and a pedophile."

Sheila was silent.

"Sheila, did you kill Kenneth Countie?"

"No, I didn't," she replied.

"Why are you burning the bed?" she was asked.

"Because I slept on it with a pedophile," she replied.

"Okay if we take that bone with us?" Cote asked.

"No, I don't want you to take it," she said. "I want you to leave. Leave my property."

Gallagher said they would leave, but he reminded her that she wasn't to touch anything while they were gone, especially not those sneakers in the cellar, and not the stuff that was in the fires. Sheila promised she wouldn't touch anything.

Suspicious, but lacking the evidence to make an arrest, the police left. The missing persons report, the bone with the meaty mass attached, and the woman's strange responses to questioning were enough to get a search warrant issued.

Police were now legally able to search the house and the grounds for the human remains of Kenneth Countie.

# "He's in that bag"

On March 25 the police raided the farm, again. This time the raid took place just shy of nine o'clock in the morning. Gallagher could see that the fire pile on the lawn had changed. The mattress was burned more completely than before. Items that had been piled on top of one another were now pulled apart. The fire looked picked through. Placed near one of the fire piles was a barrel and a chair, and on the chair was a picture of what looked to be a Native American, perhaps a Cherokee chief.

Incineration murders were infrequent, but not unheard of. Only recently in New Hampshire, in a case eerily similar to this one, Kenneth Carpenter was tried and convicted of murdering Edith Meyer, dismembering her, and incinerating her remains.

Along with Sergeant Gallagher, among those making the raid were Sheila's pen pal Chief Gregory Dodge, of the Epping Police Department, Detective Sergeant Robert Estabrook, of the New Hampshire State Police Major Crime Unit, Lieutenant Michael Wallace, and Trooper First Class (TFC) Jill Rockey, along with others.

After receiving training through the New Hampshire Police Standards and Training Counsel in Concord, Sergeant Estabrook had been a member of the state police since 1987. He received additional training in the investigation of felony crimes, including homicide, rape, robbery, and arson, through various training seminars conducted by the New Hampshire State Police, New York State Police, Toronto Metropolitan Police, and the aforementioned New Hampshire Police Standards and Training Counsel.

As police walked back onto her property, Sheila—her hair a mess, covered head to toe with ashes and soot—was walking from the barn to her house. Seeing the heat, she ducked into the house and locked the door.

Just outside the door facing the fires, Sheila had placed a large piece of luggage. The suitcase acted as a sort of altar, as Sheila had decorated it with six crucifixes, two on top and two on either side.

"Sheila, we've got a warrant this time," she was told through the door.

"Am I going to be arrested?" Sheila asked.

"No, Sheila, we just need to look around. Let's make this easy. Open the door." Sheila unlocked the door and the police entered.

"I knew you were going to be back," she said, and she started to cry. She tended to a barking dog even as she sniffled.

The first place police looked was in the burn piles, but the large bone they had spotted the previous day was gone. Next to one of the burn piles was a Wal-Mart shopping bag.

Wallace and Dodge accompanied Sheila inside the house, at which time they made a mental note that the woman now had access to a .22 long gun. Dodge noticed that there was burnt material all over the stove, and one burner was on, glowing red.

"What are you burning?" Sheila was asked.

"I was just burning my notes from Tele-Mates," she said, referencing the "dating service" through which she had met Kenny in the first place.

She was wiping ash away from the burner and her hand was touching the hot burner. Dodge grabbed her hand so she wouldn't burn herself, and asked her why she was so upset.

She said that she needed some medication and opened the refrigerator so the men could see there was actually medicine in there.

The policemen had brought a tape recorder with them, and at this point the recorder was turned on, and the incoherent conversation was memorialized.

"You are being recorded," Wallace said.

"I see that. I'm on tape," she said.

"We're just trying to make heads or tails of this, Sheila. We're trying to find Ken."

"I don't know anything about that. He's been steal-ing money from me. Look at the disorder! Look at the disorder! Between five years with a lawsuit and the state of New Hampshire, I got to tell you this, on the four-teenth, when I met Kenneth Michael Countie at the Ash-worth, I had six messages from Irish people, that's true! Can we close the front door? I'm freezing. I can't take any more stress. I don't know what to tell you. He was threatening to kill himself. He was threatening to put himself on fire, I didn't take him seriously! He started talking about killing himself right after I played that tape for Gallagher. He was a horrible person! A horrible person! A homosexual. A pedophile. You know, I hear a lot of high-powered ammunition going off on this hill."

She paced as she spoke.

"We want to know where those Irish guys put Kenny."

"I called him Adam."

"Do you think someone killed Adam?"

"I don't know. I don't know if he has been killed. He wanted to marry me. He is a heroin addict."

"Did he leave any heroin here?"

"No, just empty bottles. You know I speak the truth," she said.

"We know you speak the truth. We've never gotten anything but the truth out of you. Where's Ken?"

The woman pointed to the Wal-Mart bag.

"He's in that bag," she said, according to Sergeant Robert Estabrook. Chief Dodge only took a quick glance inside the bag before closing it. He saw a quantity of small, charred debris, but nothing he could immediately recognize as bones and teeth. They would need an expert to make that determination.

"Are these bones from a rabbit?" Sheila was asked.

"No," she replied. She, likewise, replied negatively when asked if the bones came from a horse, pig, or goat.

"Are these bones Adam?" Wallace asked.

"I don't know," Sheila answered. "There are teeth. There are teeth. Chief Dodge, are you going to arrest me?"

"No, Sheila. Of course not. I have nothing to arrest you for," the chief said. "Now, come on. Is it going to take DNA tests to ascertain if these bones are Adam?"

"Yes, it will. Because there will be no other way to ascertain if he is in the bag," she replied. "He left. He is going to a homeless shelter. He can run like a cheetah. Just kill me. Just shoot me, please. Shoot me in the back."

"Run like a cheetah? I thought he could hardly walk when he was in Wal-Mart."

"That's what I thought too."

"I think we had better continue this conversation down at the police station so that our people can work in here."

On the way out to the squad car, the police realized that they had not patted Sheila down. When they did so, they found a loaded .38 Smith & Wesson pistol.

"Why you packin', Sheila?"

"I was concerned about my animals," she replied.

"Any other weapons?"

Sheila turned to Lieutenant Wallace, the best-looking of the police. She pulled up her shirt far enough to expose her breasts to him. She pulled down her pants, but she was stopped as the police all agreed they were satisfied that she was unarmed.

"I need coffee."

"We have coffee at the police station."

"Can I bring a rabbit with me?"

The police agreed that this was okay. Sheila put a rabbit in a carrying case and returned. She got in the back of the squad car and off they went.

The search went on without her. Seized during the search of the burn pits was a large pair of pruning shears and a set of hedge shears. Tools designed to dismember. The wooden handles of each had been charred by the fire. The shears were inside the barrel, along with a silver piece of a knife, which had melted from the heat.

One of the burn piles was still actively burning. The other was still warm. Near the barrel police found more bone fragments. Near one of the pits was a number of empty fuel containers.

The search continued away from the fires as well.

Also found were several more empty yellow diesel fuel containers in the back of Sheila's green Nissan pickup truck. Between visits from the cops, Sheila had moved the truck from its usual parking spot in front of the farmhouse to a dirt road called Cilley Road, at the back side of the property. The containers appeared new and greatly resembled those that Sheila had purchased at the Epping Wal-Mart. As dusk fell upon the scene, the house was secured for the night. Police had a lot of questions to ask. They were most interested in finding out what she had meant when she said she had burned a pedophile.

Although much compelling evidence suggesting that Kenneth Countie was dead, and that Sheila had dismembered his body and burned it in the fire pits, had been discovered by police, they were still disappointed by the results of their initial search. The three-and-a-half-inch-long bone with the fleshy tissue still attached to it was gone. Also missing were the men's sneakers on the cellar floor, which Sheila had been told not to move.

Police had empty diesel containers, but no clear evidence that those containers had recently been filled with fuel. To remedy this gap in the evidence, Detective Marc Turner, of the Epping police, spoke to a representative at Irving Oil. The representative told Turner that Sheila had visited the oil company on March 17 and March 25 and had filled three 5-gallon diesel containers.

The next order of business was to have a bone expert look at the bone fragments that had been seized from the smoldering burn pits. Detective Turner and state trooper Steve Puckett took digital photos of the fragments and wired them to deputy chief medical examiner (DCME) Jennie V. Duval, of the chief medical examiner's office (CMEO) in Concord. Dr. Duval looked at the photos and promptly stated that, in her professional opinion, the bones in the photos were possibly human. To get a second opinion, she e-mailed the photos to forensic anthropologist Dr. Marcella Sorg, who was a professor at the University of Maine in Bangor. Dr. Sorg had been consulting with New Hampshire law enforcement as a forensic anthropologist since the early 1980s.

At the Epping police station, in a closet-sized and windowless interrogation room, the interview of Sheila commenced. Asking the questions were state police sergeant Richard Mitchell and TFC Jill Rockey. They were in a room with one table and bare white walls. Sitting at Sheila's feet was a cage with a rabbit in it.

"Sheila, we'd like to videotape this interview. Is that okay with you?" Mitchell asked.

"Yes," she replied.

Sheila's behavior continued to puzzle her interrogators. For example, she refused to refer to Kenneth Countie by his real name, but instead she called him "Adam."

"Why do you call him that?" she was asked.

"That was how he wished to be called," she replied. "He wished to take my last name. He wished to be known as Adam Olympian LaBarre. But we didn't legally change his last name because of the money it costs. He's confessed. He was in a desperate situation. Adam told me that he changed his name. This is typical of pedophiles. I didn't know that." Sheila began to sob.

"How did you meet Adam?"

"I almost didn't meet him. On the day I was supposed to meet him, I cut my foot on a piece of metal at my house, and everything was going wrong, and I thought I shouldn't meet him. But I did."

She related the story that police already knew, Tele-Mates phone chat, Ashworth Hotel on Valentine's Day, etc. Later she picked him up in Massachusetts and drove him back to Epping so he could live with her.

"How did he get to the hotel?" Mitchell asked.

"He has a van. I mean, I don't know if it was *legally* his van. That's the bad thing too, because who he lives with, that guy is sleeping with his six-year-old son."

"Did you like him, Sheila?" Rockey asked.

"My first thought when I saw him was that he was a pedophile. He's of legal age, he wants to chase me. He chased me, I didn't chase him, so . . . My brother Kenneth passed away September the twenty-ninth in Alabama. He was born with one kidney."

"I'm sorry," Rockey said.

"I know, I know," Sheila replied.

"Was Adam, or Ken, working at the time he came up here? How was he making money? How was he surviving?" Mitchell asked.

"He wanted to get away from something. He'd been having sex with his own mother. That also has to do with James Brackett, who is also a stalker—"

"Did you have a sexual relationship with Adam?" Mitchell said. Playing a bit of the old good cop/bad cop, Mitchell's questions were rapid-fire, while Rockey spoke more softly and sounded kinder.

"Yes, I did, but it stopped."

"Why did it stop?"

"I stopped sleeping with Adam when I learned that he was a pedophile."

"What made you think that Adam was a pedophile?"

"He confessed. He told me he'd molested several children in Massachusetts. He told me that he himself had been sexually abused for years at the hands of his own mother. He also admitted to experiencing homosexual encounters. I have a tape recording of him confessing to molesting those kids in Massachusetts. I know he was telling the truth too. I hired a private polygraphist to administer a polygraph to Adam about being a pedophile, and he passed the polygraph."

It was unknown if this actually had occurred, but those with an attention to detail recalled that this was the second time Sheila had claimed to have paid to have Kenny given a lie detector test. She made the same claim during her second visit to the Wal-Mart, the time when she pushed him in the wheelchair, claiming that she could prove he was telling the truth when he said he had been assaulted by a female Wal-Mart customer during their previous visit.

Mitchell asked, "Adam ended up in some sort of wheelchair recently. Can you tell me—"

"All that was, was I said to him, 'Do you want me to push you in a wheelchair?'" She laughed. Serious again, she said, "He's a heroin addict, he's a crack addict, and I didn't know that."

"Did he have injuries, Sheila?" Rockey asked.

"Yes, he did because of the glass pot that exploded. He refused to go to the hospital, but I tended to his wounds."

"You have an accent. Where are you from, Sheila?" Rockey asked.

"Alabama. I have a double accent."

"What do you do for work, Sheila?" Mitchell asked.

"I'm a landlord right now, with no income. All of my tenants left."

"A year ago, did you have an occupation outside the home?" Mitchell inquired.

"Get It Gone. My trash-hauling business. I'm not registered. It's just me."

"Did Adam work with you?"

"He didn't do anything except eat candy. I found out he was addicted to sugar, chocolate, heroin—or what we call smack in the South. I've never done it."

"When did you last see Adam?"

There was a long pause and Sheila said, "I haven't been at the farm in a couple of days. I've been double CAT scanned. You don't have me in the machine far enough. You ever been CAT scanned?"

"That's not the point, Sheila. When did you last see Adam?"

"You know I stopped having sex with him. I get up in the morning and I do my thing. I take care of my animals. He's afraid of horses. I cook." Whispering, she said, "He admitted to raping children. He used Vaseline on his fingers to rape children. I noticed he was looking at children. His eyes would look at little girls! Babies! Diapers! I was upset, nauseous. I said, 'You're a pedophile!' He asked me if I could save him. I said only God could save him."

"When did you last see Adam, Sheila?"

"Me and Adam went to sleep on either March twenty-first or March twenty-second, and when I woke up, he was gone. I went out into the woods to look for Adam. I thought he might be out there. I'm trying to find my way back in the dark. I'm so confused. The Irish are after me and the Secret Service. It's true!"

"Let's go back to when you tried to help Adam, help him get past this pedophilia issue," Mitchell said.

"I hired a polygrapher. Basically, the test entails him having sexual intercourse with someone who he calls mother. I have heard her voice. She is not British. She is not from England, trust me. The woman parades around naked," Sheila replied.

"How did he pass the polygraph?" Rockey asked.

"One of the questions was about he and his mother having sex. He passed that part, but it's tape-recorded, legally, to the best of my knowledge."

"Did he admit to having sex with children as an adult?" Rockey inquired.

"Not in front of the polygrapher."

"Do *you* believe that Adam's had sex with children?" Rockey asked.

Sheila whispered: "*I don't know!* God, Jesus. Jesus can be called numerous things. That's on the side of our refrigerator. Oh, the suffering, the children. Stop. Stop. You need to stop looking at them children and stop getting excited by them. I have to look at my notes, which I don't have. I have to listen to the tape, which I don't have."

Rockey said, "Okay, now, let's try to focus on one thing—"

"I know, I understand, I'm being tangential. It's the CAT scan. They gotta put me back in the machine!"

"When did you last see Adam, Sheila?"

"I fell asleep and I woke up and he was gone. I don't know if it was light or dark when he left. It was dark when I went to sleep."

"Sheila, we have some concerns about Adam and that he could potentially hurt children. Where do you think we could find him?" Mitchell asked.

"Not sure. I have CAT scan fever from too much radiation. My neurons—"

"Where can we find Adam? It's important."

"I don't know, because I've been sifting through bone fragments. I want to know what has been put in my yard. I found a tooth. I don't know. I don't *knooowww*." As she elongated the last word, her voice rose into a high-pitch whine.

"I want to know if it could be Adam's tooth," Mitchell said.

"The rabbit was dead. I was cremating a rabbit, with Adam watching."

"Why were you burning the mattress, Sheila?"

"I don't remember. I have to get an AIDS test because he said he has AIDS and he had blood coming out of his"—a dramatic pause— "*manhooooood.*"

"The bones, Sheila. What about the bones?"

"I didn't notice the bones until the police were in the yard yesterday. I'm not talking about the rabbit bones."

"What about the bigger bones? The bones too big to come from a rabbit?"

"I can't identify what they are. Maybe they came from Mercedes, the pit bull that died."

"Do you think someone made Adam disappear?"

"I don't know. I don't know. Mr. . . . the rabbit, oh, bless his heart," she said. "Sometimes I cremate my rabbits in the stove in the kitchen. Sometimes I use gasoline. The container is between my Mercedes and my Cadillac. Adam did not help cremate animals. He just watched. Ohhhhh, Skippy."

"Skippy is Adam, right?"

"Yes, that's just my pet name."

"Was he in bed with you?"

"Yes. I don't have cameras around the house, but I suspect he rifles through things."

"Did Adam ever try to run away?"

"Yes, he did leave the house. I would have to go back and get him—up the road. He is suicidal. Of course, he doesn't want to spend his life in prison."

"Why were you all covered with soot, Sheila?" Rockey inquired.

"I was discerning what was what. What was rabbit, what was not. I sifted."

"Where did you go when you realized that Adam was gone? Where did you look?"

"I went to Cilley Road. I parked and went out into the woods."

"What were you looking for in the woods, Sheila? Why did you go *there*?"

"I was looking for Adam, someone, anyone, stalkers, maybe those Irish people."

"Sheila, what were you burning on your front lawn when the police arrived?"

"I was burning trash. I know that's against town law, but I'm just trying to be honest. I was just trying to save him. I guess I have a savior complex."

"Sheila, how do you save a pedophile?" Rockey asked.

"You just talk about God," Sheila said.

"Is it possible that Adam might have hurt himself, that he might have killed himself?"

"That is possible. He stared at the gas tank. He has the potential to kill himself."

"If he tried to kill himself, where do you think he would do it? At your house?"

"Probably."

"Now those bones in the fire, they were too big to come from a rabbit, right?"

"I would think so. I have experience in identifying bones through my radiological training," she said.

"We would like to take those bones and test them."

"Well, if those are Adam's bones, he or someone else did something to him."

"Even if he killed himself, he couldn't have cremated himself, right?" Mitchell said.

Sheila didn't answer that and instead began to run down the weapons she owned. There was her .38, the one she carried in her pocket because she was out there all alone, and the .22 rifle, which Dr. LaBarre had left to her.

"Is it possible that you might not remember something, but maybe Adam tried to hurt you and you had to defend yourself against him?" Rockey asked.

"Well, I slapped him. After that, he hugged me and cried."

"Do you think Adam might be dead, Sheila?" Rockey asked.

"I don't know. It concerns me because I don't want him to come back and harm me or my animals. I have to call him all these names to get him to answer. Are you Ken? Are you Kenneth? Are you Kenny? Are you Adam? He can run like a cheetah. He's in Vermont. Or a homeless shelter. Or back in Massachusetts. I wanted him to be safe. And happy."

"Did you want him out?"

"I didn't want to support him anymore."

"When was the last time you saw him?"

"When I made the tape. When I made him admit that he molested those children. He said he was going to kill himself, so I checked my guns. He said he wanted to make his parents sorry."

"For what?"

"His mother molested him, on a schedule, Tuesday and Thursday. He claims she walks around naked. Could be public indecency. These are questions that are difficult to answer because, perhaps, it didn't end. Perhaps he went and watched TV. Perhaps I cooked. Perhaps there was no arguing."

"That sounds unusual to me, Sheila," Rockey said.

"He was an unusual person."

Both police noticed she had used the past tense regarding Kenny. "Why were you away from your farm for a couple of days?" they asked.

"I thought I might be in danger. I thought someone was in my woods."

"Who?"

"He was an Irish immigrant."

"Do you know his name?"

"No, I do not."

"Why did you move your truck?"

"Same reason. I parked my truck on Cilley Road so I wouldn't be seen, and I walked through the woods to my property. It was dark and I got lost."

"Is the jacket you are wearing not the one you were wearing then?" Mitchell asked.

"Yes, one and the same."

"How come your jacket doesn't have more debris on it?"

"This is . . . no, this isn't the jacket I wore. You are

right. You are right. I had to take off my coat and leave it behind," she said, demonstrating for the police how she had disrobed. "By the time I made it back to my house, I was in a state of complete exhaustion. I nearly passed out. I decided to burn all of my clothes."

"Tell me again what you were burning when police arrived?" Mitchell asked.

"Trash, Christmas ornaments, debris. A few cans accidentally got in there. He said he liked fire."

"You know what, Sheila, it doesn't add up," Mitchell said.

"Would you tell us the truth if something happened to Adam? Would you be comfortable?" Rockey asked.

"Yes," Sheila replied.

"Okay. You're a woman, you're out in the middle of nowhere. You've got to take care of yourself. Is it possible that something happened to Adam and you had to take care of yourself?" Rockey inquired.

"Oh yes, you are so right. It is remote," Sheila said.

The interrogators drew back at that point, then changed the subject.

"When was the last time you were with Michelle Bennett?" Rockey asked.

"She doesn't even know Adam. He doesn't even know these people," Sheila said.

Sheila told the police that she had a cell phone number for Adam, that she had spoken to his family members on the phone, and that she knew Adam liked to burn things because his dad was mad at him for burning a hockey jacket.

"What happened to the sneakers on the cellar floor?"

"I burned them too. He wanted them burned. He wanted to burn everything he had. That's the truth. It's the truth. He wanted to burn because I had a fire going in my woodstove. He knew I was allergic to cigarettes and he wanted his clothes burned so I couldn't smell it on him. He had sex with his own mother. He burned his Wayne Gretzky jacket. I burned my shoes too, the shoes I wore when I was walking through the woods. I burned them too."

At this point Sheila turned to the caged rabbit she had with her and spoke baby talk a bit. She took the rabbit out of the cage at her feet and put it on her lap. When the rabbit apparently urinated on her, Sheila calmly took a paper towel and cleaned up the mess, including wiping at the side of her leg where some rabbit urine had dripped. When done, she wiped her mouth with the same paper towel. Rockey asked Sheila if she wanted something to eat or drink, but Sheila declined.

"You have some cuts and scrapes on your hands," Mitchell said, returning to an old subject.

"Yeah."

"What happened?"

"I was picking up broken glass. I didn't want my rabbits stepping on it."

"Where should we look, Sheila? Where should we look for Adam?"

"I don't know. I seriously don't know. I'm not being cutesy with you."

"When was the last time you saw Adam?"

"You're badgering me," she said. They all laughed. "I'm just joking, but you keep repeating, repeating, repeating."

"Sometimes that helps people if they're trying to remember something and it's not quite there," Mitchell said.

"Would it help if we got that tape for you, the tape you made?" Rockey asked.

"Which one?" Sheila asked.

"How many tapes do you have?"

"A lot. A lot of them."

"Talking to Adam?"

"Yes, and sworn statements, and things like that. Singing." She turned to Mitchell and added, "I can leave if I want, right?"

"You can leave when you want," Mitchell said.

"Good. I never abandoned my animals—but with freaky stuff going on there, I don't want to stay there anymore."

"What freaky stuff, Sheila?"

"Stuttering and inversion. I've had that ever since the CAT scan. I have so many animals living with me, you know. A Dalmatian, rabbits. One got electrocuted. He tremored and shivered and shivered and tremored. I called the vet a couple of times. I've had a problem with Dr. Allen."

"What was the problem?"

"Well, he hates me. I know he wants me out of there." Crying again, she said, "He wanted me to sell part of my lot to one of his strange friends. Bruce Allen literally shot through a truck, prior to me moving here, that contained one of the sons of Daniel and Louise Harvey."

Mitchell said, "So you were at the Harveys'. Where is Ken at this time?" He had stopped calling the victim Adam.

"Back at the house. Watching television. Eating candy. He wanted to escape someone from his past. He said he would rather be dead than do what he was doing. I said,

'What happens to you? What happens to you?' He said, 'My heart starts beating faster . . . and faster. . . .'"

Rockey began talking religion with Sheila.

"What religion are you?" Rockey asked.

"I'm a Southern Baptist," Sheila said.

"Do you go to church?"

"The only thing the church wants from me is money—money to buy church dump trucks."

"I think God believes in certain things. There's a right and there's a wrong. He's got strong views on homosexuality. God's got strong views on pedophiles. There's no middle ground. God has strong views on that. It's wrong. It's wrong. That must have been hard for you dealing with Adam," Rockey said.

"It was, and it still is," Sheila replied.

"You aren't going to see Adam. He's not going to Heaven."

"I know, I know, he even looks demonic. The homosexuality was one of the last things to come out."

"How did that make you feel? I mean, the guy you were sleeping with!"

"Well, I burned the mattress!"

"I mean, those aren't little things, leaving the cap off the toothpaste," Mitchell said.

"At this point I would be happy to see him again," Sheila said.

"Why?" Mitchell asked.

"Because then he would be right here again."

"I wish he would. But I don't think he could be treated. No, you can't be cured. You can't be cured from homosexuality or pedophilia. Do you think you will ever have the opportunity to hug him again? If he walked in here

right now? Sheila, look at me, two girls here talking,"
Rockey said.

"I don't know," Sheila replied.

"If we got people out by your house and we started
looking, do you think we could find Adam?"

"I don't think there is enough food or water around
for him to survive."

"Do you think it is possible you had the gun in your
pocket? Accidents happen. Accidents happen, Sheila,"
Rockey suggested.

"Not with my gun. I guess it's possible he accidentally
caught himself on fire. I don't know. I don't know. I
wasn't there!"

"We have to ask these questions. So let me ask you this
one. Did you hurt Adam?"

"Financially!" Sheila said—and they both laughed.

"But other than financially, did you hurt Adam?"

"Well, I told him that God would probably have him
burn in Hell."

"How about physically? Did you put an end to this?"
Mitchell queried.

"No!"

"Did anything happen physically to him to end his
life?" Mitchell asked.

"Not in my presence, not in my presence. I don't know
that his life is ended, I hope not!"

"What about outside of your presence? How can we be
sure of that so he won't have access to kids?" Mitchell
asked.

"He made it very, very clear to me that he was not going
to prison. I asked him to kill me one time. I had
a mild heart attack on the kitchen floor and he didn't
care. He just stared at me! For some reason God let me

read his mind for just a moment, and he kept thinking, 'Die. Die.' He was bleeding from his urethra while peeing. I told him he had AIDS. He admitted to having sex with men without condoms. I asked him, 'What does your mother do? Does she swallow it?' He said, 'Every time.'"

"Sheila, you asked the chief to end your life earlier today," Rockey said. Sheila answered, but her words were unintelligible. She was openly weeping. Rockey repeated, "Why did you want the chief to end your life today?"

"Because I just want to be where it is peaceful," Sheila answered.

"Do you think the bones are his?" Mitchell asked.

"I can't rule that out or in. I'm not trying to be cutesy. If he did it, he did it."

"Do you help him do it, so it gets done right?" Mitchell posed.

"There's no shame in helping someone kill themselves," Rockey said.

"I didn't!"

"Those cuts on your hands appear to be only a couple of days old," Mitchell said.

"No, they are older than that," Sheila responded.

"Are there any other cuts on your body?" Mitchell asked.

"I was in the woods. I just sensed someone in the woods. At two-thirty or three A.M., the deer begin to move. That's when they feel safest. I heard some noise and I thought, 'Huh? Is that him?' You don't move in the dark woods if there's a predator."

"Did Adam have mental-health problems?" Mitchell asked.

"Absolutely. First of all, he didn't have seizures. His mother manufactured that."

"What *did* he have?" Rockey asked.

"He was mentally slow, handicapped, mentally deficient. He is not retarded. No, he didn't behave that way, to me."

"Did he shower himself?" Mitchell asked.

"He bathed, and he bled in the tub. His penis. He just started bleeding out of his penis, and I don't know why. I said, 'Are you dying of AIDS?' He said, 'I do this sometimes.'"

"Do you take any prescription medications, Sheila?"

"I take Valium due to the anxiety over the Irish people."

"What about Ken?"

"Kenneth Countie is not on any prescription medication. If his mother is saying he's on anything, she is lying."

"I think he's dead," Mitchell abruptly said.

"Why?" Sheila asked.

"You haven't seen or heard from him in days."

"What is, is," she said.

"If you had hurt Ken, who would you confide in? Who's your best friend?" Mitchell asked.

"God."

"Who's your second best friend?"

"You. I don't hang out with anyone. That's the truth."

"What about Michelle?"

"Michelle and I are not that close."

At that point Sheila began to talk about how people only befriended her because they wanted to get close to her money. She began pawing around her things, in a sudden frenzy, because she couldn't find her credit card. After the troopers got her settled down, Mitchell asked how the Epping police had first become "involved in this." She said she had called someone and had played a tape. She began pulling papers out of her bag—checks, stock certificates—and she rambled about her finances.

Rockey steered her back to the subject by informing her that police were looking through a Dumpster for the large bone they had seen in her burn pile, the one that was missing the next time they came.

"I have no idea what that bone could be," Sheila said. She recalled coming home after shopping with Michelle, finding police poking around her yard, and her last trip to Wal-Mart with Adam.

"Miss Wendy Peterson thought I was suspicious because I was taking pictures. I was photographing her aisle, the Easter aisle, where she said I squeezed his arm. I was documenting it. Even though I'm losing weight, I'm not in shape. I'm so sore from my little walk." She rambled about dieting. Vanity struck and she decided she didn't want to be videotaped any longer, and again the troopers had to calm her.

"I'm sorry," she said. "I don't want to make waves with the brotherhood."

"We need to talk about Adam," Rockey said.

"I have to get out of this room, I'm going into a full-fledged migraine. I'm not joking. I'm having a heart attack," Sheila said.

"Sheila, we found bones in those ashes, human bones. Whose bones are they?" Rockey asked. "How did those bones get in the fire?"

"This sounds like a frame! I need an attorney."

"Is it possible he did something?"

"If he tortured me, I wouldn't admit it."

"Why not? Why not? Just come out with the truth. Sheila, it will make you feel better. This is on your chest like a tremendous weight," Mitchell encouraged.

"I'm just trying to survive, please. I'm going to be sick."

By that time the smell of rabbit urine in the small

room was starting to get to all of them and the interview ended. They had been able to get her to admit doing nothing more violent than slapping the missing young man.

TFC Rockey took Sheila back to the LaBarre residence. The women entered the farmhouse together. Sheila had a couple of things she wanted to show the trooper. One was a packed suitcase and the other was a written note that Sheila referred to as her "suicide note."

*My suicide is because I cannot bear the stress of everything. I am* innocent. *Does anyone care about women in this town?* it read.

Rockey read the note and remembered it as saying that on approximately March 22, 2006, Sheila had cremated a "very large rabbit close to the front ash can." She had not killed the rabbit, however. She believed it was Adam who had killed the rabbit. The note said that Adam was a pedophile and that she had taped confessions from him, that she was a Christian, who would go to Heaven, and that on approximately March 21, 2006, Adam had left the farm. He had left either on foot or in a car with someone. She wasn't sure. In the note Sheila claimed that Adam had "threatened to kill himself and jump in the Merrimack River, or set himself on fire" if Sheila played for anyone the tape of him confessing to molesting children. She also noted that the farmhouse was haunted:

*I cremated a very large rabbit on 3.22. I've already picked up most of the pieces of my beloved rabbit. I think Kenneth Countie might have killed the rabbit. I played that tape for Sgt. Gallagher and no one cares about me. I'm close to heart attack now. The Epping police only care about killing me or getting me to kill me. He, Countie, said he was three personalities and that he was stealing cash from me. He said he had videotape of him fingering and f\*\*\*ing the pussy of a small girl. He said he would* *rather die than go to prison. I did not hurt him. To Cindy Harvey* [a neighbor], *I hereby give my horses to you. Please keep them together. Dr. LaBarre loved you. Set the rabbits free. Please please be good to them, they are all I have in this world. Michelle Bennett can verify that I've been trying to help her with her beloved dog, Mercedes. A glass pot exploded and Countie was standing close to the stove, but he did* [not] *want to go to the hospital. So he and I took care of the wounds. If he died, he did it. I have been an enemy to pedophiles. Perhaps I have been framed by one of my enemies. This house is haunted. It always has been. Countie is a pedophile. Nobody knows about the children except me.*

# The Thorough Search

On Sunday, March 26, 2006, Dr. Sorg called Dr. Duval and confirmed that the photos she had received were of human bones. Dr. Duval immediately called Sergeant Richard Mitchell of the state police.

"They are most likely from a human hand and possibly the end of a forearm bone," Dr. Duval said.

Also on March 26, Exeter District Court judge Patricia L. DiMeo signed a search warrant allowing police full access to Sheila's farmhouse and property. Local and state police began a thorough search of Sheila's farmhouse, her land, as well as some of the neighbor's land. The search of the rolling farmland and rural subdivisions would continue for seventeen days.

Police found brownish droplets on the kitchen cabinets. Those droplets appeared to be consistent with blood. The largest stain was presumptive tested for blood, and that test was positive. There were also brown droplets in the living room, on the walls about three feet off the ground. The spatter covered an area three and a half feet high and six feet long. According to a police report, these stains were "consistent in size, shape, and manner" with blood.

Assistant Commander Mark Mudgett, of the state police's major crime unit, was part of the search team, and he noted a hot-air floor register that was on, next to the spot where the bed would have been located— that is, the mattress and box spring that were found outside in the fire. Mudgett examined the register closely and smelled what he categorized as a "vomitous odor."

In a bedroom on the first floor of the house, police found boxes that were haphazardly placed on the floor. On those boxes were found two reddish brown stains, which also appeared to be blood.

Mudgett looked inside the washing machine and found a leopard-skin-patterned comforter and wet clothing. Lifting the lid, Mudgett noted a "musty, putrefied" smell. When the comforter and clothes were removed from the machine, the comforter also reeked of vomit and decomposition.

Mudgett probably needed a little fresh air at that point, so he shifted his search to the grounds surrounding the house. On the outer edge of the LaBarre property, he located Sheila's Nissan truck. In the back of the pickup were yellow diesel fuel containers. The containers were empty and smelled of diesel fuel. They looked to be the same, or certainly similar to, the containers that Sheila had had with her on March 17 in the Wal-Mart. Police noted that the diesel fuel could not have been used to operate any of the farm vehicles. The only farm vehicle on the farm that used diesel fuel was an old tractor that was currently inoperable.

Not far from the pickup truck, draped across a

stone wall, was a coat with blood on it. The coat was photographed as it was found and bagged as evidence.

Mudgett also noted that the burn piles in front of the house, where the suspicious items had been found, were new. They were far more shallow than the deep well-like pits where previous burning had taken place.

The other vehicles on the property were a black Cadillac, a silver Mercedes, with vanity plates reading CAYCE (one of Sheila's favorite pseudonyms), and a GMC pickup truck. There was also a horse trailer, and a slide-on pickup truck camper.

Though hopes of finding Countie alive were mighty slim, Assistant Attorney General (AAG) Peter Odom, when asked to comment on the search of the farm, would not verify that a crime had been committed. "We're conducting an investigation into a missing person," Odom said. "Sometimes these things turn into homicides. Often they don't." Reporters might have come to their own conclusion regarding the true nature of the investigation based on the fact that Odom was assigned to the attorney general's homicide unit. "While we do have a concern, it would be premature to talk about foul play," Odom added.

The press spoke to Countie's family, and got a statement from the missing man's dad, also named Kenneth Countie, living in Tewksbury, Massachusetts. "I've been told not to make a comment for fear of jeopardizing the investigation," the elder Countie said. "We're just hoping and praying. We don't know anything yet. It's an ongoing investigation."

Reporters got a better indication of the situation when they tried to visit the LaBarre farm. They found the road leading to the Silver Leopard Farm blocked off by police, and were informed that the entire area—the farmhouse and the 115-acre farm—was considered one gigantic crime scene.

The press and the state's attorney general's office were unwilling to give the press Sheila's name, but neighbors quickly gave her up. Her name was Sheila LaBarre, they said, but they were unclear about who the missing man was.

"She's been living there a long time and she has had quite a few menfolk living with her," said Frances Allen, a neighbor who had lived on Red Oak Hill Road (different from but nearby Red Oak Hill Lane) for more than sixty years.

Neighbor Beth Harvey, who lived on the other side of Red Oak Hill, said, "Hopefully, the kid just ran away from here and is all right."

Daniel Harvey was the previous owner of the farm, and he had sold the property to Wilfred LaBarre many years before. The sale was made sometime in the 1970s. Daniel remembered that Wilfred paid him $14,000 for the house and the land. Daniel, who with his wife, Louise, still operated the Applehurst Farms on Red Oak Hill Road, said that Sheila was a piece of work. "You haven't lived until you've met Sheila," he said. He said he'd tried to find out from the cops what was going on over there, but they wouldn't tell him anything.

When Daniel and his wife, Louise, were informed that police were looking for a missing man named Kenneth Countie, Louise said Countie was just one in a series of young men she had seen on the farm. The men were always from out of the area, in their twenties, and only remained a short time. "We've even had some of them come down here, all beat up, and she'd be all beat up too," she said. "I remember this one fellow—this was about five years ago—he came in here, cold and dirty and smelly. We gave him some tea and some food. After that? I don't know. We didn't know what to think. Maybe she threw a tantrum. We drove the man to a nearby town. I didn't see him again. That was just one of them. I couldn't tell you how many there have been, but there's been quite a few." *Quite a few.* The words were haunting.

"I talked to Sheila not that long ago," Louise continued. "She approached me and she seemed scared. I asked her what was wrong and she said that she hadn't seen Countie in a while. She told me she had sent him to feed the farm animals, but he didn't do it. He took off. She said that was about a week ago." So, according to Sheila, Countie's last task was to feed the farm animals. Was it a sick play on words?

Selectman Tom Gauthier told reporters that the town of Epping was just starting to realize that there was something going on. "Nothing like this has ever happened around here before. Nothing that I can recall," he said. "I was briefed by Chief Dodge. The police are doing a good job at this point. They've got a good handle on it."

The local grapevine was fed by curiosity over the helicopters that were hovering above the LaBarre farm, circling over Red Oak Hill and nearby Cilley Road. At least one of those helicopters was from the TV news, taking footage for the evening's broadcast. Down below, police and volunteers could be seen lined up and walking slowly over the grounds so that not a single square foot of real estate would go unexamined for forensic evidence.

# The Paquins

While everyone was talking about Sheila, the murder suspect herself was not doing a very good job of fleeing. Carrying a rabbit in her arms, she entered a PETCO on South Willow Street in the city of Manchester, twenty miles west of Epping.

Sheila had a keen instinct for finding people she could manipulate, and that instinct didn't fail her now that she was in deep trouble. In the store she met a Manchester brother and sister named Michael and Rebecca "Becky" Paquin, twenty-nine and thirty-one years old, both of whom were on disability because of a mental handicap. Michael was the more severely handicapped. He also had a seizure disorder and anger management difficulties. Sheila offered the siblings $100 to look after her rabbit for her. They took her up on her offer and she bought them a rabbit cage.

As evidence of Sheila's ceaseless ability to charm when she wanted, Rebecca took Sheila home with her, and there Sheila met Rebecca's fifty-three-year-old mother,

Pamela Paquin, who was also on disability and hadn't worked since 1991.

"It was the afternoon and I was taking a nap when they came over," Pamela remembered. "The kids told me they met a rich lady at PETCO. I said, 'Really? Who?' They said the lady bought them a cage for this rabbit. I said, 'What?' I was surprised they brought her home. When I first met her, she was really nice. I wasn't afraid of her or anything like that."

After buying a meal at KFC, Sheila offered the Paquins a total of $400 to take care of her rabbits and horses. Needing the money, they eagerly agreed—although they would later have to give up the horses when taking care of them turned out to be more expensive than they had counted on.

"I was supposed to go to her property and take care of her horses, but I couldn't do it because it cost too much money. I had to let them go. I had three of her rabbits, but I gave them away," Pamela Paquin later recalled.

On that first night Sheila ended up watching the evening news with Pamela in Pamela's room. When the story came on about the missing persons investigation for Kenneth Countie, Sheila began to weep. The woman, of course, asked what was the matter.

"That's my boyfriend," Sheila said through her tears. "He's not missing."

Sheila went on to tell Pamela, whom she'd only known for hours, that Kenneth was a guy who molested children, that he'd been abused by his mother, that she and Kenneth had been cremating rabbits, and that he might have fallen into the fire. She also said that there was a chance that he had committed suicide, or been burned. Whatever, Sheila said, she was being framed.

"It was when she started talking about Kenneth that I

first thought she was a little nutty," Pamela later said. "She told me that was why she wanted me to take care of her rabbits. She knew she was going to jail. She didn't say she did it, though."

It was Sunday night. Sheila called the cops. She spoke directly to Chief Dodge. She told him she'd been sick, slept in her car, went to Wal-Mart in Portsmouth to clean up, went to the SPCA to get her Dalmatian, and that she was going to spend the night with some "handicapped friends" in Manchester. Chief Dodge told her to keep him posted on her comings and goings, and she said she would. Sheila talked Pamela into helping her avoid the cops, and she spent the night in the Paquin home.

The next day, March 27, Rebecca Paquin took Sheila to buy new clothes at Wal-Mart, then to see a lawyer, but the lawyer wanted $50,000 up front to represent her, so she took Sheila to the bank. Business done, she took Sheila to a cemetery, where she could hide. She called the state police and told them about her strange encounter with Sheila. Rebecca was visited by TFC John Marasco and Detective Marc Turner.

At 2:15 that afternoon Pamela Paquin and her friend Sandra Sharpentier came in person to the Epping Police Department. She told police pretty much the same story, that her daughter had met Sheila at a pet store, brought her home to the Paquin residence on Hayward Street in Manchester, and how, during the course of the evening, Sheila said that the man staying with her, "Adam," was a homosexual and a pedophile who might have committed suicide or been burned. She told police that Sheila paid her and her daughter $100 apiece to watch the rabbits she had brought with her.

"She sold me her horses," Pamela said. "I have a receipt for the horses. That's why I came here. I want to claim them."

As long as she was there, police pumped her for all of her story, and she did have more details to offer.

"She told me that she had gone to see an attorney and that she and the attorney had discussed a retainer," Pamela said. "They had also discussed possible bail for different murder charges, and he had told her to not talk to the police."

Police determined that the attorney Sheila had consulted was Michael Craig, of Manchester. Craig had agreed to represent her on the condition she pay a hefty retainer. Sheila said she would return with the money, but she never did.

According to Pamela, Sheila told her flat out that she knew she was going to be arrested. Sheila said she was being "set up" for the young man's death and she was going to have to leave.

"Before I came here, I took Sheila to the TD Bank North in Manchester. I watched while she withdrew $85,778.21 from the bank. Fifty thousand was in the form of a bank check, and the rest was cash," Pamela said.

"When did you last see her?" police asked the woman.

"I dropped her off at the side of the road so she could go check on her animals. Me and Sandra are supposed to come pick her up at the same spot after a while," Pamela said.

On Monday, March 27, the bones that had been found in Sheila's fire were physically taken to Dr. Duval in Concord. Identifying bones from a photograph could only achieve a certain degree of accuracy. To be absolutely positive she would have to see the bones in person, and this was done. Dr. Duval did not have to look at the actual bones for long to confirm her opinion that they came from a human hand and forearm.

# "Are your
hands clean?"

At about four o'clock on the afternoon of March 27, police stopped Sheila, who was driving through Epping behind the wheel of the same car Pamela Paquin and Sandra Sharpentier had used to visit the police station earlier in the afternoon.

Oddly, Sheila was alone in the front seat, and Pamela and Sandra were together in the backseat when the stop was made.

"Sandra and I went to pick Sheila up at the cemetery. She was driving because the cemetery was kind of crappy, so I let her drive out. I didn't care for it. It was bad. The road was bad. We didn't like the way she was driving either. She wasn't driving very good. She was driving kind of fast and crazy and Sandra said, 'Maybe you better let Pam drive,'" Pamela later remembered. "That's when the cops stopped us and they took her from there."

As the Paquins' car pulled out of the cemetery and onto Route 27, the car was spotted by two cops in an unmarked car, Lieutenant Wallace and Sergeant Newman.

Wallace later recalled: "My assignment that day was to find Sheila. We spotted and began to follow a Toyota Camry. After driving ahead and turning around, we pulled up nose-to-nose with the Camry. Sheila was driving. Trapped, Sheila followed instructions."

Sheila was brought to the Epping police station, where she, according to the police report, *made repeated statements about the large sum of money that she had withdrawn, and stating that it was "all she had."*

All but $900 of the original amount that Pamela Paquin had seen Sheila withdraw from the bank was in the car.

Once again Sheila's interrogation was videotaped, but Mitchell and Rockey were gone. Asking the questions were Chief Dodge and Sergeant Estabrook, who read Sheila her Miranda rights and quizzed her to make sure she knew what they meant.

"It means that I can keep my big mouth shut," Sheila said. "You guys, I have to be honest with you, I'm having chest pain."

"Do you waive your Miranda rights? Are you willing to make a statement?"

"As long as I don't get the pokey, the slammer," she said with a giggle. "Can I put some lip salve on?"

They asked her again, and this time she said yes, she waived her rights. Estabrook is a no-nonsense cop. The tone of this interrogation was very different. He made it clear that he would take no guff from her. He wanted to know how she met Kenny. She told him the story of Tele-Mates, now in greater detail, how she admitted to being forty-seven and talked and talked about her life on the farm, and he never hung up on her. At one point she told Kenny she had to cut wood. She put the phone down, did her chore, and returned. He was still on the line, patiently waiting; so they met in person at the hotel bar.

"I asked him, 'What do you want with me?' He asked me if we could get a room. I said, 'Possibly.' I was nervous meeting him, because he was in a corner with a hood. The first thing that came into my head, the first thought, was 'pedophile.' I swear it was, and I should have just exited, I should have just exited. But I didn't. The music in the bar was too loud. I told him we didn't need to get a room there. He said he wanted to get away from his family, that he couldn't take it anymore. This is sad for me to think about."

"Why are you sad?" Estabrook asked.

Sheila didn't answer, but she continued with her story. Her voice was calm and her thinking lucid as she gave a detailed description of her first sexual encounter with Kenneth Countie.

"We went out and we sat together in my Cadillac. We burned a little (smoked pot). It was his, not mine. Am I going to get arrested for that? Your badge is so shiny. Do you polish it yourself?

"Anyway, he went to kiss me. I told him, 'I don't have time to play games. Homey don't play that. I don't have time in my life [to] f*** around with anyone. I hang by a thread every day. My animals are my priority. I'm forty-seven and you're twenty-five, so what do you want from me?' He said, 'I wanna be with you.' He was very aggressive sexually. He started touching me. I'm a complete heterosexual, I like men. Anyway, I started getting turned on. He started to touch my breasts and

I said, 'Wait, wait, wait. Did you bring the lambskin condoms?' On the phone I told him I was allergic to rubber, latex, and to bring lambskin, in case we wanted to have sex. He said no and that perturbed me, and I said, 'Why the hell not? I could have gone to Wal-Mart.' He was very assertive, aggressive—not violent aggressive, and he said, 'I want to touch your pussy.' I said, 'No.' He said, 'I want to touch your pussy.' I said, 'Okay, go ahead. Go ahead and touch it. Are your hands clean?' He touched my pussy with his right hand. I was already lubricated. He touched me, fondled my breast, and I said, 'Okay, stop, here's where we stop and we have to talk. What do you want from me? If it's money, you won't get it. If it's pussy . . . if it's oral, I don't suck dick until I get into a relationship. Bingo, I hit a nerve, didn't I? Now I know you like to be sucked off. Now you know I don't like to suck off. And I can tell by looking that you like it swallowed. If I like someone, I want to hear dirty talk.' This went on for some time, the back-and-forth. He persisted aggressively, you know, as a man can do some-times. Eventually I said, 'You want it, take it, I can give it. The only way we're going to have sex in this car is if I lay on my back and you lay on top of me.' He wore a size-thirteen shoe. You can't tell penis size from a shoe, that's a myth. Hey, is this going to be played in court? I would be so embarrassed if this is played in court. Anyway, he penetrated me. He climaxed pretty fast. I said, 'Are you a premature ejaculator?' He said, 'Sometimes, but you're pretty tight.' I relit what's called the roach. I was uncomfortable with my behavior, upset. I wanted to go into the house and immediately douche, but I didn't. I was afraid of VD, AIDS. We had sex again. I like that, I like men that can do that. Do it twice. I mean it's okay if they can't. He left me a clue that he was a pedophile bisexual, because he didn't kiss me while we had sex. He got in his car and I thought he was following me, but when I got home, I looked in the rearview mirror and he wasn't there. I called his cell and asked why he ditched me. He did call me back. I don't remember if it was that night."

She lost her focus at that point. She talked some about Kenny's mental breakdown, his pedophilia, and the animals on her farm, which she was worried about.

"I feel, obviously, that I've been framed. I miss Adam. I love Adam. I miss Adam. Kenny is a son of a bitch. Kenny is a pill-popping son-of-a-bitch addict. Ken is a heroin addict and a crack smoker. I said, 'There's crack in that pipe.' I asked him to leave my home after he confessed all those acts of pedophilia to me. He just went into this paranoia. He had to have a lot of sugar, candy. But if he is truly what I think he is, which is a heroin user. I don't remember how long it was between the first time and the second time. I went to pick him up. I had a lot of things on my mind. I had to pay the government a quarter of a million dollars in taxes. When his mother called, screaming at him, this woman gets louder than me, she does not have a British accent. They knew he was coming. I'm positive they knew he was coming with me and they filed what I'm *still* calling a false missing persons report. She's screaming, 'You pussy! You pussy! You're a pussy! Hey, you better get your ass back down here right now.' Or something like that. He said, 'Listen, leave me alone. I'm tired of you, I've had it with you.' And I'm thinking, big mistake. I got on and said, 'I'm Sheila LaBarre.' And she said, 'Shut up! Shut up! You're going to listen to me.' I said, 'I'm not going to listen to you at all.' I didn't curse her, I just hung up the phone. And later he wanted to change his name. Adam Olympian LaBarre. I came up with Olympian. I came up with Adam. But he wanted to change his name."

"Why did you choose that name?"

"Because he can run like a cheetah, well not seventy miles an hour, but he can run. I told him he just seemed like Adam to me, and he told me he wanted to be LaBarre. I said, 'Wait a minute, you want the LaBarre name?' He said, 'Yes, I love you.' I said, 'A lot of people don't like me in this town.' I told him I was gonna need a prenup. I said, 'That means you are not f***ing me over. I've gone through hell and high water. If you are looking for money, you won't find it here. You can help me in Somersworth, you can help me with the punch list. You can't just sit around and go *click click click click* and play hockey. He said, 'I love you.' I just went off on that. I said, 'What are you trying to get away from?' And he said, 'My. F***ing. Mother.' I said to him, 'Are you doing your mother?' And he just froze. I thought, 'Okay, he's not ready to confess right now.' You know, I have a background in surgery. Oh yes. When you see a dilation and cutterage performed every single day in every single hospital, gentlemen, *that* is an abortion."

Estabrook said, "Sheila, we're talking about—"

"So he started confessing things to me. It started coming out. So finally he confessed to me he had a very routine schedule—aww, this is horrible. He said that he—he said, his own words, 'I'm not doing it anymore, but I had a great schedule meeting my mother on Tuesday and Thursdays to have intercourse.' I said, 'I am so mad at you. If you had told me that, I would never have met you, never. But the Bible says to forgive, so I'm going to do my best to forgive. When you're with me, you're not f***ing her.' He said, 'Believe me, I don't want to be f***ing her anymore.' He mentioned Lisa, his stepbrother's daughter. They'd had her when they were fourteen. I asked him where she slept."

Estabrook wanted to move on: "Okay, he's living with you now. You have a prenup, he's going to help you in Somersworth. He can't lay around [and] watch TV," Estabrook said.

"But he did and I let him. I told him he can't live with me if he is a bastard. You know, if he is banging his mother, he really is a m-f***er. One morning I woke up and found him prowling through my house, looking for money. I said, 'There's nothing in this house except pennies, change.' You know, I gave him a polygraph. I had him tested. The polygraph man said, 'No deception detected.' Something like that. Kenneth cried during the test because he had to use his real name. I didn't stick around for the test. I said, 'See you in forty-five!' I went on a drive to the bank. You know, for years Dr. LaBarre and I only argued about one thing, how much money he should leave his children. He said fifty K apiece and I said that's not nearly enough, and he said, 'Sheila, you don't know my children.'"

"Sheila, let's get back to Adam. I would like to discuss the last time you saw Adam."

"I was up all night. I was not taking anything, but in the past I had been legally prescribed medication for anxiety and pain."

"Did you go to bed with him on the last night?"

"Yes, but I told him to stay on his side of the bed."

"Did you talk before going to sleep?"

"I asked him if there was someone who could come

pick him up. He was a pedophile and I couldn't let him stay with me anymore. When I woke up, he was gone."

"The big bone the police saw in your fire. Where did it come from, Sheila? Where did it go?"

"I don't know."

"Why did you burn the mattress?"

"Because I slept on it with a pedophile."

"When police arrived, you ran into the house. Why did you do that?"

"I was burning clothes and other household items. I ran, because I am intimidated by the police."

"Why were you covered with soot when we came to see you the next day?"

"I was sifting through the ashes, looking for rabbit bones and metal objects."

"Why did you ask the police to shoot you and take you out of your misery?"

"I was just joking."

"You weren't joking," Estabrook said, angry now. "To me, you were panicked. You were screaming. You're crying. You're hysterical. You're making it sound like a casual joke. It was not. Why did you tell us that you were burning a pedophile?"

"I didn't say that. Check the tape. I didn't—"

"Why did you tell us that Kenneth was in the Wal-Mart bag?"

"I didn't."

"You are lying, Sheila. I think you killed Kenneth!"

"No!" she said, pounding the table with her palm. "It was those Irishmen. They're out to get me. They've been lurking in my woods. They got him!" Sheila smiled a little, a hopeful smile.

Estabrook screamed, "You think it's funny that Kenny

is dead? That Adam is dead? Why did you kill him! How did he get in there? You killed him? How did he get in the bag? Why are you laughing? You told me it was him! You said, 'He's in that bag'!"

Sheila said, "We talked about teeth. Because he had beautiful teeth."

"How do you explain all of the blood in your house?"

"The only blood was on the sheet. He picked a scab on his penis."

"If he's alive, you're not helping us find him. You burned his shoes. That's not helping Kenny."

"Adam."

"You told the chief he was dead. 'He's in the bag.' Listen to what you said. You said, 'He's in the bag,' Sheila. What does that mean?"

"I did not kill him. I didn't. I mean that I did not kill Kenneth, I mean Adam. He asked to be called Adam. I did not do anything to him."

"Well, you know what, a jury will make that decision. Not us. Not you. A jury of your peers."


It was 12:40 A.M., March 28, 2006. Questioning had gone on for five hours, the longest interrogation in Epping history, police figured. They told her they had seized her car and home. She asked where she should go and how she would get there. They said they'd drop her off someplace, as long as it was within a reasonable distance.

And although the case against Sheila was rapidly growing, she was once again released into society. When Assistant Commander Mudgett last saw her, she was dressed all in black. It was 7:00 A.M. on March 28, and she was at the Mall of New Hampshire.

Police must have regretted releasing her. By the end of the day, there was an all-points bulletin (APB) out for her arrest—and they didn't know where she was.

# "'Vengeance is mine,' said the Lord."

On Tuesday, during the early morning of March 28, a three-hundred-pound, fifty-year-old man named Steven Martello picked up Sheila in his station wagon along Interstate 293, near Manchester. Originally from Massachusetts, he'd been living in New Hampshire since early adulthood. Martello was going through a rough patch. He'd just broken up with his second wife and had his nine-year-old son in the car, had to take him to school. He'd never been rich. These days he was making a living as a courier, delivering blood to hospitals.

Now it was about 7:15 A.M. When he first saw Sheila, she was standing in the breakdown lane, not far from South Willow Street. She wasn't near a disabled car, but any woman alone walking down the road waving at cars is in some kind of distress. That was the kind of guy he was. If one of his daughters was on the road and in trouble, he wished someone would stop and pick her up and help her out.

She was wearing black pants, a black top, a black jacket

with fur on it, and loafers on her feet. He would later describe her as "kind of cute," between five foot seven and five foot ten, light skin, brown eyes, and weighing approximately 160 pounds. He said her hair was long and blond, with black roots showing in the front.

Even though there was an APB out for Sheila that day, Martello said he hadn't been listening to the radio or looked at a newspaper, so he had no clue when he hit the brakes and pulled over to the shoulder. To a hitch-hiker, there's no brighter sight than brake lights lighting up, and she hurried up beside the car before the dude changed his mind.

"Can I help you?" Martello asked.

The woman said that her car had broken down and she'd had a fight with her boyfriend and she had to get to Massachusetts, where she was going to contact a lawyer.

"Dorchester," Sheila replied.

"Sorry, I'm not going that way right now." He told her he had to take his son to school. He didn't mention it, but he also had to pick up his soon-to-be ex-wife and take her to work.

"Maybe you could just drop me off someplace and take me to Dorchester later?" Sheila asked. "I'll pay you."

"I can take you as far as Derry."

"That'll be okay. Could you turn off the radio, please? I have a splitting headache."

"Sure thing," Martello said. *Click*. Off it went.

She said her name was Cayce. Later she said her name was Sheila, then Cayce again. She switched back and forth. She was well-mannered and well-dressed. There was something in the tone of her voice that led Martello to believe—correctly—that the payment was going to come in flesh rather than cash form. She was attractive and nice to him in that way women could be. Maybe both flesh and cash. Whatever, he was pretty sure he was getting laid. He pulled off the major highway and found a place to unload his passenger. He'd be back.

"I wasn't worried that she was violent because of the way she was," Martello later recalled. "She was polite and friendly. She even kissed me on the cheek when I dropped her off at a Derry Burger King to eat. I told her I'd be back in a half hour, forty-five minutes, to pick her up, and she said, 'No problem.' I dropped my son off at school and took my wife to work. I drove back to Derry, and, honestly, I didn't think she was going to be there. But she was, eating and writing a letter."

At 8:10 A.M. Sheila told Martello that she wasn't ready to leave the Burger King yet. She had to finish writing the letter and he said that was fine. She told him that the letter she had written was to a friend of hers in Manchester.

"I stayed with her last night," Sheila said. "She's watching my rabbits. You want something to eat?"

"No thanks," Martello replied. He took her tray for her and dumped its contents in the rubbish.

Sheila told Martello that she was wealthy, that she owned property in Somersworth and Epping.

"I'm going to retain a famous lawyer, the one my husband the doctor always uses. You've heard of him. His name is F. Lee Bailey," she bragged. She had to go to one of his "satellite offices" up there. She also had an interview with another lawyer, a different lawyer, because of tax issues on her property.

Martello couldn't tell if she was bullshitting or not. She could be telling the truth. She had a pocketbook and in it she had a snap change purse, and in the purse was the cash. She said she'd pay for gas and flashed that massive wad. She pulled it out and peeled off five $20 bills. They stopped for gas at a Mobil station across the street from the Burger King. She gave him $100 and wasn't interested in change. When they drove past a Derry police car on Route 102, she made an excuse to duck down. She said she had dropped something and got down, but Martello didn't hear anything fall and suspected she was hiding her face from the cops.

"I have a medical degree," she said at one point.

There was some fuss about having enough postage. One stamp wasn't enough and two was too much, so she had Martello drive around looking for the post office. When he couldn't find it, he parked the car behind a store, but Sheila said that wasn't a good idea. Cops might think they were "doing stuff." She agreed to put extra postage on the envelope. They went to a mailbox and Martello volunteered to put the letter in the box for her. When he did, he read the front. It was addressed to Pamela Paquin.

As they drove, she talked about herself, this time claiming she was a widow. Her husband had been a doctor. She owned property in the Dover area. She owned many cars. She reached in her pocketbook and pulled out what seemed like a handful of car registrations, just to prove she wasn't just "blowin' smoke."

She said that she was tired and her feet hurt, and asked if she could climb in the back and go to sleep. Martello said no, because they were going to Massachusetts, where there was a seat belt law.

"I don't need to get stopped," he said, and she agreed 100 percent. She reclined the front passenger seat, took her shoes off, and closed her eyes.

She said she'd been hiking in the woods with friends the day before and that was why her feet hurt. As she reclined, Martello looked down and could see little "bloodstains" on her ankles.

He told her about his troubles too—marital, financial. She said she might be able to help him. She said she might be looking soon for a maintenance man at one of her properties. Martello said that would be great, but he wasn't counting his chickens. After all, he'd just met the woman and they were just "shootin' the shit."

She said she liked his long hair and asked if he was a biker. He told her he rode a Honda. Every once in a while, she'd reach over and touch his leg. She told him she liked him.

Once in the Boston area, they stopped at a CVS—Sheila told the man that she needed hair dye, condoms, and douche products. She was allergic to latex condoms, so she bought the Trojan lambskin types. It was really lamb's intestines and they had an advantage beyond being a nonallergen. Lambskin was best for tactile sensation and transmitting body warmth. When a man was inside a woman, that was what was needed. *Like wearing no raincoat at all, baby.*

Martello was now positive she wanted to get laid. But did he want to? He wasn't full speed ahead. There was something odd here, a woman walking down the road alone with thousands of dollars in cash on her. While Cayce was in the drugstore, Martello called the Manchester police and told them about the woman. *Had anyone escaped from the women's prison at Goffstown? Anything robbed? Any escaped mental patients? No. No. No. Okay, thanks.* That was the best thing to do. Now he felt free to get horny.

Back in the car she told Martello that someone had tried to grab her breast in the CVS, but he didn't believe her. She told him she wanted to go to a shoe store in the same strip mall as the CVS. This time he went in with her. She bought a pair of black boots with fur on them. In the shoe store she hugged her pocketbook tightly. Made sense, considering how much money was in it, but she also acted too nice to the salespeople, sugary sweet, like life was one big act.

"That pin you're wearing is lovely," she said to the salesgirl. "Reminds me of one I own."

She left a tip. In a *shoe store*.

From there, Martello drove to a Ramada Inn in Dorchester, but "she wanted a room with a king-sized bed and they didn't have one.

"She said, 'I know how hotels work. Do you have anything on hold?'" *No. Try the Quality Inn.* So they didn't even move the car. The walked down a little service road to a nearby Quality Inn instead. *King-sized beds? No problem.* He remembered the room they were given: room 427.

"She went in and started fumbling for her ID," Martello said. "She said, 'I don't have an ID. Show yours.' So I did, and we got the room." Sheila gave Martello $120 for the room, which cost $102. She told him to keep the change.

In the room he went to turn on the TV and she told him no. She said she wasn't feeling up to television. She asked him if he wanted a cup of coffee and he said sure. She made coffee. They sat and "shot the breeze."

When the coffee was done, he declined another cup and she went to the bathroom. She came out wearing her shirt, her new boots, and a towel she had wrapped around her waist. She told him she had douched and he said that was nice. She said that she was a little bit kinky and she liked to do it with her boots on. He said that was okay with him. She didn't take the towel off until after she'd got under the covers of the king-sized bed. He took his clothes off, got in bed. The first condom broke.

She took it off, threw it away, and put a new one on for him. There was nothing unusual about the sex and they had no conversation during it. After, when she was sitting at the table, he noticed she was all marked up.

"I had touched her arm, and she yelled," he said. "She had cuts on her knuckles, up and down, and black and blues—even a grab mark." Martello didn't ask about the bruises because, as he put it, "I didn't want to know."

He was going to throw the used condom in the rubbish, but she stopped him.

"You got to flush it down the toilet," she said. "If you don't, the chambermaids find them and use them to impregnate themselves."

*Okay, whatever,* he thought silently, and he flushed the used lambskin. When he came out of the bathroom, she went in so she could douche again.

There was some more chitchat. He told her that he was looking for a place to live, that he was losing his home in his current separation. She said she was thinking about moving on also, maybe going to Florida. She said she would take him with her, but he wasn't buying it.

As the sexual afterglow faded, Sheila stopped being nice. She told him her ex had been a pedophile. Martello wasn't sure what she meant by that, but he remembered that she added, "All cops are pedophiles. How would you feel if someone touched your son?" she asked.

"I don't know."

"Would you hurt them?"

"Probably."

"Would you kill them?"

"Probably."

"Pedophiles must die," she said. It sounded like a rehearsed slogan to him.

She told Martello that he should tell no one about

their encounter, and that if he did, a sex offender would come and harm his son. The sex offender, she said, was a very powerful person, and there was no way he could be stopped.

"You know I died and came back," she said. "I talked to God and the Apostles."

Martello said he didn't know.

"You just had sex with an angel," she said.

At that point she once again went into her spiel about sex offenders and police officers, a subject that gave Martello a strong urge to flee, now that the sex was over.

"My ex-boyfriend was a pedophile. I found child pornography in a bureau drawer," she said. "I brought it to the police and they destroyed it, because they were friends of his."

He dressed hurriedly. He had to go anyway. He had to get back to New Hampshire to pick up his son after school.

She asked him to get her a prepaid cell phone and he said no. She offered to take him shopping at Target and buy some clothes for his son, because she understood he was a single dad who was struggling. But, now dressed, Martello said he had to get out of there. He had to pick up his kid and he didn't want to be late. She agreed that taking care of his son was important. She looked at the clock and said that he'd better go.

"Are you busy later?" she asked.

"I don't think so," he replied.

"Would you like to come back?"

"Sure," he said, not wanting to offend her. He gave her his cell phone number and she wrote it down backward. It was in "code," she said.

"That way if my boyfriend ever found it, he wouldn't

know what was going on," she explained. "That way he can't come and hurt your son."

With a hug and a kiss, he left her there in the hotel room and never saw her again. That evening, Sheila made the six o'clock TV news and Martello saw her photo. Despite the certain embarrassment, he decided that he should do his civic duty and tell the cops what he knew. He drove to the state police station known as Troop A. After observing that Martello was calm, and didn't appear drunk or impaired by drugs, police allowed him to sit and write a long and thorough statement regarding his experiences with Sheila. He couldn't spell "pedophile," so he used "sex offender" instead. He wrote quickly, even though he didn't have his glasses, and though he got the order of some events mixed up, he thought he did a pretty good job of telling the story of what happened.

"They told me how she stabbed a guy in the head with scissors, and I said, 'Well, I'm glad she liked me.'"

Martello wrote that Sheila had seemed pretty wacky: *She kept saying, "'Vengeance is mine,' said the Lord." She said she had died and come back. She was sent back to Earth as an angel and she talked to God and the apostles in Hebrew.*

In the meantime the search of the farm continued. Criminalist Kim Rumrill, of the New Hampshire State Police Forensic Laboratory, came to the LaBarre farm on March 28 and searched inside the house.

If there had been a TV show called *CSI: New Hampshire*, Rumrill would have been one of the stars. She had the rank of criminalist II, and her specialty was serology and DNA analysis. Rumrill was experienced in processing crime scenes, as well as in documenting and preserving evidence. Her first order of business was taking a look at the spatter in the living room, where Sheila's bed was previously located.

She observed cast-off blood spatter on the walls and on the floor. She knew that cast-off blood spatter is a pattern caused when an object bearing blood is in motion. She also saw that there were numerous blood droplets along the floor in the walkway area of the adjacent dining room.

Also in the dining room there was a chair at the base of the stairs. Rumrill observed blood droplets on the arm of the chair. The seat cushion for the chair was missing.

From the dining room Rumrill moved into the kitchen, where she found more cast-off blood spatter in and around the sink, on the cabinets, about two feet up from the floor, and also on the ceiling.

In the kitchen was a woodstove. There were droplets of what appeared to be blood on the floor next to the stove, and Rumrill also observed near the stove a heel print in blood.

Next to the kitchen was the laundry room, where the leopard-skin-patterned comforter that reeked of putrefaction had previously been discovered inside the washing machine.

Next to the washing machine was a half bath—that is a toilet and sink, but no bathtub. In the sink was a half-gallon container of laundry bleach. It was almost empty.

From there, Rumrill went up the stairs to the second floor. Up there, she discovered the full bathroom. Like in most bathrooms, the tub was ceramic and the walls were tiled. Both the tub and the walls showed cast-off spatter appearing to be blood. Looking up, Rumrill noticed that there was blood on the bathroom ceiling as well.

A second scientist from the crime lab, Tim Jackson—who, like Rumrill, held the rank of criminalist II—was also on the scéne. He worked as part of the identification unit in the lab; as part of his duties, he processed crime scenes and collected evidence. Jackson used leuco crystal violet (LCV)—a reagent that turned bright purple/blue when it came into contact with blood—on the tub and sink in the upstairs bathroom. The LCV reacted in both the sink and the tub. Revealed by the reagent were diluted stains over the entire surfaces of both fixtures.

Rumrill noted that not all of the blood spatter appeared to be the same age. Some was old, covered in a layer of dust, while other spatter appeared relatively new.

"How much blood would you say there is?" Rumrill was asked as an arrest warrant for Sheila was being prepared.

"A lot more than from an average cut" was her wry reply.

# Like Nutsville

On March 29 the bones, already identified as human by Dr. Duval, were transported to the lab of forensic anthropologist Dr. Marcella Sorg. Dr. Sorg confirmed that at least some of the Wal-Mart bag bones "were human in nature, of an adult that was under thirty-five years in age, most likely male, and most likely in its twenties."

Dr. Duval had been busy analyzing the remainder of the bag's contents, the product of Sheila's all-night sifting, and the contents of several buckets of ash that had been seized by police from the burn pits. From among this material Dr. Duval identified skull fragments, spinal bones, a rib, forearm bones, hand bones, feet bones, including toes, and three teeth, which she believed to be human.

A forensic odontologist—a dentist who specialized in making identifications of unknown human remains through dental records—was called to look at the teeth. Two of the teeth were ID'd as belonging to an animal. The third was human.

\* \* \*

In the meantime, on the outside, reporters sought witnesses who could give them fresh Sheila material. One such witness was Marcel Bruno, of Epping, who had once been Bill LaBarre's patient. "He was an intelligent man," Bruno said of the chiropractor. "He had an excellent standing in the community. But he fell under her control. He was a very good doctor, and a wonderful person—but she wasn't. I don't know what happened to him. Sheila had been a receptionist at the clinic. Neither me nor my wife, Martha, ever heard of Wilfred and Sheila being formally married, although Sheila did use his surname. Sheila took a larger and larger role in the business as the years went by. One time, sometime in the 1990s, I arrived at the clinic and found that Sheila had thrown a fit and kicked everyone out. I don't know what triggered her outburst, but just as I was showing up, they all came flying out the door."

Martha added, "But a couple of weeks later, we came back and she was just as nice as pie."

Another patient, Phil Bane, from Freedom, had no unpleasant memories of Sheila. "She was attractive, wore her hair long, and had a heavy Southern accent. She was cheerful, a little flighty, but never violent," Bane said. "She seemed like a nice enough person. I always thought she and the doctor were married."

Neighbor Bruce Allen recalled, "Police used to get called to the house all the time. I didn't know what for. There seemed to be a lot of coming and going on that road and, to be honest, I don't know what was going on. She wasn't very pleasant as a neighbor. She liked to talk about picking up men. She told me how she picked out the ones she liked and would bring them home. Tensions between me and her had been going on for a long time. It got to the point where I didn't want to walk down that road because I was afraid I might run into her."

Tom Sutcliffe, who lived one mile from the LaBarre farm, told reporters that he had only met Sheila once in his life, and that had been two weeks earlier. He admitted that he had been slightly unnerved by the experience. "She stopped by my house and ended up staying for two hours," Sutcliffe said. "I think she was on drugs. It was like nutsville. We'd never met this lady before and she proceeded to sit there and talk to us for two hours about all issues in her life. She was wearing a sweatshirt. She had a bad dye job. Her hair was pulled back into a ponytail. She told me she had footed the bill for her brother's thirty-two-hundred-dollar funeral. She said she briefly brought to the farm a man she met on the Internet. She made us promise that we would contact her family if anything should happen to her."

On the farm the search continued to be fruitful. On March 30 Assistant Commander Mudgett was searching through a hutch-type cupboard when he discovered a knife. On the knife was a brownish red substance, which he believed to be blood. Later tests would prove that the substance was indeed human blood. Mudgett also found a notebook in the cupboard. In it was writing that appeared consistent with Sheila's handwriting. Supporting the theory that Kenny had not been Sheila's only victim, the notebook contained writings dated between July and November 2005—before she ever met Countie. The notebook contained a crude drawing made up of circles of a horizontal body, under which she had written, *110 pounds, 5'4". 1. Incinerated-burned-ashes-flushed scatter; 2. Water- 3. Bury c shovel; 4. private pilot/helicopter/boat;*

*DEATH* (which was circled); *Torch* (erased but still visible). On the next page of the notebook was written *Daniel 3; fiery furnace; Hotel furnace?; Crematoriums* (this word circled); *4000F.* Police believed that Daniel 3 was a reference to a biblical passage. In that chapter of the Bible, Nebuchadnezzar set up a golden statue and commanded all to fall down before it and adore. When three children refused to do so, they were cast into a fiery furnace.

Also searching the farm on March 30 were Deputy Fire Marshall John Raymond and his dog, Clancy. The canine was trained to detect arson by sniffing out the presence of fire accelerants. Raymond told police on the scene that diesel fuel was preferable in many cases to gasoline as an accelerant because it burned longer and had a lower flash point, which meant that it wouldn't flash up at you if you were pouring it onto an open flame. Clancy sniffed around the farm and twice alerted, indicating the presence of accelerants: once in the area of the ash can, and again near the burnt mattress. In addition to these locations, two more burn piles and one ash "dump site" (basically a pile of ashes) was located on the grounds. Raymond said that these sites appeared to date back approximately to the previous autumn. In one of those burn areas, Raymond located "remnants of clothing" and a zipper. He returned to the mattress and box spring. After noticing that the springs were compressed, he concluded that something heavy had been lying on top of the bed while it burned.

A closer examination of those springs revealed a more grisly discovery. On the springs was a fatty substance, coagulated grease, that Raymond believed could be consistent with residue from some type of flesh or tissue burning.

Inside the house police discovered a document that

sent a fresh shiver down their spines. The document purported to give power of attorney for Kenny to Sheila.

According to the document, Sheila would be able to perform the following functions on Kenny's behalf: 1) talk to social services, 2) talk to any and all police departments, 3) talk to anyone regarding any and all business pertaining to Kenneth Countie or regarding any and all sworn statements Countie had made to Sheila in her capacity as his attorney, 4) receive his mail, packages, and correspondence of any nature, 5) sign Countie's name on checks, bills, bank records, or anything of any nature, 6) talk for Countie in court and any and all meetings.

The document also stated that Kenny only trusted Sheila and felt completely safe and secure in her presence. It said that she had helped him relocate, given him employment, and had provided for him "a nice place to live." It said that she had legally recorded statements made by Kenny, and that before recording those statements, she had explained to him that in New Hampshire it was necessary for both parties to consent to the taping to make it legal. The document concluded by instructing the reader to listen to that tape and to take its contents seriously. Sheila signed it, claiming that she had done so in her capacity as a justice of the peace. The document purported to have been signed by Kenneth Countie, dated March 10, 2006.

With the discoveries of March 30, police now felt they had gathered enough evidence to request an arrest warrant for Sheila LaBarre.

Wilfred LaBarre's daughter, Laura Melisi, was among the first to learn that Sheila was wanted for murder. "I plan to challenge the will that left all of my father's property to Sheila," Laura said, and then offered her condolences to Kenneth Countie's family.

She said she was not shocked by the news and had long thought Sheila capable of violence. She recalled Sheila threatening people at gunpoint. "My brother, John, and I met with Sheila's ex-husband, Wayne Ennis, not long after my father died. Wayne and my father always got along really well," she said. Wayne told the siblings that Sheila had twice asked him to kill their father so they could have the chiropractic practice and the horse farm. Wayne said he liked Wilfred and couldn't do that.

"I'm not sure if my father met Sheila in Tennessee or through a personal ad, but, either way, the second I met Sheila, I told my father not to get involved," Laura said. "She coerced him into putting her name on everything." Laura believed that Sheila's plan from the get-go was to take control of Wilfred's money. She knew he was a doctor, that he had money and property. She knew that he was emotionally vulnerable, having recently lost his wife, and that he needed help at his office.

Laura recalled talking to Sheila for the first time on the phone. As soon as the conversation was through, she told her father to get rid of her, that she was "bad news." Sheila's behavior from that point on only reinforced Laura's bad feelings.

She recalled the time that Ed Charron, also a chiropractor, used to live in the apartment above Wilfred's office with his Doberman. Since his brother owned the building, Ed was paying next to no rent. Sheila wasted no time telling Ed that his rent was being raised by $700 a month, and that if he didn't pay it, she would kill his dog.

"Three days after she made the threat, the dog—who wasn't sick—dropped dead," Laura recalled.

Laura remembered a time not long before her father died when she and he made plans to go horseback riding. Wilfred took his daughter into the living room to show her where he had hidden money for her and her brother. He explained that Sheila had taken control of his accounts, and hiding cash was the only way he could keep money away from Sheila.

Not long after Wilfred's funeral Sheila called Laura to taunt her. "I found the money," she said. "Ha-ha! How does it feel to have nothing?"

"We went to several lawyers," Laura explained. "They said that there was only a fifty-fifty chance of challenging the will. My father was neither incompetent nor unable to work. The lawyers wanted fifty thousand up front just to try."

Laura added that to further rub salt in her wounds, Sheila stiffed her for the catering and musician bills for Wilfred's funeral.

"I think Sheila intimidated my father," Laura said. "Many people tried to get him to toss Sheila out of his life, but he always said no. He said she was smart and would always find a way to outfox him."

Throughout her relationship with Wilfred, Laura explained, Sheila was around other men—boyfriends and farmworkers, and sometimes guys who were both.

"My father eventually had to move to the apartment above his office just to get away from her," Laura said. At one time or another, both Bill and Sheila had used that apartment, but not at the same time. Laura remembered that her father was a more relaxed man before Sheila came into his life. After Sheila, with the trouble she caused him, he was frequently stressed. "He began to have chest pains. I remember there were times when he had to lie down between patients," Laura recalled. "The doctors told him it was stress."

Sheila had Wilfred on a grueling schedule of hard work—sometimes manual labor—jobs better suited for a much younger man. He was past retirement age and she had him performing maintenance on his apartment buildings, painting, wallpapering, in addition to his duties on the horse farm and with his chiropractic practice. Laura remembered getting so frustrated by the situation that she would scream at her father to wake up and see the situation for what it was. He was a well-to-do older man being exploited by a younger gold digger.

Laura managed twice to convince her father to get an order of protection against Sheila, but both times he became lonely. He would cry and feel sorry for her and eventually allowed her back into his life. Laura said that her father was always highly supportive of Sheila's singing career, and he invested a lot of money in her attempts at show business. Right up until the end of his life, he used to talk to his daughter about what it would be like after Sheila was gone.

"He told me that after Sheila left, he wanted me to come back and work in his office," Laura recalled. But that day never came. Laura concluded the interview by saying, "I heard that Sheila recently tried to get a copy of the coroner's report on my father's death. I don't know why."

# The Arrest

On Friday, March 31, 2006, while Sheila hid out, Pamela Paquin—accompanied by her friend Sandra—brought to the studios of WMUR-TV the Burger King letter from Sheila. The letter read: *Dear Pamela, You are a true friend and angel. I am innocent and God knows that I am. Thank you eternally. Hold my children close each day and night.*

She went on to say that Epping police called her on March 21. She talked to Sergeant Sean Gallagher, who played an illegally obtained tape. . . . She asked Pamela to give the tape to Channel 9 news, and not give it to the police. The letter said that she was going to get "another lawyer" because "the other one" wanted a $60,000 retainer, and was signed Sheila. The handwriting appeared to match Sheila's signature on legal documents.

The station did not ID the women, but reported that one of them (Pamela Paquin, no doubt) claimed that Sheila had sold her some of her animals and had transferred control of the rental property in Somersworth to her.

Sheila herself drew up the document for the sale and transference on Monday, according to the women, and they all went together to the Raymond bank, where the document was notarized. A notary at the bank, when called by WMUR, confirmed the women's story.

On Saturday, April 1, police spokesmen met with the press and announced that they had issued an arrest warrant for Sheila on first-degree murder charges in connection with the death of Kenneth Countie. "We can't comment on what evidence we have, beyond the fact that the case reached a point that we were able to pursue and secure an arrest warrant," said Senior AAG Jeffery A. Strelzin, the state's top homicide prosecutor.

Keen-eared reporters interpreted that as meaning that the bones found in the burn pile on Sheila's front lawn had been confirmed as human remains.

"We believe that Kenneth Countie was living at the Silver Leopard Farm because of his involvement with Sheila LaBarre. We do not believe he was there to work," Strelzin said.

Asked about Sheila's whereabouts Assistant Attorney General Peter Odom said, "She could be anywhere at this point. We're looking at every possible place that she might be. We don't have any specific knowledge of where she is at this point. She has a large amount of cash with her, which gives her the ability to travel.

"We don't have any information that she is a specific threat to the public, but with a charge of this nature, she should be approached with extreme caution by members of the public, and any sightings of her should be reported to the police.

"She was last seen near the Mall of New Hampshire in

Manchester. We are focusing our search efforts outside the farmhouse. There are other priorities that we are looking at over the weekend. The entire farm is considered a crime scene.

"That is not to suggest there is evidence of a crime over every single acre. But . . . we are continuing to look at everything very carefully. Some investigators would continue searching throughout the night. Others will resume their efforts this morning.

"Search and arrest warrants and their supporting affidavits remain sealed at Exeter District Court while the investigation continues. The language in the complaint alleges Ms. LaBarre purposefully killed and incinerated his body," said Odom. "We're not going to comment on anything that has been uncovered or not uncovered."

He added that Sheila's whereabouts were unknown and that she had not been seen since March 28, when Steven Martello left her at a Quality Inn in Dorchester, Massachusetts.

Odom discussed the ongoing search of the LaBarre farm and that it was the information gathered by state and local police that led to the arrest warrant. It was too early, he said, to say if she would be facing other charges.

Major David Kelley, the commander of the New Hampshire State Police Special Investigations Unit, said, "The world is open at this point. She could be literally anywhere. We're taking all measures to locate her nationwide. We don't believe she has a car, but she could have gained access to one. She also could have left the area, using other modes of transportation.

"We've released her information to police and crime databases nationwide. We have alerted law enforcement nationwide that LaBarre is wanted for first-degree murder through the National Crime Information Center computerized database and the State Police OnLine Telecommunications System.

"We also are checking bus stations, airports, and other transportation systems and are researching relatives, friends, and any others who may have contact with her," Major Kelley said. That information instructed law enforcement everywhere to be on the lookout for Sheila LaBarre, five feet six inches tall, about 150 to 160 pounds, with brown eyes and blond hair with brown roots. "She may have changed her appearance to avoid detection," Kelley said. "She is believed to have a substantial amount of cash and speaks with a slight Southern accent. We do not have information indicating that she is armed, although we do know that she has possessed firearms in the past. The public should, nonetheless, take caution if they see her." Kelley gave the press the state police's phone number to call if anyone had information regarding Sheila's whereabouts.

On March 29 Sheila was walking across the parking lot in front of Liquidators in Dorchester on Morrisey Boulevard when she was spotted by a large African-American man sitting in his parked car. Her hair was neat and a reddish burgundy color. She looked attractive to him at that moment so he "pulled up on her" and started talking to her. After about ten minutes she got in the car and he drove. She was with him for the next three days. She said her name was Cayce, came from down South. Nashville. She was in town on business. Real estate. The airport lost her luggage. He told her he was Ken Washington, and they drove all around, got something to eat, and checked into a Radisson. They registered under his name. She paid in cash. He went out for a little while after that, by himself, and when he got back, they hung out and chilled. Smoked weed. Had sex. They spent the night together and checked out in the morning. They went to another hotel, the Ramada Inn, on Morrisey, not far from where they'd met. When he got antsy, she gave him money. Over the three days he made about $1,000. They stayed two more nights at the Ramada, had sex every night. He left on his own a few times and she would call him on his cell if she wanted to talk to him. They weren't happy with the Ramada, so on Saturday morning, April 1, they checked into a third hotel, a Red Roof Inn, near Revere. That day he left, deciding he'd had his fill, and he didn't go back. He went to his cousin's house that night, and while he was there, he saw Sheila on the news. On Sunday morning, scared that someone might think he was in on something he wasn't, Washington called the cops. At least he tried. The cop he talked to, a Revere, Massachusetts, cop, told him he would have to call police in New Hampshire to find out if there was a warrant out for Sheila's arrest. Washington couldn't believe the guy was trying to make him do all the police work. Had to be the dumbest cop ever. When he hung up, he wasn't sure his call was going to be taken seriously.

But it was. Responding to a phone tip from a male, police arrested Sheila during the early afternoon of April 2, 2006, at the Northgate Shopping Center in the town of Revere, Massachusetts. The tip said Sheila would be shopping that day, and described her unusual hair color. Responding to the tip were Sergeant Jeff Langone, an eleven-year veteran of the Revere Police Department Uniform Patrol Division, along with two other officers. All three officers arrived in their own fully marked cruisers. They knew the suspect they were after and what she'd been accused of. She was walking along the storefronts when the police converged on her, from both in front and in back.

"Drop the bags and show me your hands," Sergeant Langone said. At first, she didn't drop the bags and the order was repeated. This time she responded.

"What's going on? What are you doing?" Sheila asked.

When police first asked her to identify herself, she said her name was Cayce Washington. They asked for an ID and she said she didn't have one.

"Mind if I look through your purse, just to make sure?" Langone asked.

"Suit yourself," Sheila said, and handed over the pocketbook. No ID. He did, however, find a large manila envelope.

"What's this?"

"Please don't open that here. There's a lot of money in there," she said.

Sergeant Langone pulled out a square of aluminum foil and asked what it was.

"That's just a little bit of herb," she said. He opened the foil and verified that it contained a small amount of marijuana.

One of the officers had with him a copy of a Sheila LaBarre wanted poster, which he held up next to her head for comparison purposes.

"This you?" he asked.

"Yes," Sheila admitted. With that, she was placed in the back of a cruiser and taken to headquarters. When she was thoroughly searched, police found $83,000 on her. She had $33,000 in cash and a cashier's check for $50,000. She was booked on two charges: 1) being a fugitive from justice and 2) possession of marijuana. The pot charge was eventually dropped and Sheila was taken back to her home county regarding the other, more serious charges. Chief Dodge himself rode in the car that brought Sheila "home." She seemed in a decent mood, chatty even, considering her predicament. She joked that they were probably going to make a TV movie about her life story and she wondered which actress was going to play her. She asked the chief what actor did he want playing him in the movie. She told Trooper Rockey that Sandra Bullock wasn't pretty enough to play her.

Upon hearing of Sheila's arrest, Kenny's mom, Carolynn Lodge, read a statement: *"Please continue to pray for Kenny. He will always be in our hearts. One thing we want everyone to take with them is don't take anyone for granted. Love your children and hug them a little more every day."*

As soon as the news got to Harvey Hill, Bruce Allen said aloud what others in the community were thinking: "What about the others? Where's Jimmy? Where's Wayne? Where's Mikey?" Bruce recalled how sadistic Sheila was, the delight she took in dominating the men in her life, dishing out both physical and psychological abuse in daily doses of pain and humiliation. Bruce wondered what hold she had over them. He recalled one day, a few years back, when he'd seen Sheila and Jimmy out in the field. The two happened upon a horse pile—not an uncommon thing on a horse farm.

"That's your shit!" Sheila screamed. "You pick it up now."

No doubt about it, the woman had control issues. Bruce suspected that anyone who questioned whether or not Sheila was in charge ended up walking down the road bleeding from the face. Or worse.

Both Michael Deloge's stepfamily and his birth

mother were in despair over the news that Sheila was under arrest. To them, Kenny and Mikey seemed a lot alike, both mild-mannered men who were a little slow in the thinking department. At that point no one was certain that Michael Deloge was dead—but it didn't look good. While searching the graying white farmhouse, police found some of Deloge's belongings, but Deloge was nowhere to be found. Police went to visit Deloge's mother in Somersworth to get DNA samples that could be used in comparison with the blood and bones found on the farm. After his mother filed the necessary paperwork, Deloge, thirty-eight years old, was officially declared a missing person.

The *Boston Globe* went searching for Jimmy Brackett and received good news from one of his family members. Unlike Mikey, Jimmy was alive and well and still in New Hampshire.

Wayne, too, was found to be alive, having been deported to his native Jamaica in 2004.

There was the matter of Bill LaBarre's death. It had been assumed that the seventy-four-year-old had died of natural causes. But in light of recent developments, authorities were going to have to take another look at the chiropractor's demise.

As had been the case with Kenny and Mikey, according to witnesses, Bill had developed a sickly green complexion before his death.

# Shell-Shocked Sheila

On April 3, in Chelsea District Court, Sheila waived her right to a hearing and agreed to return to New Hampshire with the New Hampshire State Police. Because of her cooperation, Massachusetts prosecutors dropped the marijuana charge against her. The next day, as Sheila entered the Portsmouth District Court for arraignment, she and her guards had to navigate a herd of cameras and shouting reporters. She showed no emotion.

It wasn't her cool reaction that the press first noticed. It was her hair. She had a fresh dye job for the public. Her hair was now an orange-red that matched her Strafford County House of Corrections jumpsuit.

Since Sheila had dyed her hair blond before going on the lam, suspicious-minded observers wondered that perhaps this new dye job was designed to make her appear more like a habitual hair-dyer and less like she had been trying to disguise herself while taking flight.

Inside the courtroom Carolynn Lodge—because of her status as mother of the victim—sat on a spectator bench in the front row. Sitting beside her was her husband, Gerald. Occasionally, during the proceedings, she cried quietly as she held an eight-by-ten photo on her lap of Kenny. Sitting nearby were other members of the family.

The charges against Sheila were read: she had *"committed the act of first-degree murder on or about March 21, 2006, and did purposefully cause the death of Kenneth Countie, date of birth July 18, 1981, and incinerate the body."*

Judge Sawako Gardner presided over the hearing. Sheila stood amid her three defense attorneys. After the charges were read, no plea was offered, because this was a local district court, which did not accept pleas on felony charges.

After the brief hearing AAG Peter Odom said the investigation that led to Sheila's apprehension and arrest "was a remarkable, heroic effort."

The media turned their attention to defense attorney Jeffrey A. Denner, who refused to concede even that a crime had been committed. He said he had no idea if Kenneth Countie was dead or alive and limited his comments to the trauma brought upon Sheila by her arrest and incarceration. Although she appeared calm in court, Denner claimed she was in "absolute shock" and depressed.

"She is shell-shocked. She was trying—we're all trying to sort out what the accusations are. There's an allegation that he [Kenneth Countie] was on the farm with her in some capacity and he got incinerated, but I have no idea why they believe that," Denner said.

"Why was your client carrying so much money with her?" a reporter asked.

"It's her money. She can do with it what she likes.

I presume she intended to spend it," Denner said. "Perhaps on lawyers."

"Why did she change her hair color after being named a murder suspect?"

"That's a woman's prerogative. Women do like to change their appearance from time to time," Denner said. "Look, I've had this case now for less than forty-eight hours. The one thing I know for sure is that Sheila LaBarre is not guilty of any murder charges. Thank you." And he was gone.


Denner was a well-known lawyer both in the United States and abroad. A twenty-five-year veteran defense attorney, he was a graduate of Yale and of Harvard Law School. Denner's résumé included the successful defense of handyman Edmund Burke, who was charged with stabbing a seventy-five-year-old woman twenty-nine times in a Massachusetts park. Denner brought forward DNA evidence that showed Burke's saliva did not match that found on bite marks on the victim.

He represented Thomas Maimoni, who was charged with the first-degree murder of Martha Brailsford by weighting her down and throwing her over the side of his sailboat in the Salem Harbor, where she drowned. Denner argued that the woman was killed after she was hit by the boat's mast, causing Maimoni to panic before weighting her down and throwing her body overboard. Maimoni was found not guilty of first-degree murder, but he was convicted on a second-degree murder charge. He was sentenced to life with parole-eligibility after fifteen years. A true-crime book, *Counterpoint*, was later written about the case. The book was released in paperback as *A Scream on the Water*.

Denner was also credited with helping to rewrite the extradition treaty between the United States and Great Britain. Sheila's defense was in excellent hands.


On the afternoon of April 3, after court, Bonnie Meroth, a neighbor of the LaBarre farm, was taking her daily five-mile walk. Meroth was a public relations and marketing expert who had written scholarly works in history and travel, as well as for the Food Network. She knew more than the average Epping resident about serial killers, having once done research for the famous forensic pathologist, the late Dr. William Eckert.

As she walked, Meroth saw a small red sedan coming down the road. This was not as unusual as it had once been. A road that had once carried virtually no traffic was now a well-traveled one, whether it be by official vehicles involved in the intense search under way or by cars full of annoying curiosity-seekers, who wanted to see the place where "it happened." Still, it was better than before. Having Sheila locked up was such a relief. Meroth did not consider herself an "out there" person, but she did believe in crystals and karma and positive energy, and she could feel the change in the air now that Sheila was no longer free. Everyone had known that something nasty and horrible was going on over there, and now, at least, it was over. A bit of a naturalist, Meroth had loved to walk down Red Oak Hill Lane past the LaBarre home during her hikes. The dirt road was seven-tenths of a mile long and there was a heron colony at the end, but she hadn't dared walk down that road for years. Even though it was a town road, Sheila had threatened pedestrians with a gun—and no one doubted she'd pull the trigger.

Meroth watched as the red car slowed to a stop in front of her, near the spot where Red Oak Hill Lane branched off from Red Oak Hill Road, and the window rolled down.

The blond woman inside asked for directions to the crime site.

"Who are you?" Meroth asked. Snippy. It sounded like an accusation.

"I'm Kenneth Countie's mother," Carolynn Lodge replied. She explained that she wanted to see the spot where her son died.

"I told her that my heart hurts for her and her family," said Meroth, who went on to become close friends with Carolynn. "God bless her for pursuing this."

Lodge was not allowed to visit the site up close and was turned away by authorities just like everyone else. It was a crime scene, after all, and it had been cordoned off from everyone except investigators.

Down in Chattanooga, Tennessee, Sheila's brother Richard Bailey was checking the news on the Internet when he discovered, to his horror, that his sister had been arrested and charged with first-degree murder. Not long thereafter, the phone rang and it was a member of the press looking for a quote. Richard said there'd been six siblings and Sheila was the youngest. They'd been raised Baptists. "Our father was an equipment operator for the state highway department. Our mother worked in housekeeping at a hospital," he said. He confirmed that Sheila met Bill through a personal ad, and said he last saw Sheila at their brother's funeral in 2005. He was shocked by the accusations. "Sheila had mood swings but was not violent. Our church members are praying for the family of the boy, and also for my sister, that nothing she's been charged with is true," Richard Bailey said. "Just because you been accused of something don't mean it's true."

Police learned that on at least three occasions Sheila had obtained legal control over the financial affairs of a man in her life: Kenneth Countie, despite the fact that she knew the man for less than two months, Jimmy Brackett, and Bill LaBarre. Of the three, Brackett was the only one still living—and that was a matter of luck. Brackett told police that Sheila had twice fired a gun at him, missing both times, and had repeatedly threatened his life.

One week after her arrest, Sheila wrote a letter to a reporter for the local newspaper, the *Eagle-Tribune.* In it she wrote that she felt *badgered, intimidated and terrified* by police. She said she had been incorrectly portrayed by the press. *I am a devout Baptist and I enjoy my farm,* she penned. *I respect the people of New Hampshire and I have lived a simple life, not the life of a rich woman. . . . Anyone who really knows me, knows that I prefer to go around town in my old work clothes, staying close to my farm doing daily chores, feeding and loving all my animals, and cooking for friends. As a Baptist, I have complete faith in God and am always amazed at the power of the Father and Holy One.*

Police concluded the search of the farm on April 11. The next day Kenneth Countie's parents—Carolynn Lodge and Kenneth J. Countie—filed a lawsuit. In response to the suit, the parents were granted by the court a $10 million attachment on property owned by Sheila. The attachment was granted when Sheila, who was representing herself, failed to file the correct court

documents. The parents obtained a court order barring
Sheila from selling her farm or any of her other assets so
they would be able to recover $10 million due to the
"conscious pain and suffering" Kenneth endured. The
parents were also seeking the $80,000 in cash and checks
that Sheila had on her when she was arrested. The lawsuit sought compensation for the abuse heaped upon
Kenneth when he was still alive, the gash across Kenneth's nose, his swollen hands, the cuts and bruises
on his face and arms, and the ashen color of his skin.
Probate judge John R. Maher had previously validated
Wilfred's two wills, proclaiming Sheila to be Wilfred's
common-law wife and granting Sheila the bulk of Wilfred's estate, but now he issued a new order that wiped
out Sheila's control over the estate and gave Wilfred's
family a second chance at inheriting his assets.

With her son officially dead, and his alleged killer in
jail, Carolynn Lodge set about the ceremonies that accompanied closure. Kenneth Countie's funeral service—
which included a full mass—was held at St. William's
Church in Tewksbury. Seven hundred mourners attended. Most were complete strangers drawn by the
notoriety of the man's demise.

Reverend William Smith told those gathered that he
was aware that many of those in attendance were there
not because of how Kenneth had lived, but because of
the manner in which he died.

Carolynn Lodge got up and spoke, as did Kenneth's
dad and stepmother, Kenneth and Suzanne Countie.

Suzanne told those gathered, "Remember Kenny.
Remember his life. Don't take each other for granted.
Tomorrow may never come." She talked of how Kenneth

was in life, how much he loved to sing, how he loved hockey.

Carolynn Lodge could barely keep her composure as she said to the crowd, "Kenny, my son, my love, I wish you were here. My heart aches, for I know I'll never see your smiling face again."

A loved one named Kathy Durante remembered Kenny for his huge brown eyes, for how well-dressed he was, for how nice he smelled. Much better than the other little boys, who were often careless with their hygiene. Kenny always smelled great. She knew that it was difficult for him to learn; yet he was eager to learn new things, and he was so proud of himself when he did learn something new. Academics came tough, but sports came easy. Give him a baseball bat or a hockey stick and he was one of the boys, excelling as he played on the street right out in front of Kathy's home. He attended Shawsheen Valley Technical High School, where he trained in masonry as he attended special education classes. His mother worked with him, and worked with him, and he was able to get his driver's license. He tried the army, but that didn't work out. However, he hadn't given up on the military. He was no quitter. He merely thought he wasn't ready. He was going to give it a year or two and try again, and this time he was going to successfully complete basic training. He was sure of it. He had tried to make a go of it as an independent man. Things were going well with his roommate in Wilmington. He was doing okay without his mom to watch over everything he did. The big bad world was tough on Kenny, because he didn't know how to be suspicious. He thought everyone was his friend. Separating Kenny from his free will, for a predator, would have been like taking candy from a baby. And now the world was going to remember Kenny through the ugly words of his killer, and that wasn't fair.

On April 25, 2006, a probable-cause hearing was held in Goffstown District Court. For her public appearance Sheila again had changed her hair. Her long hair was now multicolored, streaked with various shades of blond, brown, and pink. She was dressed in a jail-issued orange jumpsuit.

Sergeant Estabrook testified as to the locations in Sheila's farmhouse where spattered blood had been found. The upstairs blood was covered with a layer of dust, which could mean that these stains were older than those found downstairs. Estabrook said that forensic experts had matched some of the blood from the home to a DNA blood profile taken of Countie while he was in boot camp for the army.

Countie's mother was again in the courtroom, sitting approximately twelve feet from her son's accused killer. She held a photo of her son in her lap during the hearing and cried out when details of her son's grisly demise were revealed.

Jeffrey Denner said that he was not ruling out an insanity defense. "At the very least, there will be a psychological factor in this case. At least, relating it to what in her nature made her respond to a traumatic situation the way she did," Denner said.

At the conclusion of the hearing, Judge Paul Lawrence ruled that the evidence showed there was probable cause for the first-degree murder arrest.

Sheila was injured in a jailhouse fight on April 26. That same day Captain Russell Conte, head of the state police's major crime unit, told the *New Hampshire Union Leader* that they were sifting through missing persons records, as well as the evidence gathered at the crime scene, to determine if there might have been more than one victim. "We are working with the state medical examiner and a forensic anthropologist to check the ashes found in the burn piles," Captain Conte said. "We are asking the public to give us a call if they know of anyone associated with Sheila LaBarre who hasn't been seen in a while." He noted that the most profound evidence of multiple victims was that not all of the blood found in the house seemed to be the same age.

During May 2006 it was ordered that Wilfred LaBarre's autopsy be reviewed to determine if there was a chance that he, too, was killed by Sheila. Dr. LaBarre's death certificate had been signed by New Hampshire's CME Dr. Thomas A. Andrew. In light of recent developments, Dr. Andrew agreed to take another look at the case. "As soon as this thing hit the fan," Dr. Andrew later told the *Boston Globe,* "I decided to pull the file. I just wanted to make sure that we hadn't missed something. But I am convinced that LaBarre died of natural causes."

With Sheila in jail, there was no one to take care of the animals on the farm. Pamela Paquin had agreed to take care of Sheila's animals, but she changed her mind after realizing the cost of such care. The animals were first seized as part of the investigation, then put up for adoption. State officials gave Sheila seven days to make arrangements for the animals, but she didn't respond. Either she didn't care about the welfare of the animals or she knew she was out of friends willing to do her a favor. Custody of the animals was taken by the New

Hampshire Society for the Prevention of Cruelty to Animals (NHSPCA). Seeking homes for them, Lisa Dennison, of the NHSPCA, went on local television and showed off some of the more adoptable animals, such as ten-year old Demetrious, a Dalmatian, three horses, and some rabbits.

"He's a wonderful dog. He deserves a great home," Dennison said. "The horses are in relatively good shape. They're senior horses. They all have some sort of ailment going on, but it's nothing they can't recover from. The horses place a serious burden on our resources, but the staff is ready to handle a long stay if required." There were also ponies and rabbits. She gave a phone number for anyone interested in adopting an animal.

Joy Deloge couldn't have felt gloomier. She had suspected for a long time that she was never going to see her stepson Michael again. Now she was sure of it. In desperation she wrote a heart-wrenching plea for Michael, wherever he was and whatever he was doing, to get in touch with her. She placed the notice in the local newspapers. She didn't really expect to get an answer—and she didn't. The pleas did not draw out her son, but they did draw out the press. Hot on the trail of a possible second victim, the TV stations and the newspapers were almost instantly ringing her phone and knocking on her door as they looked for the story. They talked to Joy and her daughter, Mikey's stepsister. The women were very cooperative and sadly gave WMUR-TV several photos depicting Michael at different times in his life. On the day of his wedding. Holding his baby.

Meanwhile, Mikey's biological mother, Donna Boston, told police that she had not seen her son since July 27,

2004, when both Michael and Sheila came to visit her on her birthday. She recalled that it looked as if the two had been arguing.

"She was doing most of the talking. I think they came to the apartment looking for trouble," Donna recalled. "Michael told me that he was happy with her, but I felt he had changed for the worse. Michael had changed his ways and his health and everything when he met up with her. He was pimply-faced. He looked like he had lost a lot of weight. He didn't even talk very much at all. She did all the talking." Donna remembered how the conversation went: "Sheila would say, 'Get me a glass of water,' or 'Where's my purse?' And if he didn't jump, she'd get very annoyed." Donna Boston said that she had been ill at the time and had sent Sheila and her son away. It was the last time she saw Mikey. Boston said that she still had hope that her son was alive, but she couldn't discuss it further.

Sheila again wrote the *Herald*: *I am not against being interviewed by reporters for newspapers or by television media representatives. However, naturally, my lawyers are experienced, educated professionals, who would have to be present during any interview and any and all media interviews or filming. Questions would have to be forwarded "beforehand" to Attorney Jeffrey Denner of Boston, MA and I would also have to approve.* She claimed that some of the evidence found at the LaBarre farmhouse was being misinterpreted. For example, the notebook that appeared to have notes regarding the murder she had committed was not about Kenneth Countie at all. It was, she wrote, her thoughts *about possible ways* that eighteen-year-old Natalee Holloway had disappeared in 2005 while vacationing in Aruba. The case had made sensational news for weeks. Among the notes found in Sheila's notebook were *DEATH, bury and shovel, Incinerated-burned-ashes flushed scatter,* and *"110 pounds, 5'4"*. The latter quotation had long mystified police because Countie was six feet tall. Holloway, on the other hand, was reported as being five-foot-four and as weighing 105 pounds. Sheila claimed that she took special note of the Holloway disappearance because both she and Natalee were from Alabama. Sheila wrote, *There is one thing very idiotic that Mr. Estabrook, NH State Police testified about on April 25 at my probable cause hearing. Being an Alabamian, I was heartbroken about beautiful Natalee Holliway's [sic] disappearance in the island of Aruba where I've never been! I recall praying to God about Natalee and writing a few notes about possible ways those men made her disappear. Mr. Estabrook used my notes about Natalee Holliway against me in court on 4/25/06.* She added, *I am innocent of the charges being levied against me.*

Denner subsequently told that same newspaper, "We have advised Sheila LaBarre to send no letters and to give no information, whatsoever, in relation to her case."

In July, Lynn Noojin, Sheila's sister, who worked as a court specialist at the DeKalb County Courthouse in Alabama, was contacted by the *Boston Globe* to comment on her sister's predicament.

She said, "I do not think my sister is guilty. Working in the court, I know anyone is capable of anything. Even my sister. We are just hoping for the best."

The newspaper also contacted Peter Eleey, the attorney representing Kenneth Countie's family. He said that, understandably, the family was very upset and completely denied all of the accusations Sheila was hurling that Kenneth was a pedophile and had "raped children."

Sheila had the head of a working grifter, the kind who

could see the "big picture." But what was the attraction that Sheila had over her men—Bill, Jimmy, Mikey, Wayne, Kenny—and possibly others? She had received legal control over the affairs of Bill, Kenny, and Jimmy. Bill and Kenny were dead. Mikey was missing. She had actually married Wayne, but she claimed to be Bill's common-law wife. According to neighbors, both Jimmy and Wayne had made several attempts to get away from Sheila, but they kept coming back. What was her appeal? She liked sex. Lots and lots of sex. That was for sure. She'd slept with all of them, and was often having sex with more than one of them at any given time. Neighbor Louise Harvey didn't think the question was answerable: "You never knew what hold she had on them. But these poor guys ended up sitting in her truck, all hunched down. No self-esteem whatsoever."

A hearing was held before Rockingham County Superior Court judge Patricia Coffey on August 17, 2006, to request bail for Sheila, who tried to talk to the judge out of turn and needed to be hushed by counsel. On August 21, 2006, Judge Coffey denied Sheila bail. Her defense wondered why the indictment was taking so long. The state replied that it had to do with the degradation of Kenneth Countie's body, which made scientific tests more difficult. Special tests needed to be performed by a forensic anthropologist and a forensic odontologist. The bones were in such a state that standard nuclear DNA testing was unlikely to be helpful, requiring the use of mitochondrial DNA testing. In the court order Judge Coffey wrote: *In New Hampshire, any person arrested and charged with first-degree murder is not allowed bail where proof is evident or the presumption is great. Given the sequence of events presented by offers of proof, the court finds that in this*

*case the presumption is great against Ms. LaBarre, and she*
*shall not be allowed bail.*

On Monday, September 18, 2006, after spending 130
days in jail, Sheila was finally formally indicted, charged
with first-degree murder in the death of Kenneth Countie.

# "Sheila was crazy and she will kill me."

During October 2006 Wayne Ennis, Sheila's ex-husband, who had returned to his native Jamaica after divorcing Sheila, and was living in the city of St. Elizabeth, wrote a series of letters to Sergeant Robert Estabrook, of the New Hampshire State Police, and to the *Union Leader* newspaper. The letters gave law enforcement some insight into the woman charged with murdering Kenneth Countie. The letters said that Sheila spoke often of killing Bill LaBarre. She said she hoped he would be kicked in the head by a horse and killed. She said she often contemplated killing him herself. She wanted to strangle him. Sometimes she asked Ennis to kill Dr. LaBarre for her; the two of them would inherit the horse farm then.

*I was afraid to say no to her. If I said no I knew she would turn on me,* Ennis wrote. *When she is like that, I don't trust her, I hesitate. It just can't come out. I can't do that. I am not a murderer and Dr. LaBarre is like a father to me.*

The letters said that even though the divorce papers

Sheila eventually filed against him portrayed him as an abuser, it was she who was abusive. It was just that she wanted to paint herself as the victim. He wrote that she hit, shoved, and fired guns at him and others, and often refused to let him use the phone, burned his clothes, and forced him to spend nights outside during the winter.

*She had a handgun with her all the time—she points the gun at me and shoot(s) over my head and told me she is going to send me back to Jamaica in a box,* Ennis wrote. During their fiercest arguments, when she began to get violent, he would refuse to hit her, since he had been taught it was wrong for a man to hit a woman. *She would rip her clothes off and strike herself, smile at me and call the police,* he wrote. *She said the court is not going to believe a black negro over a white American woman.*

According to the letters, the real reason for his divorce from Sheila was that he caught her one night in bed with another man. This was the incident during which the police were called and Sheila assaulted him with the cordless phone. The other man in this incident was James Brackett.

Several times Ennis tried to leave her, but he always came back. One time, he wrote, Dr. LaBarre tried to help him. Ennis wrote that Dr. LaBarre said that *Sheila was crazy and she will kill me (Ennis), so he gave me money and bring me to the bus station.* He wrote that he had returned to Jamaica because he overstayed his work permit and was deported in 2002. He noted that he had not been contacted by investigators, but he was interested in testifying against Sheila.

*I am Sheila's worst nightmare,* Ennis wrote to Sergeant Estabrook. *I see and hear too much. It does not stop with what I have written here.*

* * *

Sheila's legal difficulties became even more complex in December 2006. In addition to the first-degree murder charges, the seizing of her farm, and the lawsuit for wrongful death against her, a former neighbor reintroduced a lawsuit claiming that she stalked him in 2004.

The suit sought $10 million in damages—an amount approximately equaling Sheila's total worth, assuming her inheritance from Wilfred was legal. It was brought by neighbor Bruce Allen and had been originally filed in July 2006, but it was thrown out by a lower court. However, in light of new information regarding Sheila's violent nature, the New Hampshire State Supreme Court agreed to take another look at the suit. Allen, whose farm shared a boundary with the LaBarre farm, claimed that his problems with Sheila began when she made sexual advances toward him. She allegedly offered him drugs, alcohol, and sex—but he declined. After that, the suit claimed, she twice pointed a gun at him. "She caught me twice out in the woods with a rifle, and twice she snapped the trigger," he said. He claimed he was traumatized.

Sheila wrote in response to the suit: *He waited until I was receiving national and local news coverage, and then decided to harass me in this manner. The case arose from Allen's arrogant need for attention, fame, and money.*

Regarding Sheila's response, Allen said, "If she wants to go and speak like that, other people will come forward to the district attorney and say what they know."

On February 2, 2007, Judge Patricia Coffey met for about an hour with lawyers on both sides in her chambers in the Exeter District Courthouse in Brentwood to set a date for Sheila's trial, and to discuss the testing of blood evidence. A date was set in the spring of 2008, a year and a half away, to allow time for the labs to do their thing properly. Because of the extensive amount of lab testing that needed to be done in the case, Judge Coffey scheduled the trial more than a year later, on March 24, 2008—a date that would mark the second anniversary of Detective Cote discovering the fleshy bone sticking out of the ashes on LaBarre's lawn.

Also discussed at the meeting was the matter of whether the state would be required to open up its testing process to defense experts, a seeming necessity since, as the state had already admitted, some blood samples and bone fragments were likely to be depleted during testing.

According to prosecutor Kirsten Wilson, although a large number of blood samples were collected on swabs at the alleged crime scene, only one of those samples was large enough to determine if it was Countie's blood. That sample, Wilson said, came from a large stain found on a dining-room chair. In addition to DNA testing, the blood was also scheduled to be screened for poison. "Doing both tests is apt to use up the sample," Wilson said.

Defense attorney Brad Bailey asked that a representative from the defense be allowed to attend all testing. "We want to ensure the scientific credibility of the process," Bailey said. Bailey was a partner of Denner's and the criminal division chief of the Boston firm. He was named one of *Boston Magazine*'s "Super Lawyers" for 2004, 2006, and 2007, and "New England Super Lawyer" for 2007. It paid to be notorious. Sheila was getting a legal superteam. Still, Judge Coffey ruled that the state could use as much of the blood evidence in their testing as they wished, and a written report on those tests to the defense was sufficient.

Sheila's tumultuous existence did not cease just because she had been in jail for many months. She got into another jailhouse fight, at least her second, on February 3, 2007, and was injured. Twenty-four-year-old Jessica Hanson, of Ossipee, punched Sheila in the head causing "minor" bruises. Hanson, who was in on a probation violation, was arrested and charged with assault.

Sheila's jailhouse experience wasn't entirely hostile, however. According to a woman named Arlene Sullivan (pseudonym), who had been arrested for prostitution and temporarily shared a cell with her at the Dover jail, Sheila—being older than most of the inmates—liked to affect a "mother hen" attitude toward the others. "She called us her angels and tried to be very motherly. She wanted to 'take care of all her girls.' She would tell us that everything was going to be okay. She liked to draw cards and give them to us as presents. She drew angels on them and stuff like that."

On April 26, 2007, Sheila made a brief appearance in court. She wanted the $83,000 in cash and bank checks that was seized from her at the time of her arrest returned. She said she needed the money to feed the horses on her farm and to pay her mortgage. She claimed that the only reason she had that much money on her, in the first place, was that she was looking for a lawyer and planned to use it as a retainer. The matter of whether or not the money could be returned was complicated by civil suits filed against Sheila by Bill LaBarre's children and her neighbor Bruce Allen.

Prosecutor Jane Young said the state had no problem returning the cash and checks to LaBarre. An objection, however, came from attorney Peter Eleey, representing Kenneth Countie's family, requesting that no further action in the civil suit be taken until after the criminal case was over. Eleey told Judge Coffey that Sheila was given an opportunity on at least four occasions to have the default judgment lifted in the civil case. Each time her attempt was either rebuffed by the court clerk, because it did not follow correct procedure, or was denied by a judge. Eleey said, "There have already been four bites at the apple. Sheila LaBarre is still in default." A legal collision seemed inevitable between the children of Wilfred LaBarre and the family of victim Kenneth Countie. The victim's family would not be able to collect sums of money from the estate in exchange for Sheila killing Kenneth if that money and property never belonged to Sheila.

During the month of June 2007 police complained that keeping trespassers away from the farm had been a problem ever since Sheila was arrested. As often happens when a grisly crime takes place in a small town or rural area, the location of the crime takes on a "haunted house" status, and becomes a strong attraction for the curious and those seeking a thrill. Epping police chief Dodge said that although there had been no evidence that teenagers in the area had used the farmhouse as a "party spot," there had been a problem of trespassing on the land. He said that police had found beer cans on the property, but that it was impossible to tell how long they had been there. The police had been called several times by neighbors, who reported that cars were going into the area. In March a carload of young girls had to receive police assistance when they drove up the LaBarre driveway on Red Oak Hill Lane and their car got stuck. When police came to their aid, the girls explained that they had wanted to "check out the scene."

Dodge said, "People might be thinking the place is haunted and that might be part of the drive for visitors to seek out the home."

A next-door neighbor said, "The problem here is that the police are not there twenty-four/seven. They don't know how many people come in and out. Actually, they are hardly ever there. I know, I live next door. I see the people come in and I see them come out. I hear them at two A.M. and at four A.M. I see carloads of kids come in, I see moms and dads in their minivans, the people on horseback, the kids on their bikes, the people walking their dog. On the average there are six or seven cars a day visiting that property."

The story of the trespassers on the LaBarre farm was big news in the local newspaper and on its Web site. One person who was infuriated by the coverage was Joy Deloge, Michael's stepmother. She wrote into the Web site complaining, *Why don't you write about why no one is looking for Mike Deloge instead of this insignificant bull about partying on the farm? I am Mike Deloge's step-mom and he most likely died at the hands of Sheila, but nobody seems to care!*

Sheila's defense team filed notice during August 2007 that they were contemplating an insanity defense and asked that the trial be conducted in two parts. Under

New Hampshire law, a jury in this case could be divided into two parts, one to determine guilt or innocence and another to determine, if guilty, whether she was sane.

In preparation for the possible insanity defense, Sheila was evaluated by forensic psychiatrist Dr. Roger Gray, who agreed to provide his services pro bono—a necessity, since Sheila's assets were frozen.

Due to alleged misconduct, Judge Coffey was put on paid leave on August 30, 2007. Judge Coffey was off the Sheila LaBarre case for good, replaced by Judge Tina L. Nadeau.

On October 3, 2007, Judge Nadeau declared Sheila indigent. Sheila's legal team took a huge pay cut, from $500 to $60 per hour, with a cap of $15,000 in total attorney fees for the entire case. Sheila's legal fees were going to be paid by the state's indigent defense fund. Sheila's legal superteam came on the taxpayers' dime. In most cases in which a defendant was broke, the court would appoint that defendant an attorney, usually one who worked out of the public defenders office. Occasionally a lawyer in private practice would be assigned such a case, if everyone in the public defenders office was busy. But rarely would a firm of Denner Pellegrino's stature take on such a case.

On October 22, 2007, Sheila's defense team filed court documents questioning the admissibility of the prosecution's "blood spatter" evidence, claiming that the report was too vague, too grisly, and too graphic, and not based enough on science. They wrote that the report *purports to divine a series of troubling events surrounding the shedding of blood in the LaBarre household at an unspecified time.* The report in question was filed by Dr. Marilyn

T. Miller, a spatter expert working for the state, who performed her analysis on a number of items that had been removed from the LaBarre home and taken to a state police hangar, as well as on a police photo of a bloodied dining-room chair. Police had been thorough in preserving the blood evidence, and there had been a "large number" of stains to preserve. An entire living-room wall and kitchen cabinetry had been removed and relocated in the hangar. Police had earlier theorized that Sheila had murdered Kenneth Countie with poison, basing this theory on the sickly appearance. The blood evidence, however, with its "arterial gushes" indicated that the end, for Kenneth, may have come swiftly and brutally.

On Monday, November 19, 2007, Sheila LaBarre, now forty-nine years old, appeared in Rockingham County Superior Court before Judge Nadeau to determine whether police improperly interviewed her and seized evidence. If the defense had its way, all evidence seized before the implementation of the search warrant would be suppressed.

Sheila was like Lon Chaney. She had a thousand faces. And she wasn't shy about flashing all sides of her personality. She laughed loudly and made jokes with her defense team. She tried to melt the small grouping of TV and newspaper reporters in the courtroom with an angry glare. She flirted with her favorite photographer. *Boom, boom, boom.* She had put on weight since her last public appearance, and her hair, last seen matching her jumpsuit, was now dark brown with gray streaks. During the hearing she furiously scribbled notes and whispered comments and questions to her counsel.

Also in the courtroom was a large contingent of Countie's family, including mother Carolynn Lodge, who had become a fixture in the courtroom whenever a hearing regarding her son's murder was held.

During the hearing prosecutor Jane Young introduced photos of Sheila pushing Countie in a wheelchair at the Epping Wal-Mart. Stacked on Countie's lap were yellow diesel cans. Similar cans, the prosecution noted, were found outside LaBarre's farmhouse and near the burn pile, where it was believed she incinerated Countie's body. The photos were not shown to spectators in the courtroom but were rather held up briefly as they were described and handed over to the judge.

Epping police chief Gregory Dodge, questioned by James "Jim" Boffetti, testified that when he first arrived at her farm with the search warrant, he found Sheila LaBarre covered with ashes. She told him that she'd been burning rabbits throughout the night, and that she'd been saving some of the bones in a white Wal-Mart bag for police to look at. Dodge interviewed LaBarre in the kitchen of her house as police outside prepared to execute a search warrant. An audiotape of that interview was played. On the tape Sheila said, "Just shoot me because I don't know if I can take any more stress. He was thinking about killing himself and was threatening to set himself on fire."

Epping police sergeant Sean Gallagher took the stand and testified that he and Detective Richard Cote had visited Sheila the day before that taped interview, on March 24, a well-being check for Countie. He'd been reported missing by his mother, and was last seen in the company of Sheila LaBarre. They found two burn piles on her front lawn. He described the phone call the previous night and the tape she had played for him, the one on which Countie "confessed." In the first burn pile they found a burning mattress. In the second pile they found a knife with a melted handle, a pair of hedge clippers, and what looked like a flesh-covered human bone. The bone, he said, stuck out of the ashes, in plain view. Sheila told him the bone belonged to a rabbit or a pedophile.

Under Bailey's cross-examination Gallagher testified that they had got onto Sheila's property by climbing through the rungs of a gate that she'd placed across the road. Gallagher said that, despite the gate, the road was a public thoroughfare and not a driveway, and legally continued through the LaBarre property, going directly past the spot on LaBarre's front lawn where he had discovered the two burn piles.

Sheila had seemed in a good mood. She invited the police onto her property and said that they should look around as much as they liked. "She was very happy, boisterous," Gallagher said. "The only way I can describe it is that I felt like I was on a tour."

Bailey told Gallagher that the police did not seem very concerned about Countie's well-being. Despite the fact that Gallagher had responded to the Wal-Mart on March 17, 2006, because of Countie's sickly appearance and Sheila's bizarre behavior, the police did not show any interest in Countie again until they went to the farm following the second missing persons report filed by Countie's mother, and the troubling sounds on the audiotape Sheila had played over the phone. "You didn't do anything proactive regarding Kenneth Countie," Bailey said. "You didn't go to Red Oak Hill Road in that six- to seven-day period."

"My concern was growing," Gallagher responded. "But, yes, we didn't check."

Bailey noted that even after they found the bone, police

still did not detain Sheila but rather left. Gallagher explained that they didn't want to spoil the case and felt the prudent thing to do was to return to town, get a search warrant, and return the following day for a more extensive search of the property. Though Sheila had been "happy" and "inviting" upon their first visit, her mood was very different when they returned the following day with the search warrant. He said that she was "panicky" this time.

Prosecutors completed the day by playing a videotape that showed Sheila being interrogated by police in the Epping police station. She was read her Miranda rights.

Everyone was back in court the following day, Tuesday, November 20, 2007. It was a cold, misty day with the temperature just above freezing. The first witness was Epping road agent David Reinhold, who testified that the road going past the LaBarre farm was indeed a public road and not a driveway, and that the town maintained it. Reinhold testified that—despite the fact it was a public road—Sheila clearly considered it a driveway and part of her private property. How else to explain the gate she had put across the road to prevent cars from going past her house? The gate, he noted, was usually closed.

Chief Dodge also finished his testimony on Tuesday morning. He told the court about the statements Sheila had made to him and Lieutenant Michael Wallace in the kitchen of Sheila's farmhouse. Among her more bizarre statements was a request that when she came down to the police station to be questioned, was it all right if she brought her rabbit with her? "That was just Sheila being Sheila," Chief Dodge said. She had written him a letter on February 7, 2006. The letter concerned a polygraph examination she said she'd given to James Brackett and her claim that she'd been questioned by the Secret Service the day before. In the letter Sheila wrote, *I've been threatened by a dangerous gang member from Ireland who told me I would disappear if I reported him to the Secret Service.* She added that the Irish gangsters were rapists, and since she was in danger, she asked Dodge if she qualified to have a permit to carry a concealed weapon.

Lieutenant Michael Wallace was called to the stand and was asked by Jane Young if Sheila had been delusional when she said that members of an Irish gang were harassing her. Lieutenant Wallace said that this was not necessarily so. There had been an actual case in which Sheila had had something to do with an Irishman being deported. After the hearing the prosecutor told reporters that she had no specific details regarding this incident, only that Sheila's statement was not evidence of mental illness but apparently based on an actual occurrence.

Wallace said that Sheila had been armed when police first arrived, but when asked, she turned a loaded pistol over to Dodge.

"I asked her if she had any more, at which point she lifted up her shirt and exposed herself and started to undo her pants, when I told her that wasn't necessary," Wallace testified.

"Did you ask her why she was armed?"

"Yes, ma'am. She said that there were Irish gangsters after her, men who raped women and their mothers."

"Was that unusual behavior on the part of Sheila LaBarre, as per your experience, Lieutenant Wallace?"

"It was not. I've dealt with her for eighteen years."

"And how would you characterize her?"

"She was manipulative and flirtatious."

On cross-examination Wallace described LaBarre's sooty appearance when officers arrived with the search warrant. Asked for his observations of the yard and the area outside the house, Wallace noted that he found it unusual that there was a pile of luggage and crucifixes just outside her front door.

Bailey asked, "You've got the crucifixes and a woman crying—did you question her sanity at that point?"

"I wouldn't call her crazy, but I did think some things were bizarre," Wallace replied.

The original affidavit to suppress the evidence gathered during the initial search of the farm included the claim, by the defendant herself, that she had been intimidated by police into cooperating with them. To refute this charge, the prosecution called Trooper First Class Jill Rockey to the witness stand.

TFC Rockey, it was established, interviewed Sheila at the Epping Police Department. She described Sheila as "calm and very aware mentally of what was going on. I found her to be very intelligent and very articulate. She seemed to have a grasp of the law."

Through Rockey's testimony, Kirsten Wilson pointed

out for the court that Sheila was in control of herself and her situation.

The next witness was Cindy Harvey, a postal carrier who had lived in Epping for fifty years. She testified that the gate crossing the road at the entrance to Sheila's property was usually closed, but was sometimes open. It was there, she said, to keep the horses from escaping. She said that the road, known as Red Oak Hill Lane, was a town road past the farm, but farther on narrowed and couldn't be used by a motor vehicle. "You could get through with a horse, but nobody's ever driven through there," Harvey said.

The last witness called during the hearing was Epping resident Michelle Bennett, who had been with Sheila LaBarre when the three police officers had made their first visit to the farm on March 24, 2006. Bennett testified that she was not in court that day of her own free will, that she would, in fact, prefer to be anywhere else. She had been subpoenaed to appear in court so she had come, and that was the only reason. She testified that she was at Sheila's house when police arrived on the night of March 24 because she and Sheila had just returned from shopping at the Stratham Market Basket. When the police arrived, she had sat in a truck at the end of the farm property and had watched the interaction between Sheila and the law officers from afar. She had no idea if the officers had entered Sheila's house without her permission.

"Isn't it true that you're afraid of Sheila LaBarre?" Boffetti asked Bennett.

"A little bit," Bennett said. As Bennett left the stand, she avoided making eye contact with Sheila, who smiled when looking at Bennett.

At the conclusion of the two-day hearing, Judge Nadeau said that because of the quantity of evidence, it would take her a few weeks to make her decision on whether the evidence in question should be suppressed.


On Wednesday, December 19, 2007, Judge Nadeau granted a motion by Sheila's legal team asking for a split trial. That meant that the unusual proceedings would be bifurcated. A first trial would determine her guilt or innocence. If she was convicted, a second trial would determine whether she was criminally insane.

Regarding the suppression hearing, Judge Nadeau did, as promised, take several weeks to make up her mind, but on January 22, 2008, she denied all parts of the defense request to suppress statements and evidence they claimed were obtained through an illegal search of Sheila's property. The charred bone and flesh in the burn pile—in. Sheila's pleas to kill her—in. Sheila flashing her breast to a cop—in. The judge based her decision on several points. There were exceptions to certain privacy and trespassing laws in cases where emergency aid is being given, and the police were at the farm in the first place because they had strong reasons to suspect Kenneth Countie was in trouble. The strong reasons were that his mother had reported him missing, and he was obviously sick and injured the last time he had been seen in public.


Around the time of Judge Nadeau's decision, Sheila penned a letter to WMUR-TV complaining about the treatment she was receiving in jail. She wrote that the most painful thing was she wasn't allowed to wear her religious necklace. She termed that restriction an *emotionally painful oversight,* and complained that she cried daily about it.

# A Change of Plea

The case shifted dramatically on February 12, 2008, when Sheila changed her plea to not guilty because of insanity. But that was not the biggest bombshell of the day. The court hearing began with new charges in the case. The prosecution announced that it was now prepared to prove that Sheila LaBarre, in addition to killing Kenneth Countie, was also the murderer of Michael Deloge.

The older blood found in the farmhouse—that is, the blood that was covered with dust—had been proven to belong to Deloge. Likewise, the blood found on the coat located near Sheila's pickup truck was also Deloge's. Bruce Allen finally had the answer to his question, first asked when he heard that Sheila had been arrested: *"Where's Mikey?"*

Following the announcement of the new charges, Sheila changed her plea. At her side in the courtroom was her defense team, Denner and Bailey, and two Exeter lawyers named Rich Taylor and Alex Yiokarinis, both of whom were former New Hampshire public defenders. They were brought on board by Denner to help.

Sheila now admitted to killing both men, but she claimed that she was not legally responsible because she was insane at the time. By changing her plea, Sheila no longer had to face a jury assigned to determine whether or not she committed the crimes. But she would still face a jury to determine her sanity. If she was found sane, she would be sent to prison for the rest of her life without chance of parole. If she was found insane, Judge Nadeau would decide if she needed to be sent to the state mental hospital. Although an extremely unlikely prospect, if the judge determined that she was *no longer* criminally insane, Sheila could be released immediately back into society. Once in a mental institution, she could, if declared cured by doctors, be released in as little as five years.

The changing plea altered the case in yet another way. In a normal murder trial, it was the prosecution's burden to prove that the defendant committed the crime. The defense did not have to prove the defendant's innocence, but merely had to create a "reasonable doubt" in the minds of the jury. But this trial was different. In this case Sheila's defense team had the burden of proof. They had to prove via clear and convincing evidence that Sheila was insane at the time she killed Deloge and Countie.

The defense needed to demonstrate that Sheila suffered from a mental disease or defect, and that the murders were a *product* of that mental disease or defect. Neither "mental disease" or "defect" had been defined by the New Hampshire Legislature or its courts. The jury would decide what those terms meant and if the evidence indicated those things were present.

Because of the shifting burden, the order of events at the trial would be different. Normally, the prosecution presented its case first and its final arguments last. In Sheila's trial the defense would present its case first and would be the last to speak.

Judge Nadeau asked Sheila if she understood what was going on, and she said she did.

"I'm here to tell the truth," Sheila added. "No one, meaning no professional, has said to me, 'This is your diagnosis.'" The defendant spoke in a low voice and a couple of times became emotional. Judge Nadeau interrupted her and asked her if she wanted a glass of water, but Sheila declined.

During the hearing gruesome details of the crimes were revealed, details that proved to be too much for the mothers of the victims—Carolynn Lodge and Donna Boston—both of whom were sitting in the Brentwood courtroom's front row. Both moms cried, hid their faces, and eventually had to be escorted from the courtroom.

Michael Deloge, it was revealed, was beaten, killed, and burned, much in the same manner that Countie had been killed and incinerated. In addition to discussing the bones found in the Wal-Mart bag, and in the burn piles on the farmhouse's lawn, a familiar fact to those following the case, prosecutors also said that bones were found in the farm's septic system and in burn buckets. Prosecutor Kirsten Wilson said that bone experts were able to identify a cranium, hand, foot, pelvis, spine, and lower arms, even though many bones were degraded beyond the point of identification. Such deterioration indicated the bones were burned at temperatures hotter than those found in a campfire. Based on size, the bones were identified as those of a man under the age of thirty-five. The burn piles, prosecutors said, tested positive for accelerants.

Wilson said, "Based on the evidence, the state is

convinced that Sheila LaBarre was sane at the time of both killings. She sat by the fires, carefully adding fuel, and turning the bones as they burned. Based on the degradation of the remains, someone would have had to supervise with accelerants and turn the bones." Both victims were a sickly color and suffering from wounds when last seen. A Buck knife that had been found in a farmhouse hutch—the blood on that knife belonged to Countie. Vomit containing nicotine and Countie's blood had been found in an air vent in the living room. Countie did not smoke. A journal had been found containing suspicious notes.

Two witnesses, both men, had told investigators that Deloge also looked sickly before he disappeared, and they had seen Sheila beat Mikey. According to one of those farmhands, Sheila said, "You think I killed him, don't you?"

DNA from blood spatters found in the house was matched with a DNA profile for Deloge, which had been supplied by his mother. The farm's septic system was cleaned twice by authorities, and investigators found Deloge's birth certificate, a bullet casing, bone fragments, and what police say were cell phone fragments. Those fragments were still being analyzed. Deloge was last seen during the fall of 2005.

Also found by police was a letter written by Deloge and, bizarrely, notarized by Sheila. In the letter Deloge admitted to being a pedophile. He further wrote *There is no hope for me. I've even tortured this kind lady's baby rabbits.*

Kind lady? Deloge's mother was outraged at the wording. When that letter was read aloud in court, Donna Boston couldn't stay in the courtroom any longer and had to leave.

What was clear was that Sheila not only wanted to know

if her future victims were pedophiles, she wanted to document their admissions. Why else have Deloge's admission notarized? Why else tape-record Countie's supposed confession? She wanted everyone to know what these men were. But why? Was it because, if she was caught, she wanted to be forgiven? Did she really believe that she was doing God's work, and that she was doing the world a favor by eliminating pedophiles? If so, that might be considered by a jury evidence that Sheila was actually insane. On the other hand, perhaps she was crazy like a fox. This conniving woman, who had gotten control of Wilfred LaBarre's considerable estate, might have been smart enough to place in advance her insanity defense so that she'd never have to go to prison if she was caught.

"Remember," Boffetti said in court, "there is an important distinction between being diagnosed with a mental illness and being legally insane. There are a lot of people diagnosed with mental illness and personality disorders, but only a very small percentage that are legally insane. Being eccentric doesn't mean you are insane. Having unusual behavior doesn't mean that you are insane. It could be indicative of it, but you can't strictly equate them." In other words, Sheila's defense team had a long row to hoe.

And yet the hoe was already busy. Jeffrey Denner argued, "Sheila looked at the world through a very different lens than you or I. Suffice it to say, she killed these people because she is utterly insane. Sheila LaBarre is a very, very sick individual. She needs a lot of help and she cannot control her behavior."


After three and a half years of being missing, Michael Deloge was officially dead. Michael's stepfather, Gordon

Boston, sat in his Dover apartment and quietly played a game of solitaire as he recalled for reporter Gretyl MacAlaster his earlier memories of the boy he now knew was gone for good. "I first met Michael when he was nine. We got along well. I met his mother, Donna, when we worked together in a shoe shop in Somersworth. I married her and I treated Michael like my own son. I remember teaching him how to drive," Gordon said wistfully. Donna was three years younger than Gordon. As a teenager Michael suffered a personality change. He began to follow what Gordon referred to as "sadistic teachings." He did drugs. His problems were exacerbated by the marital difficulties being experienced by Gordon and Donna. When they divorced, Michael went off the deep end. He ran away and lived from time to time in homeless shelters.

"In 2004 Donna and I gave our relationship another chance," Gordon remembered. "That was about the time Michael met Sheila. She was good-looking and fun to be around. I could see what Michael saw in her." She used to hang around with the family—drink a few beers and play a few country songs on the guitar. But she had a mean streak, and she and Michael would fight all the time. Michael was no longer a kid. He was thirty-seven years old when he went missing. At first, Donna and Gordon believed he'd just taken off, like he had when he was younger. But after news reports of Sheila and the disappearance of Kenneth Countie, they knew what had happened to their boy. Not long after Michael disappeared, Donna and Gordon separated again, this time for good. The stress of Michael going missing was at least in part responsible for their separation. "Donna loved Michael," Gordon said. "She was suffering over it. I do realize it's hard for her to lose her son." Although he and Donna had been together for twenty-five years he admitted that it had been more than two years since he'd spoken to her.

The papers seemed surprised that Sheila had admitted to two murders rather than one. Gordon felt no shock. "I wasn't totally surprised," Gordon said. "She's right on pleading that she's insane, because she is. She's a very smart insane. That's what makes her dangerous. Michael and Sheila would do drugs and study sadistic material. Both Donna and I tried to talk him out of staying with that woman. The last time we saw the two of them together, they were having a fight." The fight was over an incident that had allegedly occurred years before. But he wouldn't be specific. Did it have to do with pedophilia? We know that Sheila forced Countie to confess to pedophilia before she killed him. In court prosecutors had discussed a note that appeared to be in Michael Deloge's handwriting in which he, too, admitted to pedophilia. When asked specifically about this, Gordon Boston clammed up.

"I'll admit my stepson made mistakes in his life. Life's bad that way sometimes—but he didn't deserve to be murdered" was all Gordon would say.

When the same question was asked of Donna Boston by phone, she said, "I'm not giving the papers anything," then hung up.

Did Gordon care if Sheila spent the rest of her life in a prison or in a mental institution?

"It doesn't make a difference to me," he said. "You don't kill people. It just doesn't work that way."

A few days later, Donna Boston gave her first public statement to a reporter from the Associated Press. "Up until [Sheila's admission]," she said, "I didn't know if he was dead or alive." But after Sheila admitted to killing him and throwing his parts in a fire, Donna at last felt a sense of closure—as well as more than a little anger. She handwrote an obituary for her son and sent it to the *Foster's Daily Democrat* newspaper. In the obit she said that she was planning a private memorial service for her son, but as of yet no date had been set.

Donna added, "It's too sad it had to end this way. But there is a lesson to be learned from my son's death. Pick the people you want to spend your time with. Don't spend time with people just because they have money."

What did Donna think of Sheila's new plea—not guilty because of insanity?

"I don't want her in the psychiatric unit," Donna said. "I want her to know exactly what it feels like for us mothers who have to deal with this."


On March 17, 2008, the *Eagle-Tribune* newspaper petitioned Judge Nadeau to have the previously sealed portion of Sheila's arrest warrant unsealed. Nadeau granted the request and the public learned for the first time new details regarding the case. Much of the new material pertained to how police first learned of Michael Deloge's death. According to a police affidavit, Mikey told his mother in 2005 that he thought Sheila was trying to kill him. An entry in Sheila's notebook appeared to describe the cremation of someone about Mikey's size. Witnesses saw Sheila cruelly beating Mikey. After he was gone, Sheila said, "He left and his family doesn't want anything to do with him."

One witness claimed that he was with Sheila one time in Hampton during her marriage to Wayne Ennis. Ennis was inside their apartment and had the door locked. When he refused to let her enter, Sheila fired a shot through the door.

During the investigation efforts were made to contact all of Sheila's known ex-boyfriends and husbands. Jimmy Brackett told them that Sheila had threatened to kill him three times, fired a gun at him twice, and had frequently scratched his face.

# The FBI Profiler

During the weeks leading up to Sheila's trial, the prosecution hired a former FBI criminal profiler, and now private consultant, named Mark E. Safarik to file a report and possibly testify at the trial. After seven years as a police officer, Safarik had served as an FBI agent for twenty-three years, and had acted as supervisory special agent for the FBI Behavioral Analysis Unit in Quantico, Virginia, from 1995 through 2007. His principal training was in crime scene analysis. He had conducted hundreds of crime scene assessments, published and lectured on the analysis and interpretation of violent crime scene behavior, and in 2008 was the executive director of Forensic Behavioral Services International. He had been an expert witness at the trial of several serial killers, and his work had been featured on the Discovery Channel, CNN, and CourtTV.

Safarik wrote a letter on March 5 to the prosecution in which he said, *By definition, the homicides of Countie and Deloge would be captured under the definition of serial murder. Most serial killers are not psychotic. They are in touch with reality. Their response to the challenges of continuing their killing is what allows them to elude law enforcement scrutiny and focus. They clearly know that what they are doing is against the law. They simply choose to ignore both the moral and legal implications.*

The profiler came to the conclusion that Sheila's known murders—that of Deloge and Countie—showed signs of "serial" behavior. Thus, jurors were to believe these were not the acts of an insane woman. His logic was that since Sheila was a serial killer, and serial killers were sane, Sheila was sane.

When Sheila's defense team learned of Safarik's report, they objected to Safarik being called as an expert witness at the trial, questioning whether the former profiler used "reliable methodologies" in preparing his report. The defense called Safarik's opinions "highly prejudicial." The objection was voiced during a half-hour, behind-closed-doors meeting with Judge Nadeau.

Brad Bailey protested that Safarik had no background in psychiatry or forensic science. "He merely purports himself to be an FBI profiler. Safarik's scientific opinions are speculative," he said. Bailey asked that a Daubert hearing be held on whether Safarik's "serial murder analysis" relied on "real science" and could be used against Sheila's insanity defense.

Jeffrey Denner added, "There are a lot of issues that need to be brought in front of the judge. We are not comfortable with the assumption that this is a serial killer case. We believe that this woman is clearly insane. That her mental illness prevents her from doing what serial killers do, which is to repeatedly kill, according to a certain MO, certain deliberation, a certain premeditated pattern. We don't think that happened here at all."

He added, "We don't believe what they are seeking to introduce has a scientific basis."

According to behavioral-unit-type thinking, a serial killer is a person who commits three or more murders with a "cooling-off" period between. Without the cooling-off period, the murderers of three or more are called "spree killers." Sheila's defense team wanted it to be known that, by that definition, Sheila should never be referred to as a serial killer.

To that, prosecutor Jane Young replied that the state had never used that term to describe the defendant and that they were "not going by any definition."

The prosecution also said they wanted to add to their witness list three attorneys who worked with Sheila near the time of the killings. Those attorneys were Lynn Morse, who was the Exeter town attorney, Michael McCarthy, of Hampton, and Michael Craig, of Manchester. Sheila met with Morse and McCarthy between the murders of Deloge in 2005 and Countie in 2006. The stated purpose of those consultations was to discuss a rental property in the town of Somersworth that Sheila was managing. Sheila met with Craig in the days after Countie's murder. She met Craig on March 27, 2006. She left his office promising to get money for his retainer and return, but instead she hired Jeffrey Denner. Local papers noted that Craig was the son of former Manchester police chief Louis Craig.

Young said the state needed to talk to the lawyers to help their case that Sheila was sane at the time of the murders and was making calculated moves to help her cause.

Denner objected to those witnesses, saying, "We simply don't believe that the attorney-client privilege is waived simply because an insanity defense is presented in the case."

Bailey added, "The attorney-client privilege is an absolute privilege and we have not waived it. The defendant's assertion of an insanity defense does not act as a carte blanche waiver of the attorney-client privilege."

When the meeting was through, Judge Nadeau assured the public that nothing had occurred that might jeopardize the trial schedule, and indicated that the meeting was held in secret because it dealt in part with "communication issues" between Sheila and her defense team.

On April 7 Judge Nadeau granted one prosecution wish during the meeting. She said that, first thing, before any testimony was heard, jurors would be allowed to tour the LaBarre farm as part of the proceedings, including the spots where the state claimed Sheila incinerated her victims. Stops on the tour would include the exterior of the farmhouse, the back woods locations where Sheila's truck and bloody coat were found when investigators arrived, and the Epping Wal-Mart where Kenneth Countie was last seen alive. Jurors would not be allowed inside the farmhouse, where blood spatter from the dismemberment of the bodies was found, Judge Nadeau ruled. The judge said she made this decision because of "deteriorating and unsafe conditions inside the house."

If her defense team approved, and it did, Sheila would be allowed to accompany the jury on the trip, but she would have to keep her mouth shut.

Upon learning that jurors would be visiting the farm, *Foster's Daily Democrat* reporters Gretyl MacAlaster and John Huff went there to get an idea of what the jurors would find. What they found was pretty depressing. Although it was true that the farmhouse and the farm itself had gone downhill between the time of Wilfred LaBarre's death and when Sheila was arrested, that change was nothing compared to the deterioration that had occurred between Sheila's arrest and the spring of 2008. The fields were untilled and covered with dead hay. The farmhouse wasn't just abandoned, but had been vandalized as well. Months of teenagers visiting the "haunted house" had taken its toll. The windows were all broken, probably by thrown rocks. The inside of the house, where kids held séances looking for Captain Shaw and the ghosts of Sheila's victims, was far more trashed than it had been when Sheila was neglecting the housework. On either side of the house were cars and trucks that had been abandoned, their windows smashed in, bullet holes in their bodies, their tires slashed, their bodywork pocked with dents. A closer look showed that someone had got inside the vehicles and slashed the seats with a knife. A peek through the broken windows of the house showed the rooms to be littered with paper and artwork. The floorboards were moldy and rotting from the dampness of exposure. The house's screened-in porch, once a place to sit and enjoy the coolness of the night air, now housed discarded furniture and appliances, which had been haphazardly heaped into a pile.

One thing that struck the journalists was just how secluded the location was. From the vicinity of the farmhouse, the only other buildings in sight were the rundown barn and a couple of other smaller buildings, which belonged to the property. There were no visible neighbors.

The reporters searched in vain for the spot where the burn piles had been. What hadn't been removed by police investigators had been destroyed and covered up by the weather and time.

One indication that something very bad had happened here was discovered by the reporters at the very entrance to the property. It was a makeshift memorial. A large drawing of Kenneth Countie had been attached to the trunk of a tree, while at the base of that tree trunk were the remains of flowers, several written messages expressing love, glass pebbles, seashells, figurines of Christmas scenes, a small statue of a rabbit with large eyes, a couple of baseball caps, a hockey stick, and other sports equipment.

The reporters weren't the only people visiting the site. Also scouting the location was Sheila's defense team. The lawyers were bothered by the memorial to Kenny on the tree trunk, and at the first opportunity made a motion to the court that the memorial be taken down before the jury's visit to the farm, making the case that the large photo and the flowers would be *unduly prejudicial to the defendant*. The motion added that the memorial provided *no relevant evidence* and served *no purpose but to inflame the jury*.

Peter Eleey, the attorney who was now representing the families of both Deloge and Countie, subsequently announced that he had talked to Countie's family and they had agreed to temporarily remove the memorial before the jury visited the site, but that it would be restored afterward. In a separate interview Eleey warned everyone that he would be attending every day of the trial and would be prepared to counter any evidence presented by either side that implied that his clients were sexually deviant and had participated in incest and pedophilia.

\* \* \*

Judge Nadeau ruled on April 11 that the state could talk to two lawyers, Lynn Morse and Michael McCarthy, who had dealings with Sheila after she killed Kenneth Countie, and that those lawyers would be allowed to testify at the trial if the state wished to call them. The judge ruled, however, that no verbal or nonverbal communications between Sheila and those lawyers would be allowed in the testimony because that would violate the lawyer-client privilege. The subject of those meetings were Sheila's real estate holdings. The testimony, she ruled, would be limited to "the appropriateness of the defendant's conduct." Judge Nadeau was still contemplating her ruling on whether or not FBI profiler Mark Safarik would be allowed to testify.

Also that day the state released a list of 140 possible prosecution witnesses. There was Sheila's family, neighbors, police, and the guy from the septic tank service who sifted the contents of Sheila's tank for evidence. The defense countered with a list of seventy potential witnesses of its own. The two lists had forty-three names in common.

Journalist Lara Bricker's article on the unusual nature of the upcoming trial appeared in the New Hampshire Bar Association newsletter a week later. She pointed out that in most cases when a defendant is declared indigent, he/she is appointed a public defender. However, in this case attorneys Denner and Bailey, of Boston, asked Judge Nadeau to allow them to defend Sheila. The case was complex and they'd been with Sheila from the start. They couldn't "abandon Sheila midstream." Denner told Bricker that an insanity defense for his client was the game plan from very early on, that "there was a very legitimate insanity, lack of criminal responsibility issue here." He said that he felt Sheila had come to trust him and Bailey, and since they had promised to stick by her side throughout the legal process, they were not going to break that promise because of monetary considerations. "I love working in New Hampshire. There's a pace of life that reflects itself a little in the pace of the courtrooms that is a lot more attractive to me," Denner said. "There's a nice collegiality that you sometimes lose in the more metropolitan areas." Sentencing, however, he said, was tougher in New Hampshire.

Near the end of April, questionnaires were sent to approximately five hundred potential jurors. Of those, a pool of about three hundred were expected to arrive at Rockingham County Superior Court on Monday, May 5, 2008, for the first day of jury selection.

Jim Boffetti said that five hundred potential jurors was not an unusually high number in a first-degree murder case—especially one with this much notoriety. Boffetti predicted that eighteen jurors would be chosen—twelve to serve on the panel and six alternates—because of the predicted length of the trial. Which six of the jurors were to be alternates would not be revealed until the jury was sent to deliberate.

"The reason you do that is if in the middle of a trial a juror has a health problem or a family issue, you have enough people, so at the end you have a jury of twelve," Boffetti said.

Whittling three hundred jurors down to eighteen was an orderly process. The first cut would come when jurors who had a personal knowledge of any of the lawyers, or any of the witnesses, were dismissed. After that, the voir dire process would begin. Both sides would have the opportunity to interview the potential jurors. These interviews would last about five minutes each, and the goal was to remove any potential juror who was biased in one direction or the other. Both sides had the right to "strike" as many jurors as they liked on the grounds that that person could not be fair and impartial. Each side could also strike fifteen jurors without a stated reason. This was called a peremptory challenge.

# No One Knows
# Whose Toes

On April 29, 2008, the public got an inkling of the topics that had recently been discussed during behind-closed-door meetings between the lawyers on both sides and Judge Nadeau. One question answered was why FBI profiler Mark Safarik could so definitively refer to Sheila as a serial killer, even though she was known to have killed only two persons. (A minimum of three kills is necessary for a murderer to be classified by the FBI as a serial killer.)

In an admissibility ruling Judge Nadeau wrote that Safarik's analysis of the case had been based on evidence including *toes discovered at the defendant's property belonging to an unidentified male whom the defendant murdered.*

This quote was the only mention of the toe bones in Judge Nadeau's statement, so it remained unknown precisely where on Sheila's property, or when the bones had been discovered.

Almost two years after the search of the farmhouse and its property, it was revealed for the first time that there were bones found that belonged neither to Kenneth

Countie nor Michael Deloge. That brought Sheila's known kills up to three, thus classifying her as a serial killer. And, of course, the locals were convinced that Wilfred LaBarre had also been a victim.

Judge Nadeau's ruling was that the FBI profiler could not testify at Sheila's trial, stating that his testimony would be "more prejudicial than helpful" to the jury. In her decision she noted that the admissibility of expert opinions was governed by New Hampshire Rule of Evidence 702, which said that scientific, technical, or other specialized knowledge would assist the trier of fact to understand the evidence or to determine a fact in issue. Expert testimony must, therefore, *rise to a threshold level of reliability to be admissible.* Judge Nadeau ruled that though the FBI profiler's analysis might have been relevant if the trial was determining Sheila's innocence or guilt, that matter had been settled by Sheila's insanity plea.

*Although Safarik possesses specialized knowledge in the area of crime scene analysis . . . [he] does not possess qualifications in psychiatry and psychology,* she wrote.

The judge believed, however, that the profiler's analysis of Sheila's psychology was not relevant in the case. According to her written decision, she felt that the profiler's testimony would only confuse the jury.

*The Court agrees that Safarik is not qualified by experience or training to give an expert opinion relating to sanity and his testimony is therefore irrelevant,* Nadeau wrote. *In sum, because Safarik's testimony is not relevant to the issue of sanity, it is not admissible. Moreover, the State is precluded from offering testimony through Safarik or any other witness that unidentified toes were discovered at the defendant's property because the Court finds that the unfair prejudice of this testimony will far outweigh its probative value.*

Prosecutor Jim Boffetti refused to comment on the toes. Since it was known that DNA testing and other forensic techniques had been used to positively identify the remains of Countie and Deloge, the fact that the toe bones didn't match either of those profiles definitively categorized them as belonging to a third, and unknown, victim.

Brad Bailey also had no comment, although it was clear that the judge's ruling was a major victory for Sheila's defense team. His argument that the FBI profiler's methodology in defining Sheila as a serial killer was flawed must have carried weight with the judge. Serial killers, the FBI profiler had said, take steps to avoid being caught, thus proving that they are sane.

In her decision Judge Nadeau also declared that, in her opinion, Sheila failed to meet the criteria of being a serial killer, in that she lacked the ability to blend into society, and although she was similar to other serial killers in that her victims were dependent on her, she differed from Safarik's profile in *her methodology and alleged motive.*

As jury selection approached, Jeffrey Denner said he did *not* expect the process to go smoothly.

"Normally, in a high-profile case with as much exposure as this, you'll find people come in with a lot of preconceived notions. Certainly, it's a concern," Denner said. "I suspect we'll go through a lot of potential jurors before we finally find a jury."

Using the questionnaires that the jury pool had filled out, Denner said, "We will be able to get a feel for them and they will be able to get a feel for us."

The court would be drawing upon its pool of six

thousand jurors that appeared on its annual list, names chosen from the Department of Motor Vehicles and local voting registration. Jurors that were selected would be paid $20 per day—plus mileage if they lived outside of Rockingham. Employers were not required to pay their employees during jury duty, but by law, they had to guarantee that the jurors' jobs would be waiting for them when the trial was over. Potential jurors were allowed to opt out of jury duty if they could show a financial hardship.

# Jury Selection

Monday morning, May 5, was a perfect spring day in New Hampshire. The temperature was in the sixties, and the modern Rockingham County Superior Court building looked great against the cloudless sky. Out front were forty flowering white dogwoods and a riot of azalea. The building was busy, as well as beautiful. The courthouse was bustling.

About ninety potential jurors reported to the court for the morning session, and another 110 reported in the afternoon. Carolynn Lodge and several other of Kenneth Countie's relatives were in court watching the proceedings. Only family members and the press were allowed in the courtroom for the process.

Sheila was there, of course, wearing a black jacket over her green prison jumpsuit. She wore black horn-rimmed glasses, and she tended to look over the top of them. When she complained that she suffered from migraines and needed caffeine, she was allowed to sip on Pepsi.

Sheila's hair was what appeared to be its natural color, dark brown, and she wore it down and loose. It covered her face from the sides and prevented most courtroom spectators from seeing her expressions.

The process of interviewing prospective jurors to weed out those with a possible bias is called voir dire. It is common in most states, but in New Hampshire it only takes place before first-degree murder cases.

Each member of the jury pool was questioned by Judge Nadeau, by members of Sheila's defense team, and finally by prosecutors. Asking questions for the defense were Brad Bailey, Jeffrey Denner, and Lauren Thomas. Jane Young, James Boffetti, and Ann Rice questioned for the state AG's office.

Initial questions asked of the jury pool were:

1) Do you have any connections with any of the persons associated with the case?

2) Do you accept the possibility that Sheila may have been insane when she murdered her two known victims?

If any jurors answered yes to the first question, or no to the second, they were promptly dismissed.

Those that passed that round were asked: What does the term "insanity" mean to you? What factors would you consider in determining insanity? And do you feel there is a difference between mental illness and insanity?

Those who thought that insanity and mental illness were synonymous were dismissed by the prosecution. Those who expressed opinions that insanity was something that people "faked" were let go by the defense.

Defense attorneys asked the prospective jurors if they believed police were more likely to tell the truth than a layperson. Those who said yes were rejected.

Judge Nadeau said that though it may be appropriate for jurors who believed the word of police to carry more weight than the word of other citizens to be dismissed, she wanted it known that, in her opinion, it was reasonable to expect the police to be truthful.

How easily shocked a juror might be had to be determined before they were put on the panel. Jurors were warned by the defense that those chosen for this trial would have to be emotionally strong, that testimony would be emotionally draining, involving "a variety of fairly ugly issues," containing evidence of "sadomasochism, incest, pedophilia, and sexual abuse."

As these words were spoken, Sheila turned to the photographers at the back of the courtroom, narrowed her eyes, and glared. Her mood was not universally foul, however, as she flashed her prettiest smile for photographer Mark Bolton, of the *Union Leader*. Because her hair was pulled back into a ponytail, it was easier for spectators to see her face.

One juror answered the question about sadomasochism by saying that she fainted when she thought of other people in pain. The juror was dismissed.

Defense attorneys' questions implied that their argument would hinge on the theory that Sheila's insanity was triggered by certain events, most likely her delusional belief that her lovers were sexually abusing children.

One woman was asked if she thought outside influences could trigger an insane reaction. She said yes and was chosen to sit on the jury.

Some members of the jury pool failed to fit the bill because of their preconceived notions of criminal trials in general. One man, who happened to be the last juror interviewed on Tuesday, was dismissed when he expressed his intense distaste for all defense attorneys. He didn't know why, he just didn't like 'em. This made everyone in the courtroom, including Sheila, laugh.

Most of the jurors who were dismissed were done so "for cause," which meant that both sides found them inappropriate. One juror, for example, said that she thought the whole trial was a waste of taxpayers' money because she "didn't believe in no insanity defense."

Others were dismissed by one of the sides for a specific reason. Several were let go because they were aware of the unidentified toe bones that had been found on Sheila's farm, indicating a third victim.

The process went smoothly, and by noon on Tuesday, four jurors had been selected. By the end of the second day of selection, two more panelists had joined their ranks. Both sides were pleased with the pace.

On the third day of jury selection, Sheila maintained the same color scheme, now wearing a black sweater over her jumpsuit, and the proceedings maintained their crisp pace. Twenty-five candidates for the jury took their turn in the courtroom's witness stand, answering questions from Judge Nadeau, and from prosecutors and defense attorneys. It was a day of opposites. Prospective jurors seemed either eager to be chosen or to be dismissed. Not everyone got their way.

A music teacher wanted to serve. When asked, she explained that she put on an end-of-year production, and, yes, that might be a distraction for her.

"But I think I can put it aside," she said hopefully.

She was asked about her children and admitted that she had a son who was approximately the same age as Kenneth Countie. She admitted under questioning that this case was an emotional issue for her, at which point she was dismissed for cause.

Another eager-to-be-chosen juror was a simple man who claimed to have heard nothing about the case. When asked if he had read anything about the case, he

Sheila LaBarre's first identified victim, Michael Deloge, grew up in West Haven, Connecticut, a blue-collar town, living with his father and stepmother. *(Photo courtesy of Joy Storer Deloge)*

According to his stepmother, Michael Deloge dreamed as a boy of being a songwriter. That would have been something that he and Sheila LaBarre had in common. *(Photo courtesy of Joy Storer Deloge)*

In 1993 Michael married his girlfriend when she became pregnant.
*(Photo courtesy of Joy Storer Deloge)*

Michael and his son Aaron. After Michael and his wife divorced, his family lost touch with Michael's son and ex-wife. Michael, who had a long history of problems with drugs and alcohol, took off for New Hampshire to start a new life. *(Photo courtesy of Joy Storer Deloge)*

Michael had aged poorly by 2005 when Sheila LaBarre videotaped him
accusing his family of allowing him to be sexually molested as a child.
*(Photo courtesy of Joy Storer Deloge)*

Michael Deloge was living in the Cross Roads homeless shelter in
Portsmouth, New Hampshire when he met Sheila. He eventually moved in
with her at her farm, and she subsequently murdered him. *(Author photo)*

Sheila's final victim, the mentally handicapped Kenneth Countie, had only lived away from his mother for a few months—including a short-lived attempt at serving in the military—when he met his killer.

Sheila and Kenneth's first date was at the Ashworth-by-the-Sea Hotel in Hampton Beach, New Hampshire. *(Author photo)*

After sitting in the back in a corner at the Ashworth lounge, having drinks, Sheila and Kenneth went to her car in the parking garage and had sex twice. *(Photo courtesy of Anne Darrigan)*

Sheila LaBarre combined paranoia and sexual perversion with deadly results. But was she criminally insane? *(Photo by Don Clark)*

Sheila's closest relative was her older sister Lynn, who was willing to talk about the horrible abuse they had endured as children at the hands of their father and his friends. *(Photo by Suzanne Danforth)*

Dr. LaBarre, seen here in a hat, with his horse and buggy, was a beloved member of the Epping, New Hampshire community. He gave rides on his buggy to children and, on this occasion, led the funeral procession for his friend and neighbor Bert Allen. *(Photo by Catherine Casavant)*

Following Sheila's arrest, Bert Allen's widow Frances *(pictured)* said, "She's been living there a long time and she has had quite a few menfolk living with her." *(Photo by Catherine Casavant)*

Red Oak Hill was a purely pastoral place until Sheila arrived. Neighbors didn't like the flashy Sheila from the start. They had no idea of the grief she would eventually cause. *(Author photo)*

Dr. LaBarre's chiropractic office in Hampton, New Hampshire. For a time Sheila lived in the upstairs apartment, where she once stabbed a lover in the forehead with a pair of cuticle scissors. *(Author photo)*

In an incident that was bizarre even for her, Sheila took a badly beat up Kenneth Countie to the Wal-Mart in Epping and tried to convince employees there that the eventual murder victim had been attacked by another female customer. *(Author photo)*

The LaBarre farm was at the end of a long dirt road through the woods. The nearest neighbor was too far away to hear the screams of her tortured victims. *(Author photo)*

Sheila came to pick up Kenneth Countie in her Nissan pickup truck. Kenneth told his roommate he'd be back the next day, but he never returned. *(Author photo)*

The LaBarre farmhouse where Sheila killed at least three men: Michael Deloge, Kenneth Countie, and a third victim who was never identified. *(Author photo)*

After Dr. LaBarre's death, the farmhouse fell into disrepair, but the barn where the horses were kept remained orderly and clean. *(Photo by Anne Darrigan)*

The LaBarre farmhouse was sealed as evidence but that seal was quickly broken by a steady parade of teenagers and curiosity seekers using the "haunted house" as a site for parties and séances. *(Photo by Anne Darrigan)*

Following each murder, Sheila started a big fire. The victims' bones were later sifted out of the ashes. Only the unidentified victim's toe bones were found. *(Photo by author)*

The farm's chicken coops doubled as jail cells for Sheila's lovers when they had misbehaved and were in need of discipline. *(Photo by author)*

Prosecutor James Boffetti convinced the jury at Sheila's sanity trial that there was "an important distinction between being diagnosed with a mental illness and being legally insane." *(Photo by Suzanne Danforth)*

In the prosecution's opening statement, Ann Rice said, "Actions the defendant took after each killing will make it clear that she knew what she was doing, and she knew it was wrong." *(Photo by Suzanne Danforth)*

Defense attorney Brad Bailey was named one of Boston Magazine's "Super Lawyers" for 2004, 2006 and 2007, and "New England Super Lawyer" for 2007.
*(Photo by Suzanne Danforth)*

Defense attorney Jeffrey A. Denner argued, "Sheila looked at the world through a very different lens than you or I. Suffice it to say, she killed these people because she is utterly insane." The jury, however, did not buy it.
*(Photo by Suzanne Danforth)*

Before the trial started, the jury got on a school bus outside the courthouse and toured the Wal-Mart and the LaBarre farm, so they would be able to better understand testimony. *(Photo by Suzanne Danforth)*

Though the evidence presented at trial included the ugly and spurious accusations of molestation and incest hurled by Sheila, Kenneth Countie's mother Carolynn sat with her chin held high in the courtroom every day, sending a silent message to the jury. *(Photo by Suzanne Danforth)*

Kenneth Countie's mother and prosecutor Ann Rice embraced and the jury's verdict sent Sheila to prison for two lifetimes. *(Photo by Suzanne Danforth)*

On the road leading to the LaBarre farm is a memorial to Kenneth Countie prepared by his mother and other loved ones. On the tree is a hockey stick, a note from mother to son, flowers, and other items honoring the victim and expressing the loved ones' grief. *(Author photo)*

answered, "I don't read. I drive to work and I listen to music."

"You never heard anything about the case?" Bailey asked incredulously.

"No," the man said, insistent.

"Tell me what you associate with the name Sheila LaBarre?" Bailey asked.

"I associate it with, I don't know how to put it, I associate it with someone who killed a person," the man said.

The defense repeatedly asked the same questions. Do you associate insanity with hiding from responsibility? Do you associate insanity with trying to pull the wool over someone's eyes? Can you be insane if sometimes you are normal, but you go in and out of that condition? Is it in your thought that some people with a serious mental illness can sometimes appear to not be so mentally ill to the outside world? Do you understand what is meant by the words "domination" and "abuse"? Do you understand that in some relationships there is a dominant and a submissive? Do you or any member of your family attend Alcoholics Anonymous meetings? After all, drug use and "other types of addictions" were going to be testified about during the trial.

The prosecution also maintained a theme in its questioning. "What kind of information would you like to hear to help decide whether or not she was insane?" Boffetti frequently asked.

One male prospective juror, when asked about the insanity defense, gave an opinion that seemed to reflect how many locals felt about the subject: "I think—for lack of a better phrase—it's the last line of defense. I would be looking for a history of mental disease." Although he said that he did believe there were legitimate insanity cases, he felt that, far more often, insanity was a last-ditch attempt to escape responsibility.

Prosecutors wanted to make sure that the jurors understood the law, asking questions such as, "If it is the defense's burden of proof in this case and they need to show that the defendant is insane, what would the state of New Hampshire need to prove?" The correct answer was nothing. Many jurors were unable to give an adequate answer. "The state has to prove she is insane" was a common—and wrong—answer.

An older female schoolteacher did understand. When she was asked to define as best she could what "insanity" meant, she said, "Insanity is no control over behavior, the inability to tell right from wrong." She said that she had taken a keen interest in the case right from the start because of how unusual it was to find a woman who could dominate a man. The juror was dismissed for cause.

Although the majority of potential jurors had excuses for not wanting to serve—"My father was murdered," "I am hard of hearing," "I am self-employed," "I have plane tickets in June"—the number of jurors chosen to serve rose to ten by the end of the third day.

On day four, the golden sunshine over New Hampshire had been replaced by a gray drizzle. Sheila's mood appeared to have darkened with the weather. She was less willing to turn around and face the press photographers, who wanted to take her picture. She didn't even partake in her favorite courtroom pastime, glaring at Kenneth Countie's family.

By the end of court on Thursday, fourteen jurors had been chosen. Two were from Boston, one a scientist and the other a lawyer. One was a housewife who was married to a lawyer, and another was an older woman who spent her winters with her retired husband in Arizona.

One man said that he thought at first that he could be a good juror but after some "soul searching" he realized he could not, that he was biased in favor of the prosecution, that he didn't think insanity could be the cause of both the murder of Kenneth Countie and Michael Deloge, because those two murders took place at different times. He said he had come to the conclusion that Sheila's insanity defense was a "ploy."

Another said she was uncomfortable with New Hampshire law. She wouldn't mind Sheila being found insane and going to a mental hospital instead of a prison, as long as she could be sure that Sheila was going to remain inside the walls of a secure mental hospital for the rest of her life. The fact that she could be proclaimed "cured" and released back into the world made her uneasy.

On Friday, another rainy day, Sheila was back to her more animated self. She reached out and touched the hand of one of her attorneys when she agreed with something he said, and laughed at one point, appreciating a humorous moment with her defense team. Friday turned out to be the least productive day of the week. Perhaps it was because the remaining members of the jury pool had been waiting all week for their turn to be questioned, but only one new member of the jury was chosen, thus necessitating a sixth day of voir dire.

The lone new member of the jury was a man who had only moved to New Hampshire in March and knew nothing about the case.

Those dismissed on Friday included a woman who said she was a spiritual teacher and a psychic. She said that because she was self-employed that six weeks serving on the jury would cause her a financial hardship. Another woman was dismissed when she said she was a member of the clergy. Although she said she could try her best to follow only the instructions of the court, she couldn't ignore her own personal beliefs.

Because the pool of prospective jurors was shrinking down to a precious few, Judge Nadeau ended the week's proceedings by saying that she was willing to start the trial with sixteen panelists, twelve jurors and only four alternates, rather than fall further behind schedule by calling a new pool of jurors to the courthouse. As it turned out, that wouldn't be necessary.

And so on May 12, as a nor'easter walloped the region, the job of picking a jury for Sheila's insanity trial continued. Ann Rice did the questioning for the prosecution. She asked the prospective jurors if they knew anyone who was quirky, outrageous, or wacky. Did they know anyone who was opinionated, difficult, confrontational, or dominant? Did that mean they were insane?

For the first time the prosecution was taking full advantage of the fact that the defense had the burden of proof in this case. "We don't have to prove anything," they were saying now, loud and clear.

In response Bailey was giving a lesson in New Hampshire law disguised as voir dire. He said that when it came to burden of proof in this trial, things would be different than other trials that perhaps they had seen in TV. The defense did not have to prove Sheila was insane beyond a reasonable doubt, but only that clear and convincing evidence indicated that she was insane *when killing* the two victims. Bailey told prospective jurors that they were going to hear expert witnesses on both sides, and those witnesses were going to contradict one another, and when that happened, it was okay to believe the one that "made sense."

During a ten-minute break between prospective jurors, Carolynn Lodge had an intense conversation with attorney Jane Young. Kenneth's mother held on to both of the lawyer's wrists as she spoke.

Just before noon the job of picking a jury was completed. The last to be approved was a man who worked in a nursing home in Merrimac County. Ten woman and eight men had been chosen. Judge Nadeau gave the jury its instructions. She told them that, unlike in most cases, the burden of proof in this case was with the defense. "That means that when you begin your deliberations, you must assume that the defendant was sane. It is up to the defense to prove that she was insane." The judge told the jury that first thing the next morning, they were going to be taken to the Wal-Mart and to the farm, to view those key locations. When they returned to the courtroom, opening statements would begin. Sheila was within her rights to go along on the view the next morning, and Sheila said that she would like to exercise those rights. The judge informed the defendant that that was okay, but she was going to have to wear a stun belt under her clothing. Not that anyone thought she was going to go running off into the woods or anything, but if she did, she would receive a mind-numbing shock.

Sheila spoke right up in her high and light voice. "Well, actually, this is the first I've heard about it. I just want to be sure someone doesn't"—she paused and shook her head—"shock me"—again she paused— "arbitrarily. I can guarantee you I have no interest in fleeing."

Judge Nadeau explained that the stun belt was the best option for her because it meant she would not have to be seen by the jury shuffling around in her shackles and chains.

"Anything else?" Judge Nadeau asked.

Sheila raised her tiny hand—surprisingly tiny, everyone noticed—and began to speak, but Bailey jumped in to stop her.

"Why don't you address your attorney first. That is usually what I ask people to do," Judge Nadeau suggested.

After some discussion Sheila's defense team successfully talked her out of asking her follow-up question.

When proceedings were through for the day, reporters peppered Denner with questions and he fielded them deftly, like a legal shortstop.

"Why does Sheila get to go along on the viewing?"

"Because the viewing is a critical stage in the proceedings, and defendants are allowed to attend critical stages."

"Are you worried about Sheila's reaction to the property, given the state it is in?"

"It will be the first time Sheila has seen her farm since she was arrested two years ago. It may be an emotional moment for her, but it is important for her to see what is going on."

"Who will be doing the opening statement?"

"Bailey. I'll be doing the closing. Thank you."

# First Day

The trial began on the morning of May 13, 2008, with something that looked like a parade. After a speech from prosecutor Jane Young, in which jurors were told to make note of the vastness and remoteness of Sheila's property, the jurors rode in two small yellow school busses, while Sheila and others drove in cars. The convoy toured the Epping sites that the jurors would need to visualize as they listened to evidence.

One of the sheriff's deputies carried the "button," which if pressed would shock Sheila so hard that she would be unable to run.

The parade passed the Wal-Mart, where Sheila twice visited with Kenneth Countie, although it did not stop so that jurors could see the inside of the store.

From there, the caravan traveled to the farmhouse, where Sheila killed and dismembered Countie, Deloge, and possibly others.

Here, the motorcade stopped and everyone got out. The jurors were allowed to wander around the grounds and familiarize themselves with the area. Sheila, along with Kenneth Countie's family, also got out, but they didn't move around much. They stood near the separate vehicles that had brought them and watched the jurors.

The defendant was stoic at first, wistfully gazing out over the land. About ten minutes after they arrived, as jurors were boarding the bus to leave, Sheila briefly cried, perhaps realizing that this was probably the last time she would ever see her former home.

Next, everyone proceeded to the spot where Sheila's blood-spattered coat was found, and the spot where Sheila had last left her Nissan pickup truck.

The parade returned to the courthouse in Brentwood, and after a recess, the trial began. The right side of courtroom #2, the prosecution side, was full. The press sat on the right side, behind the prosecution. Four rows of seats, the back two reserved for press, were filled. On the left side, the defense side, there were only a handful of spectators. It felt like a wedding in which the groom was a lot more popular than the bride.

The first order of business was the reading of the charges: two counts of first-degree murder. Judge Nadeau gave her instructions to the jury.

"My job is to determine what the law is," she said. "Your job is to determine what the facts are. When the trial is over, you will not be allowed to take a transcript of the testimony with you. When a witness is on the stand, that is your one and only opportunity to see and hear them. Listen carefully to what they say. Observe carefully their demeanor. Remember, while the trial is going on, you are not allowed to talk to anyone about it—not even each other.

"You may take notes during testimony, but not during

the opening and closing arguments. I discourage copious notes. It is better to listen closely to what is being said. Too much note-taking can distract you. Your job is to determine the credibility and reliability of each witness. Listen not just to what is being said, but how it is being said. Any notes you do take will be collected and destroyed after your verdict to preserve the secrecy of your deliberations."

The judge issued to each juror a steno-style notebook. She said that all notes had to be written in these notebooks, and that the notebooks would be collected at the end of each day.

The opening statement for the defense was given by Brad Bailey. After introducing himself he explained that he and Denner would be taking turns examining the witnesses. He told the jurors that they had each been selected to serve because they had promised to be fair and to keep an open mind. He said he planned to hold them to those promises.

"You have promised to detach yourself from the fact that our client isn't contesting two murders in this case. This case is not about punishment, sentencing, or is anyone going free? It is about insanity." He told the jurors that there were a couple of key questions they had to ask themselves as they listened to the evidence. "Was our client insane at the time of these murders? Was she suffering from some sort of mental defect when she committed the alleged acts—and were those acts the product of her mental disease?" Bailey said.

The defense, he said, would argue that Sheila's behavior before, during, and after the time of the murders was full of moments that painted a clear picture of insanity.

He told the jury a little of what they should expect to hear from the prosecution, that Sheila destroyed evidence to avoid being charged, that she knew the difference between right and wrong. He urged the jury that while they listened to that evidence, they should not lose their common sense.

He asked the jury a series of questions:

"Does someone who is sane try to cover up her crimes by placing her bruised and dazed and beaten victim in a wheelchair and [bring him] through a public store, lifting his shirt and causing a scene, drawing the attention of everyone in that store to her—mere days before his end?

"Does someone sane cover up a crime by playing a tape for her local police, playing them a tape of one of her victims retching and vomiting while she is accusing him of faking his symptoms, cajoling him into confessing to crimes he never committed, just a mere matter of days before she kills him. Is that someone who is sane?

"Does someone who is sane cover up her crime by burning a body within steps of her own front door while placing a picture of a Cherokee chief on a chair next to her burn pile and leave the picture in the burn pile for all who are there later to see it?

"Does someone who is sane cover up her crime by leaving a human bone visible in the burn pile by her door, and when confronted about it, say that the bone belongs either to a large rabbit or a pedophile? Asked moments later, immediately saying she never said that.

"Does someone who is sane cover up a crime by greeting the police on her property with ashes and soot on her face? With crucifixes strewn on items on her lawn?

"Does someone who is sane tell the police officer that

her victims' remains are in the bag nearby and then points out that bag?

"Does someone who is sane, when asked to come with the police, ask one question—'May my pet rabbit come with me?'

"Does someone who is sane cover up her crime by keeping the remains of another victim in green bags in the trunk of her car for two weeks?

"Does someone who is sane cover up her crime by agreeing to give five different statements to police in which she refers to the victim as a pedophile, and suggests he might have fallen or jumped himself into a fire pit, all while denying knowing what happened to this person?

"Does someone who is sane flee a crime by dying her hair red and purple, thereby assuring that she is not going to blend in, but rather stand out?

"Does someone who is sane flee by meeting two men, having sexual relations with each of them, and telling one afterward that he just had sex with an angel, an avenging angel?

"Does someone who is sane cover up her crime by saying things so alarming that he actually calls the police to inquire if someone in the area has escaped from the mental institution?

"Does someone sane kill two people within six months based solely on the same delusions about things that never happened? Does someone who is sane keep acting on those same fictitious delusions when they aren't true?"

Bailey paused and let that sink in. When he started in again, his tone was softer as he tried to pry from the jury's minds any lingering misconceptions about what is and isn't "insane." As Bailey spoke, Carolynn Lodge and

Donna Boston, the mothers of the two known victims, sat together in the front row of the spectator section, sometimes holding hands.

"This isn't the type of case where there will be evidence where someone is parading around naked or howling at the moon. Although it is true that Sheila could maintain a seemingly ordinary day-to-day life between murders. She could go to court, pay bills, write letters, and lodge complaints. Her insanity always emerged when it came to her relationships with men.

"This is a deeply troubled woman, a woman who beat her men with sticks. Even in front of other people. This is a woman who thought the men in her life were pedophiles, child molesters, and child abusers. She believed that the men in her life, including her last two boyfriends, had sexual relations with their own mothers and were the victims of incest. She believed that the men with whom she shared her bed were hurting her animals, killing her animals, sometimes in preposterous ways.

"She believed that there were people who lived in her woods who were out to get her. The whole world was out to get her. That the men were having homosexual relations with each other. She believed that a ghost lived in her house and attacked her. She believed that she had died and come back to earth.

"This is a woman who sincerely believes she has been told by God himself, even though she's died in a car crash several years before, to return to earth for, and I quote her, 'find the reason why.' I want you to think of a woman who polygraphs her lovers, forces and compels these men to admit things that they never did or never happened, a woman who believes being a notary public gives her special powers, who believes those powers give her the ability to be the judge, jury, and executioner.

This is a woman whose insanity grew as she got older, and she became more aggressive toward each man she encountered. She nearly killed a few of her boyfriends before she finally succeeded in taking a life. One ex-boyfriend now drives a car with vanity plates that read 'I'm Alive.' This is a woman who truly believes that she is an angel, a spirit walking among the living, who has returned to earth for a special purpose. This is a woman who honestly believes that her two victims thanked her for killing them. When it is all taken together at the end of this case, I submit that you will know insanity is there," Bailey said. "And you will see it. As elusive as it may sound to you, you will know insanity when you see it, and you will see it in this case. You will know insanity when you see it, and it is looking right at you. It won't even be close. It will be staring right back at you. All you need to do is look. Maybe at first you will see it there under the surface. Listen to her words. By the end of this case, you are going to see it boiling right out and over the top."

After a break Ann Rice gave the opening statement for the prosecution. She said that the prosecution would argue that the murders of Michael Deloge and Kenneth Countie were not the actions of an insane woman.

"Actions the defendant took after each killing will make it clear that she knew what she was doing, and she knew it was wrong," Rice said. "She destroyed the evidence, burned them, sifted their ashes, and lied about their whereabouts. She told people they had left on their own accord and that she was glad to get rid of them. When she learned that police were onto her, she ran, she looked for an apartment in Massachusetts, she cut and dyed her hair, she used a false name—all acts designed to avoid detection."

The defendant, Rice argued, had an abrasive personality, and that there were many times when she acted perfectly rational.

"Her day-to-day behavior will tell you that she is not insane. She maintained a hauling business, rental properties, negotiated the sale of real estate, hired people to help her on her farm. She shopped, paid bills. Defense experts will tell you they never met her before her arrest. No one questioned her sanity. Not the police. Not the doctors. Not the people who saw her day to day," Rice said. "You will hear other words to describe her—weird, violent, vindictive, seductive, manipulative, controlling, calculating, outrageous. Witnesses who use those words to describe Sheila go as far back as the late 1980s. But they will also tell you she was well in control, that she was intelligent and articulate.

"The question will be, did she kill her victims impulsively or cunningly?" Rice told the jury. "Violent aggressiveness was a constant theme well before Michael and Kenny came into her life. Her violence against them was neither isolated nor unexpected.

"During the state's case, you will hear from fifty people who have known her in the last ten years. The resounding message is that the defendant was and is sane," Rice said. Dr. Albert Drukteinis would testify that Sheila had a mood dysfunction and a sexual disorder. He would say that she was hypersexual with exhibitionist tendencies and sadistic behaviors. He believed she was delusional when it came to pedophilia, but that the delusion was wrapped up in her urge to dominate and humiliate. She was a sexual dominant, a sadist.

"She had constant sexual urges and fantasies that are

beyond the norm. It's all wrapped up in the defendant's need to control men, dominate them, and humiliate them—and at the same time derive sexual satisfaction out of it," Rice said. "It is Dr. Drukteinis's opinion that the murders were not a product of that mental illness, and that is what is required for you to find the defendant insane."

For the first time a possible manner of death for Michael Deloge was publicly stated. Rice told the jurors that Sheila claimed to have killed Mikey by beating him over the head with a four-foot chain. She began beating him, she claimed, because she believed he had started to harm the farm animals. Sheila also claimed that she killed Kenneth during a fight over money and that he had died when he fell and hit his head on the tub. Rice told the jury that the state did not believe these scenarios to be true, that Sheila had fabricated them after the fact.

"Experts will tell you that her own accounts don't make sense, that she has woven the stories to fit the evidence," Rice said. "It was only eleven months after she was arrested, after filing a claim of insanity, that the defendant first told her story that she thought Michael was killing her rabbits, that she thought of her rabbits like children, and that a voice was telling her that Michael was going to kill her next, so she'd better protect herself. The same voice told her that Michael was evil and needed to die, that she hit him with a chain and saw blood, that she wanted to take him to a hospital, but he refused, that he became increasingly ill until he died, that she built a funeral pyre and cremated him.

"When it came to Kenny's death, she had fabricated two stories. First she told her attorneys that she beat him to death with a sledgehammer. In the other story they were enjoying sadomasochistic sex. She had beaten him with a belt before sexual intercourse and they had fallen asleep naked. She woke up with his hands around her neck—or, in another version, she woke up and he was going through her purse. Either way, when she woke up, he ran upstairs to the bathroom, where she said two thousand dollars was hidden in the wall. They fought, he slipped in the tub and fell and hit his head. She claimed she administered CPR, cut a hole in his neck, and tried to insert a straw through it in an effort to save him. Later, in a dream, she claimed she heard Kenny's voice telling her that he didn't want his mother to touch his body again. She said she never meant for Kenny to die. It was all an accident. Of course, her account is inconsistent with the physical evidence found at the house. Days earlier, Kenny had been seen so weak, so ill, that he couldn't run up a flight of stairs and fight her."

As Rice spoke, Sheila did not look at her, but rather scribbled notes furiously on a pad of paper in front of her. She noisily ripped off the paper with the note on it and shoved it into a pocket of her prison jumpsuit.

Rice described for the jury the defendant's MO with men. She chose men in the first place that could be easily dominated. "It was no coincidence that both men she killed were mentally disabled," Rice said. The defendant gained power of attorney over them. They didn't even understand what that meant. She distanced them from their families. She killed them, incinerated them, and "pulverized their bones."

Rice explained that not all of the defendant's boyfriends ended up dead. Some managed to break her spell and get away. One, James Bracket, left after the defendant smashed his teeth with a basting brush. They were also going to be hearing from one of the survivors, a man named Yvon

Blais, of Derry, who broke off his relationship with the defendant after only a couple of months. The defendant responded by coming after him. "She went to his mother's house and kicked down the door," Rice said.

Rice offered an overview of the case's backstory. Sheila met Wilfred LaBarre, gained control of his chiropractic office, assumed his name—even though they were never married—and gained complete control of his sizeable estate. Other tumultuous relationships ensued. Two of her boyfriends were dead. When abusing Michael Deloge, the defendant allowed Mikey to visit his mother only on the condition that he did not hug and kiss her. She forced Mikey to write a letter to his father in which he confessed to being a lost-cause pedophile, and that the defendant was the only person who could save him. Rice told the jury that they would be hearing from witnesses who observed the defendant beating and humiliating the victims, with a stick designed to inflict damage. The police finally broke the case when they responded to the missing persons report and found the fleshy bone in the fire. After being questioned by police, she took off. She was innocently helped along the way by the Paquins, Steven Martello, and Ken Washington. She was eventually arrested in Revere.

Rice gave the defendant's mental history, that she had once attempted suicide when she was in her early twenties, that she had never been diagnosed with a psychiatric disorder or was prescribed psychiatric medications. Her disorder was sexual. She had paraphilia—a long history of reductionism and exhibitionism. It was not uncommon for her to expose herself to men. She spent hours on phone-sex lines, talking dirty to men; she met strangers regularly for sexual trysts. She felt sexual pleasure when she talked about her fantasies of S/M and incest. It turned her on—yet simultaneously angered her—to get other people to talk about incest.

"We concede that the defendant is mentally ill, but we will clearly show that she also knew that what she was doing was wrong and was therefore sane when she murdered Michael Deloge and Kenneth Countie."

Keen-eared observers noticed that Bailey had never once used the names of the victims, and Rice had never once used the name of the defendant. Tricks of the trade.

Following a break, the defense called their first witness, Lynn Noojin, Sheila's older sister. Lynn bore some facial resemblance to Sheila, but she was taller and slimmer. She was also far more neatly coiffed. Her black hair was styled and teased up, and she wore glasses as she sat on the witness stand.

"Where are you from?" Bailey asked.

"I grew up in Fort Payne, Alabama. I currently live in Dawson, Alabama," Lynn said. "For the past thirteen years, I have worked as a court specialist doing domestic violence cases at the DeKalb [County] Courthouse."

"Do you recognize the woman sitting in the front of the courtroom in the jumpsuit?"

"I sure do." The witness mouthed the words "I love you" to the defendant.

"Could you identify her for the court, please?"

"That's my baby girl, Sheila," Lynn said.

"She's your sister, correct?"

"Yes."

"Younger or older."

"Younger. My baby sister. She is four years younger."

"How many brothers and sisters do you have?"

"There were three brothers and another sister. Jimmy,

Judy, Kenneth, Richard, me, and Sheila. Jimmy and Kenneth are deceased."

"When was the last time you saw your sister Sheila?"

"September 2005, at my brother Kenneth's funeral—but we have stayed in touch with phone calls, cards, and letters."

"Did you ever visit Sheila when she lived at Red Oak Hill?"

"Yes, I did. First time was in 1989."

"Did anything unusual happen during the 1989 visit?"

"Well, there was an incident where Sheila was bringing Bill, Dr. LaBarre, a beer, and he already had one. He said he already had one, just casually—but it irritated her and she threw the bottle across the room and stormed out. The bottle broke."

Bailey showed Lynn a series of photos of Sheila as a younger woman and had her identify each one as the defendant. He showed her a more recent photograph of Sheila, and Lynn began to cry.

"As far as you know, how many times has Sheila been married?"

"I believe she has been married three times. There was Ronnie Jennings in the early eighties. That lasted maybe a year, not sure. Then John Baxter, maybe 1984, '85, not exactly sure. That didn't last long, maybe six weeks. Then Wayne Ennis. I don't know the date, sir. She brought him to Alabama. She told me he was from Jamaica. I don't know how long that one lasted. She has no children."

The sister testified to the hardships the family had to endure when Sheila was a child, including an abusive father.

"Sheila was abused?"

"Yes."

"Sexually?"

"Yes."

"How do you know?"

"On at least two occasions, I saw Sheila being sexually molested," Lynn said.

"By your father?"

"Yes, and by a family friend."

"Please tell the court about that."

"Sheila was the last born of the family. Our parents were pretty old at this time. My mom had already started going through menopause. Sheila as a baby just cried all the time. You couldn't comfort her. She just cried all the time. The incident happened when she was three, four months old. I walked in and it was daytime. My dad was in the bed and Sheila was in the middle, and my mom was on the other side. As I walked in and toward the bedroom door, I heard my mother yell out, in an aggravated tone."

"What did you think was happening?"

"Well, I don't know if it was a 'think,' I pretty much know it was happening. I think my dad was doing something to her sexually."

"And the incident with the family friend?"

"Well, I was outside and I came in the house. When I came through the door, to my left, we had one of those old ugly turquoise vinyl couches. My dad was sitting on it and Sheila was there and another gentleman. Daddy called him uncle to us. Sheila, I think she was in his lap, and she was squirming, trying to stand up, and I could hear him saying, 'Ahh, Sheelaaaahh, that's a Spanish name.' He had his hand around her and his hand was up her dress. She was maybe two, maybe three years old. She looked like a little baby doll. She always wore these cute little dresses. She was probably the only one in our family who was that cute. I told my mom. She came in there and she didn't say anything. She just grabbed Sheila by her little left arm and kind of walked her fast out of the room."

"Were there any other occasions?"

"Yes. We slept in the same bedroom, us little girls. There was a frightening incident when we were sleeping together. I was probably five or six, maybe seven. So Sheila was three or four. Lights were on, we were playing on the bed. She always slept on the left side, it was closer to the windows. She looked toward the big window and screamed, a man's face at the window. We ran down to our parents' bedroom. And, of course, they didn't believe us. Made us go back to bed. The next day Sheila and I both went out, at that window there was a cement block and it was turned up in ways like someone had stood up on it to look in the window. We told our daddy again. Naw, he didn't believe us. We got moved to a different bedroom. Sheila was a little nervous after that and wanted to make sure the windows were locked.

"Father hurt Sheila in 1964 when she was six. Our dad was pretty bad to drink on weekends. He had come in drunk and really violent, really violent. He destroyed the inside of the house. We heated the house with a big iron stove. There was no fire going, he turned that over and pulled the pipes out of the wall. Tried to turn the fridge over, but couldn't, so he threw the groceries around. We were scrambling to get out—Mom, Sheila, and me. We got out the back door, gave Mom the car keys. Sheila and I both got in the front seat. She started backing out and the car went dead. The window was down, and he didn't know, because he drew back with his fist to break the window, but instead of punching the window, he pitched forward into the car over our mother. We tried to scramble out the right side of the door, all three of us.

I was holding Sheila's right hand and trying to run. He picked up a can of antifreeze, and slung it with force toward us. And it hit Sheila. It caught her in the side of her head. She reached up like this to try to stop it. Her four little fingers were dented in from the ridge on the bottom. He was going to pick it up again, and I didn't want him to throw it again and hit her again. I jumped up on his neck and tried to wrestle him. Of course, he threw me off, but that gave Mother and Sheila time. There was a cornfield aside the house. He was running, catching up to me, and when I got to the edge of the cornfield, I dove into the cornfield and laid still. It was dark. I heard him rustling through the cornstalks. Then he went to the house. I was calling for Mother and we found each other in the cornfield. Sheila was with her. We started walking through the cornfield toward my brother Jimmy's house. Five miles."

"Was your father ever arrested for any of these incidents?"

"Nope. Not charged or prosecuted."

Lynn's vivid description was rich in specific and realistic detail, so it is unfair that some in the courtroom might have found the end of Lynn's story familiar. In the popular movie *Forrest Gump*, there is a scene in which a little girl in Alabama escapes her sexually abusive father by hiding in a cornfield.

The questioning jumped ahead to Sheila's adulthood and the time of her marriage to Ronnie Jennings. Lynn described Sheila's suicide attempt in the early 1980s and subsequent stint in a mental hospital. "She had a car accident and it was close to my house, and the local law enforcement, knowing me from the court system, came to my house and told me she had had an accident."

Lynn described how she picked up her mother and

drove to the accident site. She saw her sister's car, off in a deep ditch, and the paramedics were still trying to remove her from the vehicle. "I got out and walked up as close as I could to the car. Her body was over from the front seat. Her head was in the backseat, but her body was arched over the seat. One paramedic was in back and one in front. We couldn't tell if she was dead or alive," Lynn testified. She heard one of them say Sheila had a pulse. She was unconscious. They thought she had a head injury, but they couldn't find any obvious sign, but they thought it had to be a head injury due to the fact she was unconscious. "I watched them load her into the ambulance. They handed me her purse, and I went to where Ronnie worked. It was a small little restaurant, a Sonic. I pushed the button to order and told Ronnie to get outside. Asked him if he and Sheila had had an argument. He said yes. I asked, 'Did she take something?' He said she took a handful of Placidils. I screeched out from the Sonic and flew up to the hospital, and they had already called a helicopter to transport her to Birmingham." They were still thinking she had some type of head injury. Lynn told them as soon as she got there that Sheila had taken something, and they immediately started pumping her stomach. "I could see this red stuff coming out of her. She was still unconscious. She was airlifted to the University of Alabama at Birmingham. Neurological Intensive Care. I visited her there. For eight days she was in a coma." After Sheila regained consciousness, she was taken to the psychiatric ward of the hospital. "I tried to visit her there. They wouldn't allow anyone to visit. I think she was there for thirty days before she was released."

"Did your sister tell you about anything unusual happening to her during her stay at the hospital"

"Yes, she said that an orderly tried to rape her and that she had to constantly fight for survival."

When Lynn said that, Sheila expelled a loud sob and lowered her head to the defense table.

When Sheila came out of her coma, she told Lynn that she had had a near-death experience and that she had been sent back to life. Lynn said, "She told me there were men with long white beards and the bright light, and they were waiting to take her with them, but they sent her back."

"Sent her back to where?"

"To life. They told her she had died." Sheila said she had been reincarnated. In a previous life she had been a Salem witch.

"Were there any thoughts about Sheila's mental health around the time of her accident?"

"Yes. Well, the situation with Ronnie. They wasn't a real good union. She was pretty despondent most of the time, and I knew she wasn't happy. I sure knew she wasn't happy after she tried to commit suicide. After her stay in the psychiatric hospital, she had trouble getting along with people. She was angry. Angry and paranoid." After breaking up with a boyfriend, Sheila visited him and pulled a gun on him. In another incident Sheila embroidered the back of a denim jacket for a boyfriend, and when she got mad at him, she destroyed the jacket. Sheila was impatient with service in restaurants. She took personally things that other people might let slide. Sheila had a loud, hysterical, and often inappropriate laugh. She believed that the ghost of a sea captain lived in her house. To prove the house was haunted, Sheila sent Lynn a photograph of the house in which it looked like there was a person in the window. Sheila began to tape-record all of her phone conversations and became preoccupied with people stealing from her or breaking into her house. She carried a tape recorder on her person.

After Bill died, Sheila was nervous about staying alone in the farmhouse at night. That was perhaps why she had so many men around. Sheila was obsessed with finding the money she knew Bill had hidden and felt elation when she found it. Sheila began to treat rabbits like her children and allowed the animals to have the run of the house, which Lynn did not approve of.

"Do you remember Jimmy Brackett?"

"Yes, I believe Sheila brought him with her to our brother Jimmy's funeral."

"What was your opinion of him?"

"I wondered what was wrong with her that she would have somebody with her that looked like—I hesitate to say anything derogatory—but he seemed to be slow. There wasn't much interacting, he stayed right by her side. Just like a spring—down down, up up, when she did. She didn't let him speak unless she told him to. Sheila told me once she threw James's clothes into a creek. To get the clothes, he had to wade into the water. It was deep. It was up to his chin. He couldn't swim. She thought it was funny. Later, Sheila told me that James owed her quite a bit of money. She wanted me to help her find him so she could file a suit."

Sheila's problems worsened when Bill LaBarre died. Sheila used "that telephone service" to talk to people. One day Sheila told Lynn that pedophiles were drawn to her; if she talked to someone for long enough, she could tell if they were a pedophile. "She just seemed obsessed with talking with that type of person," Lynn said. "She had taped a few of these conversations and played a few for me."

Another of Sheila's obsessions troubled Lynn. "She said she had met this group of Irishmen. I think there were four, maybe five of them. She dated one of them briefly. One or two days." According to Sheila, the Irishmen had come to the farm and she thought one of them had stolen some money out of her purse. She went to wherever they lived, maybe Boston, to confront them about this. And she slipped at the doorway and fell backward and hit her head. They wouldn't even let her use the phone to call for help. I told her to go to the hospital, but I don't know if she went. She said they also said they threatened the president, and that wasn't right, and she was going to see what she could do to get him deported. The one that she dated told her he was going back to Ireland, that his girlfriend was pregnant. As soon as I answered the phone, I knew she was upset. She screamed out, 'I hope the baby dies.' She'd only known him briefly. Most normal people don't wish for a child to die like that."

Lynn told of an incident that had happened many years before.

"I was eighteen and Sheila was fourteen. I had just gotten married and she said that my husband had shown his penis to her. It pretty much ticked me off. I eventually established that it wasn't true."

"How did you do that?"

"I talked to her years later and we were talking about men's anatomy. I made a comment about my husband's penis. She said, 'If I could see it, I would know for sure.' I thought, I don't know, 'I don't think she saw it.'"

Lynn said that nothing was off-limits when she talked to her sister, that she talked to her four or five times a week, and that Sheila frequently said strange things. "She'd tell me to hold on and lay the phone down and she'd say, 'I think I heard someone.' Demetrious the dog would start barking. Afraid someone was trying to break in, she'd go get her gun, go to the door, and fire off a couple of rounds. I could hear her yell, 'You better get out of here! You're trespassing!'" If someone came over to her house, the odds were good that, at some point, Sheila would think they were trying to steal something.

During one of Lynn's visits to Sheila at the farm, right after Kenny had come to stay with Sheila, Kenny brought Sheila a mixed drink while she was on the phone, and he accidentally spilled some of it. "Sheila berated him. She said, 'I'm going to make you lick that up.'"

Lynn described a troubling phone call she had received from her sister just before the time of Kenneth Countie's death. According to Lynn's best recollection, Sheila had called late at night, sometime near the end of March 2006. "She said my name in a whispering, guttural type of voice. I wasn't sure who it was at first. She repeated my name three times. She seemed distressed. I asked her where she was, and she said that she was sitting naked on the floor underneath a table. I asked her, 'What's the matter with you?' And she said, 'He's looking at me with demonic eyes.'"

"And who was she referring to when she said 'he'?"

"Kenneth Countie."

"Did she say anything else?"

"Kenny got on the line, and I said, 'What's the matter with her?' He started to say something like, 'She won't let me . . .' She started screaming. 'Tell her!' she screamed. 'Tell her your mother has been f***ing children!' He got on the phone and he got out the words. He got out the words, 'My mother . . .' You know. Sheila got back on the phone. I tried to talk her into letting Kenneth leave, but she started talking in a baby voice, saying,

'Mommy scalded me.' She said it was too cold and too dark for Kenneth to leave."

Lynn told her sister to get up off the floor and to eat something, to eat some soup and put on some pajamas.

Sheila said, "I don't sleep in pajamas."

Lynn said, "Well, put some on. Go to bed."

Lynn called her a day or two later and Sheila sounded kind of perky. It was a brief call.

"I'm okay, everything's okay," Sheila said.

Lynn Noojin testified that in addition to Sheila's bizarre behavior when she was younger, that it was after Wilfred LaBarre's death that her mental condition seemed to deteriorate into bouts of paranoia and delusion. Between 2000 and 2005, Lynn estimated, Sheila put on about seventy-five pounds. She also stopped dressing in fine clothes. At their brother Kenneth's funeral, Sheila's mother, who could "be kind of crude," called Sheila fat. Sheila screamed at her mother, all of which was inappropriate for a funeral, Lynn thought.

Bailey asked, "Did you and others have a nickname for Sheila when her mental health deteriorated?"

"Yes, we did."

"And what was that nickname?"

"We—well, we called her 'Crazy Sheila.'"

She testified that, despite her sister's problems, Lynn never sought mental help for Sheila.

That concluded Brad Bailey's direct examination of Lynn Noojin.

Day two began with Boffetti cross-examining Lynn Noojin. During this process Boffetti established several points that were helpful to the prosecution: Lynn loved her sister and would do anything to protect her; it wouldn't be unfair to describe Sheila as controlling, manipulative, high-strung, aggravating, etc.; none of those personality traits involved insanity. Attempts by Boffetti to establish Sheila as a liar and an actress were objected to by the defense, and sustained by Judge Nadeau. But this exchange was allowed into testimony:

"Sheila made false accusations against your husband, correct?"

"Yes."

"She accused him of showing her his penis?"

"Yes."

"And that accusation followed an incident in which he would not allow fourteen-year-old Sheila to go to the beach with a much older man. Is that true?"

"Yes."

Boffetti sought to demonstrate Sheila's controlling nature by showing that she had acquired power of attorney over various family members, but his efforts were at least partially undone when it turned out he didn't have his facts straight.

"Sheila acquired power of attorney for your mom?"

"Yes."

"And your dad?"

"No."

"She acquired power of attorney for James Manuel Bailey, correct?"

"That's my brother, not my father," Lynn snapped.

Seeking yes-or-no answers, Boffetti got Lynn to corroborate the many ways in which Sheila was functional in society, right up until the time of her arrest, that she ran a farm, had a hauling business, managed rental properties, etc. Yes, Lynn knew Sheila smoked pot. Yes, that she took pills also. Yes, she might have been wasted on some of the occasions when her behavior was strange. But

Lynn drew the line when talking about the phone call she received from naked Sheila under the table.

"That wasn't a phone call from someone who had taken pills and smoked a joint," Lynn insisted.

Boffetti established that Lynn had been interviewed on tape by police for two hours in January 2008, and that at no time did she mention incest or pedophilia; that, as far as Lynn knew, Sheila had not had a psychiatric exam between the time she was hospitalized after her suicide attempt and her arrest for murder, a period of twenty-five years. And that Lynn got rid of many letters Sheila had written to her, for fear that police would read them.

"There were a lot of personal things about Sheila being sexually abused that I didn't want them reading. There were also some things in those letters that pertained to me," Lynn said.

After the morning break the court listened to an audiotape of a long phone conversation Sheila had with Lynn while in prison. On the tape Sheila sounded normal, bright, and coherent. Some old bugaboos emerged, however. Predictably, Sheila was convinced her cellmate was stealing from her. Sheila wanted a watch so that she'd know what time it was when she was in lockup.

"Do you think you could go to Wal-Mart and get me one of those I-don't-give-a-shit plastic ones?" Sheila asked. Lynn said she would. Sheila complained that she was having a rough time, felt on the verge of a nervous breakdown, and was upset with her attorneys because they promised to get her new meds and hadn't. "My nerves are just shredded weak," she said. When Sheila explained that her lawyers didn't want her too medicated before the trial, Sheila fumed and threatened to "call a press conference." Lynn tried to distract Sheila by talking about how frighteningly thin their mother had grown, but Sheila wouldn't change subjects.

To explain her predicament, Sheila said, "I went insane and I wasn't responsible. That's the law." When Sheila complained about the never-ending noise of prison, Lynn told her to take her mind to a different place. Typical sisterly advice for an abuse victim.

"But they have a complete f***ing nut in with me. She is going to drive me to hurt her, because she keeps provoking me. I mean, I'm a very in-control person, but waking up with her on the floor staring at me? Wouldn't that freak you out?" Sheila asked.

On redirect examination Brad Bailey got Lynn to emphasize that Sheila's complaining about her cellmate stealing from her was very familiar, and that it was, indeed, common for Sheila to believe people were stealing from her.

"What do you hope is the outcome of this trial, Lynn?" Bailey asked.

"I hope she is able to get mental-health treatment," the big sister said. "I don't think she can live with this in her. Things erupt. If you've not been molested, I don't think you can understand what it does to you."

"Are you talking from personal experience?"

"Yes," Lynn Noojin said.

"No further questions," Bailey said, and the witness was allowed to leave the stand.

Lieutenant Charles West, of the state police, who had served on the major crime unit for six and a half years, was sworn in. It was Lieutenant West's role to introduce into evidence the more than three-hundred cassette audiotapes, almost a thousand hours' worth, found during the search.

Every minute of those tapes had been reviewed by police, he said. Among the taped material's common themes were discussions with men about pedophilia, bisexuality, and homosexuality, and heated arguments involving business and relationships. Sheila hadn't just taped herself arguing with car dealerships about money, and with tenants about rent, but she had also memorialized violent arguments with Bill LaBarre, Wayne Ennis, and Kenneth Countie. According to West, Michael Deloge also appeared on several tapes, but none of them depicted violence. "Sheila seemed to feel that most of the people on the East Coast were pedophiles and homosexuals," West said.

Sheila recorded songs she had written too. The lyrics tended to be macabre, dark, West said. She sang of violence, chopping people's hands off, killing a cat, dropping a baby in the river, and things like that. There were also songs about suicide.

That concluded the direct examination of the witness. Lieutenant West was cross-examined by Jane Young. West admitted that during his career he had encountered other individuals who had recorded their conversations. But, he added, "not to this volume." He noted that in New Hampshire all parties needed to know they were being recorded in order for recordings to be legal, and that on many tapes, Sheila clearly informed the other party that they were being recorded. On each tape Sheila had a point that she was trying to make, a specific point, and that she focused that point throughout the conversation. Talking to a local Mercedes-Benz dealership, she focused on the lemon law, for example. Talking to tenants, she focused on the rent that was late. Young's point, of course, was that there was nothing insane about it.

And what about the phone-sex chat lines? Sheila would leave a recorded message on the chat line and later would play back the answers she received. It was West's opinion that when a male respondent sounded assertive, Sheila deleted the message. When a man was soft-spoken and submissive, she would follow up. She used fake names: Nova, Silver Leopard, Falling Star, Angel, Desire, Desiree. This was role-playing. She was always the dominant and she controlled every conversation. She would chastise people. She called herself the Black Widow once and said to a particular guy: "I'm Black Widow, and I can devour you without even mating." If males tried to dominate, she grew pushier. She eventually took control of every situation.

"What were some of her common fantasies?"

"There were two. Sometimes she said she was looking for a male lover for 'James.' Other times she said that she was looking for a female lover for herself. She wanted to have sex with a woman while her man watched. There were no taboos. One conversation was of the defendant having phone sex with a woman."

"Graphic?"

"Very, very graphic."

"Were there discussions of incest?"

"Yes. There was a period of time when there were a lot of phone calls in sequence in which she always discussed males and their mothers. She was still domineering and in control of these calls. If the conversation would drift away from incest, she brought it back. She talked about adopting children, both male and female, for sexual purposes. She wanted to 'get young boys,' get them at a young age and shape them."

"Did she play different parts?"

"Yes, she could sweet-talk, then turn angry. In one tape she made a point that she did not have a multiple personality disorder, and that all of those people were stupid."

"No further questions," Young said.


Bailey established on redirect that Sheila also talked on tape about having died and being brought back to earth. She could berate merchants for a long time.

West said he was surprised that more people didn't just hang up on her. If someone called her crazy, she would quickly anger. Among those who called her crazy on the tapes were Bill LaBarre and James Brackett.

On one tape Sheila complained about a plane leaving without her. The airline representative noted that she had arrived late, and Sheila screamed that the plane should have returned to the gate to pick her up. When she didn't get her way, she talked to the CEO of the airline and reported hearing a "racist remark" by airline personnel. Claims she made on the phone were that she was a pilot, a private investigator, a drug informant, a friend of the Bush family. She purported to be someone who knew Oprah Winfrey, knew Al Gore, knew Steve Forbes, and that she was a multimillionaire. Her most common claim was that she was a notary public, a claim she would make even when it was irrelevant. West said he believed she used this title to give herself a "badge of respectability."

West said that among the tapes were her interrogations of Deloge and Countie during which both confessed to incest and pedophilia. The conversations, West thought, were very similar to the role-playing conversations she'd had on phone-sex lines.

After a brief recross in which Young established that Sheila's claims of knowing famous people to get what she wanted was cunning rather than insane, West was excused from the stand and the court broke for lunch.

Dr. Malcolm Rogers had been a forensic psychiatrist since 1993. He was examined by Denner, whose courtroom demeanor contrasted sharply with Bailey's. While both men were tall, Bailey was stout and Denner was slight. Bailey had a booming voice, while spectators sometimes had to strain to hear what Denner was saying. Dr. Rogers took the stand that afternoon, and the witness chair became a second home to him for many days.

His specialty was forensic psychiatry, Dr. Rogers said, "as it related to legal issues, both civil and criminal." More specifically, he helped determine criminal responsibility, competency to stand trial, and psychological conditions that may have resulted from injury or negligence. He matched up legal standards with psychiatric conditions. He had testified at about sixty trials and said that 95 percent of his work was for the prosecution. He said he was getting paid $5,000 for his services in this case, far below his normal rate of compensation. Twice he had examined Sheila to evaluate her criminal responsibility. To make such an evaluation, he had to consider a combination of factors: the circumstances of the events, and observations of the person's mental state at the time of the event. For a person to be insane, their criminal conduct had to be a product of their mental disease. To a reasonable degree of medical certainty, Rogers believed Sheila was insane when she killed her victims. He based this conclusion on police reports and interviews conducted by Epping and state police. He listened to about twenty of the recordings Sheila had made of her own conversations, including those of her on sex chat lines. He reviewed the evaluations of two other psychiatrists and one psychologist who had examined Sheila. He spoke with Lynn Noojin. As a result of all that information, he formed the opinion that Sheila suffered from a mental disorder at the time she killed Kenneth Countie and Michael Deloge.

When Denner asked which mental illnesses Sheila suffered from, the doctor replied in part, "She has a psychotic level of disturbance, which I believe was there, is there. Schizoaffective disorder and a related thing called delusional disorder."

Schizoaffective described a patient with a mixture of a major mood disorder together with a disorder of thinking and reality testing. She suffered from depression, mania, hypomania, as well as disturbance in thinking or reality testing. Thinking disturbance existed even in the absence of the mood disorder. There were different types. Hers was the paranoid subtype, because of the prominence of paranoid symptoms. One or the other is always there, but they can be there in different intensities.

Sheila perceived for at least several years that many men, if not most men, were pedophiles. "That perception was a specific factor in murders that occurred," Dr. Rogers said. "In reality some people *are* pedophiles. It's not on the face of it a totally unrealistic idea that someone could be, but in the circumstance of her life, and the people in her life, it was beyond what was realistically possible.

"There was concern and preoccupation with pedophiles that went back to 1999 or before. In the more recent years, this became more than just a preoccupation, it became a belief—an unrealistic and firmly held belief and it became an influence of reality."

"How does sadomasochism, homosexuality, and bisexuality fit in?"

"A lot of relationships were sexualized. That was a part of who she was, who she is. Her own life experience probably has some bearing on that, being an area of particular concern and focus. She has a history of sexual abuse, molestation done to her as a young child, perhaps as an infant, at least two other sisters subjected to sexual abuse within the family."

"Would physical abuse contribute to her mental problems?"

"Yes. Her mother avoided conflict, did *not* come to her assistance to stop it. Her father was an alcoholic, actively intoxicated at times, and the mother couldn't control him. That experience in some way contributes to the personality disorder, to the particular form her schizoaffective disorder has taken. Afraid in this world, everyone is out to get her. Early experiences affected her sense of trust and her vulnerability in relationships. This is evident also in the personality disturbance she has."

"And what about the belief that she has died?"

"That was the coma instance. She perceives that experience as having died, gone to Heaven, and come back as an angel. The degree has gotten worse—her belief in this—and is now paired in recent years with ridding the world of pedophilia and other evils."

The court took its afternoon break.

After the break Dr. Rogers said that one piece of evidence that proved Sheila believed her delusions occurred on March 17, 2006, when she paid a polygraph operator to test Kenneth Countie and confirm that he was a pedophile.

At this point the defense played the tape of Sheila interrogating Michael Deloge. As soon as the tape started to play, Sheila began to behave strangely in the courtroom. She breathed heavily, louder and louder, until Judge Nadeau noticed her reacting and abruptly halted court proceedings.

"She collapsed in on herself," defense attorney Rich Taylor commented.

# The Tapes

Sheila was back in court on Thursday morning, and on her best behavior. While everyone else on the defense team had other tasks to do during the day, Brad Bailey's job was to never leave Sheila's side. There were numerous times where Sheila would turn to Bailey, or Bailey would independently lean in and speak to her. Bailey was alternately trying to validate Sheila with vigorous head nods, and explain something to her, something he had to frequently repeat. He walked the line between empathizing with her and paternally keeping her in line. Equipment for a multimedia presentation was in place.

Dr. Rogers was on the stand and tapes were played of Sheila interacting with Michael Deloge. Sheila could be heard saying, "He bears the mark of Cain. He is. Not treatable. He is never going to change. He is not safe to have around. Do not be taken in and do not feel sorry for him. If you have any children in school, call the school police, the police in your town so everyone knows what he's like, what he did and what he may do again.

Think of all the little children, think of all the little children. Turn your back on Michael Deloge before it's too late. May God watch over all of you."

On another tape, recorded on St. Patrick's Day, 2006, Sheila—now with Kenneth Countie—could be heard saying, "I made a horrible, horrible, horrible mistake. I have allowed an evil paranoid-schizophrenic pedophile—polymorphous perverse—rude, crude twenty-four-year-old white male, from Wilmington, Massachusetts, into my life. I consider him to be dangerous. Not fit to be in the public view in any way. Kenneth Countie is looking right at me right now. He wants to drink his own blood and I've watched him do it. He's admitted to me that he has pranced and paraded naked in front of a four-year-old girl." She named the child and her parents, and specifically revealed where the parents worked. "I'm extremely upset and extremely angry with Kenneth Countie, and as a justice of the state of New Hampshire, I make a motion that he be brought before a grand jury in the state of Massachusetts and indicted on charges. He has admitted to, quote, f***ing, unquote, Carolynn Lodge, his own natural mother. He has admitted to shooting his cum inside her pussy. He has let her, quote, suck his dick, unquote, and she swallowed his cum too many times to count. When I met him at the Ashworth in the lounge, I was upset and suspicious of him. I woke up yesterday morning with this man trying to strangle me. He claimed he was trying to get comfortable. Yes, we had intercourse. Yes, I made a horrible mistake. Yes, I will testify in court against him. Kenneth Michael Countie has told me that he is turned on by young girls and young boys. I have witnessed him looking at young kids out in public. He, quote, claimed that his mother was unfit, unstable, etcetera. Well, I agree. What type of woman would screw her own son? What type of son would screw his own mother? It is a serious problem and it has to be stopped. I've been angry to the point of slapping his face. I wished and hoped that Chief Dodge would come into my home and blow this guy's brains out. *I think he needs to be in prison, not in an institution.* He says his mom is faking a disability. I don't believe any of it. Listen to me carefully, because I—I want my freedom from this situation. I want my life and my home restored. Every single night I have been awake. He has been tortured psychologically, mentally, and sexually by his own mother. Kenneth, Kenny, and Ken are the names of his father's three personalities. I feel that Kenneth Michael Countie is a paranoid schizophrenic. He needs to be imprisoned. Not in a mental institution. I feel that he may kill me, and I may have to shoot in self-defense. He says he wants to commit suicide. He'll blame me for his injuries. He caused a scene at Wal-Mart recently. I feel personally he invited it in some way. I don't know. And I don't care. What I care about is children and animals. He told me he, quote, loved it, unquote. He told me he *loved* f***ing her pussy. These children need to be polygraphed. These children need to be found. They need to be located. He and I had numerous arguments over him staring at numerous children, boys and girls, very, *very* young. God bless America and God bless President and Mrs. Bush, and senior President Bush and Mrs. Bush. Please understand, anything I do is in self-defense. And I should have called the police yesterday morning when he was trying to strangle me to death. If anyone finds this tape and I am deceased, contact Anthony McAnelly. He will inherit each and everything I own. Anthony McAnelly is my common-law husband. You know the road I walk. You know. Protect me from this demon. Amen."

Anthony McAnelly was one of Sheila's first boyfriends back in Alabama, the childhood friend with whom she "rode bicycles and dated a little." As this tape played, Carolynn Lodge broke down in tears, but she waved off an attempt to comfort her.

Afterward, Dr. Rogers gave his interpretation of the tape, stating that the claims of incest and pedophilia that Sheila repeatedly made were "outlandish" and "hardly believable."

Another tape was played. Each tape had the same theme. In one tape Lynn Noojin's husband was the pedophile. On the next tape she discussed waking up from her coma in 1983 "with a black man staring over me at my breasts, breathing very heavily like he had an erection." A nurse tried to give her a sedative and she was raped by three male nurses.

After each tape Dr. Rogers explained how Sheila's monologue or dialogue specifically demonstrated her various mental problems. The doctor was asked why the victims agreed with Sheila's perverse accusations, and he replied, "In the relationship the force of her belief, I think, overcame their (Countie and Deloge's) own ability to stand up to it. I think the power of this was she believed it herself."

On another tape Sheila could be heard talking to Wayne Ennis, saying, "Huh? Huh? You want to be in my pants, but you don't want me in yours. You know something? You know something? Let me say something to you. Oh, really? If she exists, if this woman does, in fact, exist, I'm going to put an ad in the paper, I'm going to flush her out. I'm going to find out. I'm gone to be investigating you. You know where you're going? You know where you're going? You're going to jail."

After the lunch break Sheila was heard calling a bar, the Electric Wave, complaining that a patron there grabbed her breast. At least that was the way the tape started. It lasted for nineteen minutes, and by the end she was talking about how she didn't want her husband hanging around in the Electric Wave, that she had power of attorney over Wayne, and that she was an immigration specialist. It ended with her saying, "I don't know who this guy is, I can't keep him out of here if I don't know who he is. He's my husband! My husband is psychotic. My husband beat me."

Following the tape, Dr. Rogers commented, "That's a very patient manager on the other end of the phone." The tapes, he said, gave a clear indication of how Sheila thought in terms of the law. She sought power of attorney over just about everyone. Her arguments always had a litigious quality. She was documenting wrongs that had been done to her, and that payback would be like a juicy episode of *The People's Court*. But, Dr. Rogers noted, there was a key component missing to Sheila's psyche: self-knowledge. She had *no* realization of why she had been wronged, no self-reflection of her own role in the difficulties that had occurred. She was grandiose: She said she was a lawyer, a doctor, an immigration specialist, and she assumed that the person she was speaking with was interested in all of this information, this detail. The notion that she was an angel on earth on a mission was especially grandiose. Her language was diffuse and excessive. She could accuse a stranger of having sex with someone else's wife and having HIV one second, and flirt with him the next.

Another tape was played, this one of Sheila talking to one of her boyfriends, Yvon Blais, who, at one point, could be heard crying on the other end of the line. Sheila said, "Hello, my sugar pie, this is Sheila—the one you think is not so smart. You are never going to out-smart me, baby. I am a witch and I am an angel, I am dead. I can get anybody's number. I. Am. Not. Human. What's wrong with you, Yvon? Why are you doing this to us? I want to apologize for hating you, but I am an angel, and I am going to get out of these charges because they are not going to stick. Are you listening to me? Are you scared of me? God sent me to you. God let me live. Yeah, well, listen, Yvon, I'm no threat to you. I want you to be happy. What you did, you did. You never realized it, but, um, I'm an angel. Angels can have tempers. Angels can have problems because they have to act like humans be-cause they have to blend in. I'm not human, I'm just not. You needed me and you still need me to guide you out of the darkness. If you'd only listened to me, you could have been perfect. Die? I don't want to die! Do you want to die? I'm going to let you go, as you wish. If you are going to kill yourself . . ." She giggled. "I have this amaz-ing knack for reading people's minds—it's a genius I have, high-ranking things, things from companies, I have found out. All this shit. I've got these asshole moth-erf***ers on tape. I saw what they did, I heard what they did. Death is nothing to fear. It's a part of life. It's a part of nature. It has to be. It will always be until God decides differently. My own personal death was wonderful."

Dr. Rogers said that one theme in Sheila's tapes was

that she projected her own psychological problems onto the person to whom she was speaking. She didn't really identify anything as being a problem in herself. Other people were ill, psychotic, disturbed, untruthful—a whole range of things. Other people had been abused as children, turned into perverts. She lacked a realistic sense of her self and her role in things.

"She picked men who were vulnerable and who lacked the intellectual power or personality to stand up to her, so they were more vulnerable," Dr. Rogers said. The tapes covered a time range of eight to ten years. "In the later tapes she is single-minded. The focus on the evils of sexual abuse and pedophilia is much more dominant, has much more force than in these earlier conversations, where it's a theme but not such a dominant one."

The next tape was of Sheila on a chat line talking to a stranger named Nick. Nick seemed fairly pleasant and responsive. He tried to be part of the conversation. Following her lead, he discussed pedophilia—talking about when he was an eleven-year-old boy and a woman in her late thirties "brought him off" with intercourse, oral sex, and anal sex. But Nick's part in the conversation ended abruptly when Sheila launched a perverse filibuster. Her theme was what turns you on as a child continues to turn you on throughout your life. You can never be "satiated." Eventually the "sex chat" went badly. Nick was evasive about giving Sheila his home phone number, she metamorphosed from flirtatious to angry. She decided Nick was dangerous and the rest of the world needed to be protected. After hanging up, she called the phone service back and left a message warning other ladies not to talk to Nick. The tape ended with Sheila singing in a high-pitch voice, some distance from the microphone, the sound too garbled to understand any of the lyrics.

Dr. Rogers observed that Sheila had no objectively valid reason to be afraid of Nick. He had tried to play her game, but was understandably reluctant to give his phone number. Court ended for the day and the next morning Dr. Rogers said that the tapes, if taken chronologically, demonstrated a progression in Sheila's delusions and paranoia.

Rogers said, "I think that her perception of reality was significantly impaired, most impaired in the degree of pedophilia in most of the population and, in particular, the men she became involved with." What progressed was the level of misperception of reality and the degree that she distorted what was happening in the world. Rogers said, "By 2005, 2006, I think her mental illness has progressed in terms of the intensity of the expression of her delusional thoughts." She lacked the capacity to function in a daily manner. The circumstances of her life were different. Dr. LaBarre died, the loss of someone who had a reality check on her to which she responded. There were other losses after that, her brother and the loss of her own father. Circumstances had affected her mental state. She was living essentially by herself except for the men at the farm. She was isolated from people and unchecked—functioning poorly. "By the end of 2005 to 2006, my understanding is that there were not tenants left in the rental apartments. Many had left because of their difficulty in dealing with Sheila. Images of the inside of the farmhouse seemed very chaotic and kind of disorganized. Lots of animals living in the house, rabbits in the house, and her appearance had changed. Her sister had expressed concern."

\* \* \*

During a break caused by technical difficulties, Sheila shot a look at a man sitting on the defense side of the courtroom. She pursed her lips and began to take off her coat slowly, one . . . sleeve . . . at . . . a . . . time, moving deliberately, as if doing a striptease. When the coat was off, she shook it out and turned to sit in her seat, flashing her prettiest smile at the jury. With the tape recorder fixed, the jury listened to more tapes. One was of a call Sheila made to a Hampton police captain in 2000.

When the captain requested she not record the call, she overreacted and hung up. She said directly into the microphone, "I wonder why you didn't want to be tape-recorded." Later she said, "I feel very intimidated by this Captain Sullivan. I feel he has a vendetta against me. I have to do what needs to be done to protect my rights. I am being discriminated against. It is not right. It is not fair. Each time I have called the chief of police, he has not returned my call. I don't consider that professional. I'm going to call my doctor right now, the doctor treating me for heart problems."

On another tape Sheila could be heard yelling at James Brackett's boss, accusing him of sleeping with Brackett, of being a pedophile, and threatening legal action. Her speech was rapid-fire and scattered. She would start a thought with a sexual accusation and end it by saying, "Are you a corporation or a limited partnership?" Her rant continued, "I am hot and I am bothered. Are you involved with my boyfriend? He has also attacked me. Another stupid body shop. Okay? Why? You? I have to talk to my attorney, but he is in court. I demand a copy of James Brackett's file. You have to do it. Oh, don't laugh at me. That's right. I am not desperate for

AIDS. I am not desperate for other men. I don't like that. I will call the f***ing police. Pardon my language. I will file a suit. James Brackett is a loose cannon. And you hired him? Is that true? I have a big strapping guy in the air force that will restrain him before he does something. I have power of attorney over him. He's a dangerous man. He stabbed me. I'm not trying to be a bitch. I could send the cops up there right now. I could have the guy arrested. He's a lousy boyfriend. Other people from the clinic have tried to attack me because of him. He is a pedophile. He shows patients his penis. There's something clearly wrong with him. Have a good day." The tape went on for more than ten minutes, and, amazingly, the guy on the other end of the line never hung up on her.

About that tape, Dr. Rogers said, "My reaction is that this is just totally bizarre. And any sort of veneer of normality is missing in this conversation."

On the tape of Brackett and Sheila arguing, Sheila screamed, "I've had enough of your abuse. Go ahead, Jim. Say whatever you want. You are being recorded. I am asking you for about the twentieth time to get out of my front yard."

"You broke my teeth," he screamed back. "You're crazy, you know that?"

As he was saying this, she repeated, "Coffee, hot coffee, coffee, hot coffee, coffee with extra cream in it, coffee, coffee" over and over again to demonstrate that she was not listening.

In the courtroom, listening to herself, Sheila laughed loudly. Later on that tape Sheila could be heard screaming for Brackett to get off her property.

"You bitch. You f***ing cunt!" Brackett yelled. Calmer, he said, "You have a mental problem. You need help."

"You're a pedophile," she screamed at him. "You fist f*** rabbits."

"You kill everything," Brackett replied.

"I don't want to kill anything."

"You killed that dog out back."

"I told you that dog should be killed. The black one will be killed too. I told the police that either I or Dr. LaBarre would kill that dog if it attacked one of our patients. It will be with a gun or a hammer." After a pause she said, "You are going to Hell."

"No," Brackett said. "I am already in Hell."

"Why don't you do what I have asked you to do a thousand times and get out of my life?"

"I will, after I pack," Brackett answered.

"I straightened your credit out and you ruined it. I've supported you since 1996."

"You're a f***ing pothead."

"I have never molested an infant or a child. Never! What about it? If you say that again, I'll never see you. I'll be talking to your boss. I won't chase you—you dumbass."

"You're lying now."

"Wanna bet? Wanna bet? I'm not taking you to work, so start walking, damn f***ing homo."

Dr. Rogers commented, "It certainly implies anger, and that if she could kill a dog, she could certainly kill him. In some ways this relationship has all the elements of what happens later to Mr. Countie and Mr. Deloge. Mr. Brackett somehow manages to leave. One suspects that had he not, he might have been another victim."

* * *

On a short tape recorded not long before Sheila murdered Kenneth, she said, "Hello, I am a notary public and a justice of the peace in the state of New Hampshire. My name is Sheila LaBarre, Esquire. In the room with me is a guy who has threatened to kill President Bush. I am investigating an assassination attempt of President Bush. Together with the government he says he wants to kill President Bush. He has a gun, some kind of high-powered sniper rifle and he's going to use it. Sitting here in the room with me is Kenneth Countie. If I become deceased, please let it be known, he has raped, molested, and murdered various young children in his course as a registered nurse in the state of Massachusetts. I will have been raped, sodomized, vaginally raped, raped in the mouth, and murdered by a man by the name of Kenneth Countie, son of Carolynn Lodge. Currently I've placed him under citizen's arrest. He's sitting in a rocking chair perfectly safe. He's nearby. I'm holding a revolver for my personal defense. I fear for my own safety, although I don't fear anything. I have animals to consider, children to consider, I believe all pedophiles should be shot on sight. I wish President Bush would enact that into law. Thank you."

About this tape Dr. Rogers reiterated his diagnosis that Sheila was expressing delusional thinking, and that she was suffering from either a schizophrenic or a delusional disorder. "This tape was made, apparently, while Kenneth Countie was in the room and she had a loaded gun in her lap. It seems to me her mind is in a psychotic state as she's making this tape," Dr. Rogers said. That ended the first week of testimony. Sheila's defense team had to feel pretty good about the proceedings so far. What juror, having listened to those tapes, wouldn't think, *This woman is nuts!*

* * *

On May 19, 2008, more tapes were played. Sound quality varied. Some recordings were so bad that jurors were supplied with a transcript to read along. The press was given one copy of the transcript, which they were supposed to share. In one tape the batteries on Sheila's tape recorder were apparently failing and the tape had slowed down when she was recording. The result was something that sounded like a perverse episode of *Alvin and the Chipmunks.*

With Dr. Malcolm Rogers still on the witness stand, the tape played on that Monday morning was the most heartbreaking of all for Carolynn Lodge. It depicted Sheila harshly interrogating Kenneth, forcing him to confess that he had been abused as a child. She accused Kenneth's mother of abusing not just him but another young girl, and Countie meekly agreed that it was all true. She did all of the talking, firing accusations at him while he said yes to each of her questions in a barely audible voice.

"Do you hate your mother?"

"Yes."

"Do you want your family to leave you alone?"

"Yes."

The rhythm and tone was that of a lawyer deposing a witness. Lodge shook her head vigorously and cried.

After the tape Denner asked, "Keeping in mind that there is no evidence that Countie committed any of the acts that Sheila is accusing him of, and that there is no evidence that he was ever abused, what does this tape tell us about Sheila's state of mind at the time it was recorded?"

Dr. Rogers replied, "She is projecting her psychological state onto Mr. Countie and his mother. Again, this goes back to her personal story of being molested as a child and perhaps in some unconscious way of being robbed of her own childhood. On the tape, when Ms. LaBarre says that Mr. Countie's mother controlled or dominated him, she is essentially talking about herself. As I've said, her thoughts, feelings of paranoia, and irrational accusations are symptoms of mental illness."

"Dr. Rogers, do you believe that Kenneth Countie believes that the accusations are true?"

"No, I do not."

"Why, in your opinion, does he say they are?"

"I believe he is playing along to appease her. It's pretty clear that Mr. Countie is just passively repeating what she has really pushed him into doing. Whether this is conscious or not, this is an effort to alienate Mr. Countie from his mother."

"Does Sheila believe what she is saying on the tape?" Denner inquired.

"Yes, I believe she does."

"And what was the basis for that conclusion, Dr. Rogers?"

"As I hear this tape, I considered the possibility that Ms. LaBarre doesn't believe anything she says, that she is just making this up for the purpose of dominating and subjecting the individual to her own abuse. I just don't think that is possible. Fundamentally, what is significant is Ms. LaBarre acts on the basis of her delusional beliefs. It's one of the ways you can determine if someone believes the delusion in a real way or they don't. If she didn't believe the accusations were true, she would not have paid a polygraph expert to administer Mr. Countie a lie detector test."

\* \* \*

The other tape played on Monday morning also seemed to affirm that Sheila believed her own accusations. After getting Kenneth to tell her the name of the four-year-old girl his mother supposedly abused, Sheila called Child Protective Services in an attempt to report the abuse. The tape was dated February 25, 2006. Kenneth had known Sheila for eleven days.

At first, the operator thought Sheila was with the girl, and was understandably troubled by Sheila's never-ending, rapid-fire speech. Sheila kept repeating that she was with Kenneth Countie, who was twenty-four years old, and that his "psychotic mother," whom she named, was dangerous, from Massachusetts, guilty of incest, and there was a four-year-old girl in danger. The operator was confused. Why was Sheila reporting a Massachusetts crime if she was in New Hampshire?

"I live in the state of New Hampshire and I have never met this woman. This woman has walked around naked," Sheila said.

"Stop, stop, stop," the operator interjected, in an attempt to get a word in edgewise. Finally the operator convinced Sheila to give her name and location, and admit that she "didn't witness any of these acts."

"Okay, okay," the operator said.

Sheila continued, "'She's unstable, dangerous—she's violent. I don't want any contact with her. I don't want that woman to get my information.'"

In the background Kenneth could be heard crying.

"I've been abused too," Kenneth called out.

"He hasn't been around his mother since Valentine's Day," Sheila said. "He is an adult and he is safe and sane. *S-A-F-E* and *S-A-N-E*." She began reading from a "sworn statement" supposedly written by Kenneth, verbally noting the quotation marks: "*My natural father has trained me repeatedly to quote, stay away from her, unquote, and, quote, to cease communication with her, unquote. She has paraded in front of me naked. Recently she called me on my cell phone to tell me, and I quote her verbatim, the baby is in the womb and we are having sex, unquote.*" She expressed concern for Kenneth's eighteen-year-old stepbrother. "Is he still living at home with Carolynn? I need to know."

The operator asked who was the four-year-old's legal guardian. Sheila asked Kenny, who said that she had a mother who was eighteen. Kenny became agitated and Sheila said to him, "You can have anything you want, just calm down now, just try to calm down." She continued to read from Kenneth's affidavit: *"I am living with a very decent and very respected female. My mother is insane."* She emphasized the "very decent . . . female" in her Southern voice. Again, Kenny was agitated and she said to him, "You're a grown man, stay away from this woman. If I feel someone is violating the law, I have to report it. I know it hurts. I know, I know, you did the right thing. It's okay to cry. A four-year-old girl. Ohhhh, I get chills thinking about that four-year-old girl." When Sheila completed her call, she hung up and broke into song, an old-time gospel, *"I saw the light . . . no more darkness . . . now I'm so happy."* In a spoken voice she said, "Praise the Lord," and, *click*, shut off the tape recorder.

Dr. Rogers told Denner that this tape showed the same bizarre, delusional process, in which Sheila projected herself onto her image of Kenneth's mother.


The next tape, recorded during the evening of March 16, 2006, was of very poor quality. The quality of the tapes was starting to get on Judge Nadeau's nerves. On this tape Sheila called a health club in Billerica. She pretended to be inquiring about rates, but her real purpose was to spread nasty rumors about Kenny's mother.

"Hi," she said with a Southern lilt. "What's your name? John? I'm Lisa. What are your monthly rates? What hours are you open? Is there a shower? What part of town are you in? I'm in Boston right now. Are you close to a police station? Do you have a tanning booth? Do you do a criminal background check on members?"

"No, we don't," John said.

"Do you know Carolynn Lodge?"

"Who?"

"Carolynn Lodge."

"No, I don't know her."

"But you know who I mean. I know you do."

"I don't know who she is. Is there a problem with her?"

"If she's still there, I'm not coming there, and do you know why? Because she's a pedophile. Really. And she's had sex with her son when he was underage. In fact, he's right here with me." She said to Kenneth: "What's your name?"

"Kenneth Countie."

"Is your mom a pedophile?"

"Yes."

Speaking to John again, she said, "I'm not coming there, and you have a nice night."

Dr. Rogers commented that the tape showed Sheila's ongoing efforts to alienate Kenneth from his mother, while, by slandering Carolynn, creating problems for her. Yet she sounded reasonable to a point.

"She can sound reasonable and still be psychotic?" Denner asked.

"Oh yes. She is articulate, bright, kind of officious, and she brings all of that to bear on this conversation.

Even if it were true, it would be a pretty bizarre way to deal with it."

The next tape, recorded soon after police first came to the house to look for Kenneth, was particularly hard to listen to. Not because of sound quality—because of content. It depicted Sheila verbally abusing Kenneth in a relentless manner.

Her voice was horrible as she said, "Apparently, you don't get it. I'm sick of this. Number one, I don't give a f*** about you. There is *nothing*! What is your f***ing problem? I am the only woman on this earth. You need to cut the cord. Why don't you just admit it? At your age? They are both doing the same thing to you. Something horrible is going to happen. You didn't do everything I said. You are severely mentally ill. You wanted to fight in the infantry, but you failed. What have you accomplished by the time you are twenty-four? Nothing! No, you're the problem, buddy. I'm not going to have arguments with men."

"I want to be with you. I want to be with you," Kenny said.

"You are a screw-up. Don't you ever, ever come anywhere near my property. Why would you not want to grow up? What's wrong with you? I'm cold!"

"I want to be with you."

She screamed something about an erection and the tape ended.

Dr. Rogers commented, "She is much angrier here. There's an intensity to her anger and a volatility that we haven't heard before. She has much less control of her emotional responses."

"And how does the notion of control enter into insanity?" Denner asked.

"Sane persons have the capacity to conform their behavior to the requirements of the law. The capacity to control one's own behavior is part of the consideration of whether one has become insane. Sheila's delusional thought process is driving her level of anger and rage. She is responding to that misperception of the world," Dr. Rogers replied.

On Tuesday and Wednesday, the court watched videotapes of Sheila being interrogated at the Epping police station on March 25, 2006, by TFC Rockey and Sergeant Richard Mitchell, and on March 27 by Sergeant Estabrook. These were the interviews during which Sheila insisted on referring to Kenneth as "Adam."

On Wednesday, Robert Ducharme, who taught an abnormal psychology class at Portsmouth High School, brought two dozen students to observe the courtroom proceedings. The teenagers got an earful as this was the day that the videotape was played on which Sheila gave her sexually explicit description of her first face-to-face encounter with Kenneth Countie.

The day ended before the tape was finished, so the last hour of the tape was shown to the jury on Thursday morning. When it finished, Denner asked for Rogers's interpretation and turned the witness over to be cross-examined by Boffetti.

"Dr. Rogers, does a lack of criminal responsibility mean a psychotic level of illness?"

"Yes."

"If a person isn't psychotic at the time they commit a crime, they are not likely to be insane. True?" Boffetti inquired.

"That's probably true."

"You cannot determine when the defendant's psychotic state began, can you?"

"She was in a psychotic state as far back as the year 2000, and there were threads of focus on pedophilia that predate even that," Dr. Rogers answered.

"Are you operating on the assumption that the defendant was sexually abused as a child?"

"Yes, based on my interviews with the defendant, and the testimony of Ms. Noojin."

"Yet there are no other sources for that, true?"

"Her sister Lynn observed it happening, and I took that as a clear enough indication."

"You take that account that Lynn Noojin says as something that actually happened?" Boffetti asked.

"What I found reliable in what she told me was that when the defendant was three, and Ms. Noojin was seven, that she saw a person known as [an] uncle with his hand between the defendant's legs, and the father was also in the same room. There was additional information that there were other females in this family that reported being sexually abused by another family member, as well as the father, so these were not the only instances."

"And all of your information regarding these instances came from the defendant and her sister?"

"Yes," Dr. Rogers replied.

"Do you consider the defendant [a] reliable reporter of the events of her past?"

"No, but the corroboration of her sister's testimony makes the information more reliable."

"Isn't it true that all the details about how Michael Deloge died come from the defendant herself, in part because she so successfully covered up her crime? And what she said to you and others might have been said in [an] effort [to] put herself in a better light."

"Yes. But she destroyed the evidence in a bizarre manner. She burned Countie's body in a fire only a few steps from her front door. And her attempts to cover up were sporadic. She would deny killing the victim in one breath and say, 'He's in that bag' in the next. If it's an effort to cover up her crime, it's such a pathetic effort and such a bizarre effort. If she is a sane person trying to destroy evidence, having a big fire by the house would be bizarre."

"The burning of Kenneth Countie's sneakers, would that be considered an effort to cover up?" Boffetti posed.

"It may have been. I don't know."

The prosecution had a tape of its own to play. On this one, Sheila screamed at Wilfred LaBarre that she would kill him and his horses and burn down his house if she didn't get what she wanted. Her problem was a disagreement with a secretary at Dr. LaBarre's chiropractic office. When Dr. LaBarre refused to back down, she threatened to cut his hands off.

"Bill! Hey, Bill! If you want to live, you better leave me alone. I want you to decide if you want to live or die," she said.

"Isn't it true that the defendant, on this tape, sounds more mean than psychotic?" Boffetti asked.

"I think being nasty is not the same thing as being crazy and psychotic, and I think she subsequently becomes psychotic and delusional. If it were simply a volatile, angry person, I would not view her as insane. I view her as insane because of the psychotic processes," Dr. Rogers replied.

Boffetti asked if it wasn't true that the defendant never received psychiatric treatment the entire time she lived in Epping, and Dr. Rogers replied that this was because people were afraid of her.

"I think people avoided confronting her because they didn't want to provoke her anger, so they left her alone," Dr. Rogers said. "It would have been difficult to treat her for her mental illness. It would be difficult even now. I think it's a combination of this nasty response and her not ever being open to being told what to do. And the fact that she doesn't have any insight into the fact she's psychiatrically ill. And I still don't think she does."

# Law Enforcement
# and the
# Wal-Mart Witnesses

That Friday, and for most of the next week, the defense called a series of police officers who had been part of the investigation just before and after Kenneth Countie's death.

First on the stand was Sergeant Sean Gallagher, who, while questioned by Bailey, testified regarding the second Wal-Mart incident, the late-night phone call during which Sheila played the tape of Kenny "confessing," and his visit to the farm during which he saw the fleshy bone sticking out of the fire on her lawn.

Jurors were shown a photo of Kenny in a wheelchair with yellow diesel cans stacked on his lap. They were also shown a photo of the shirtless victim, taken at the farmhouse, in which he was covered with cuts, some still bleeding.

Gallagher testified that in 2001 he had responded to a complaint at the farm, and while he was there, Sheila had shown him photos of herself naked and in various "compromising positions." He had told her to knock it off, then left. Thereafter, two officers always responded when a complaint came from the farm.

On cross-examination Boffetti used a model of the farmhouse and surrounding grounds to help jurors better visualize where things had occurred. He induced testimony that Sheila had never, in Gallagher's presence, called herself an "avenging angel," or complained that any of the men on her farm were "pedophiles." When Boffetti asked if he had ever considered having Sheila committed to a mental institution because of her mental illness, Gallagher said no.

"She always had her faculties about her. Her complaints always made sense. She told a story with a beginning, a middle, and an end. She never made threats to harm herself or anybody else," Gallagher said. Sheila's appearance had not changed dramatically during the time he had known her.


Detective Richard Cote testified that he had accompanied Gallagher to Wal-Mart and the farm the following day. Sheila, who had been animated throughout the day—playing with her hair and glaring at prosecutors—laughed loudly when Cote testified to the squalid condition of the farmhouse. Cote's testimony contradicted Gallagher's when he said that during the Wal-Mart incident, he neither remembered any conversation with Sheila, nor seeing Kenneth Countie walk.

Ann Rice performed the cross-examination. She took the detective through all of the calls Sheila had made to the police over the years, several complaining about Jimmy Brackett doing damage to her house, several complaints about strangers parked near her house. Rice asked Cote if any of the calls had to do with incest or raping children. He said they did not. Cote agreed with Gallagher that although Sheila had put on a few pounds over the years, she looked pretty much as she always had.

Chief Gregory Dodge, questioned by Bailey, testified that his police staff had answered one hundred calls over the years for problems involving Sheila. Sometimes she was doing the calling, other times someone was calling about her. She tended to conceptualize circumstances in terms of civil and criminal law. Her letters listed her problems, framing them as infringements of the law that the police chief could solve by making the necessary arrests.

"Isn't it true that Sheila, in a letter, asked you if you had burned her at the stake in a previous life?"

"Yes."

"Did that statement make you question her mental status?"

"Not at all," Chief Dodge said.

Bailey showed the chief a notarized document the police received in February 2006 that was signed by both Kenneth Countie and Sheila, the one that started, *I am an adult, safe, sane and very happy.* It went on to say Kenny trusted Sheila alone, and that his mother was unfit. Bailey made Dodge say aloud who he thought probably wrote that document, and if the wording sounded, at all, like it might have come from Kenny. Dodge knew that Kenny was mentally handicapped. Carolynn Lodge had told him so. Dodge agreed that Sheila wrote the document and confirmed that he took no action to protect Kenneth Countie after receiving it. There was also the document that granted Sheila power of attorney over

Kenny, the one that contained the line *I only trust Sheila LaBarre and feel safe and secure in her presence.*

"Did you have any concerns that this was a voluntary statement?" Bailey asked.

"Well, yes."

Didn't that make the chief think?

Not in terms of taking any action. "She didn't seem like a danger to herself or others," the chief said.

But Bailey got Dodge to admit that he knew Sheila was trying to take control of Kenny's life, that he needed assistance, that Kenny was in need of medications he didn't have, and that he didn't function very well in life, out on his own.

"We were investigating," Chief Dodge said.

"In one letter Sheila referred to you as the 'only one I can count on.' Is that correct?"

"She was prone to saying things like that, yes. She wanted to count on my support."

"Chief Dodge, how did Sheila react when you mentioned Wal-Mart?"

"She reacted angrily. It's clear that she does not care for Wal-Mart."

"Does it tend to make her crazy?"

"I wouldn't say 'crazy.' The topic makes her angry."

"Is that a button you have learned not to push with her?"

"Yes."

Bailey read into the record a suicide note written by Sheila on March 25, 2006, only hours before Chief Dodge arrived with the search warrant. In the note she complained that a physician she knew enjoyed giving exams to small boys and girls. She talked about the scary Irish guy and President Bush. She said she had cremated a "large rabbit" three days earlier. She thought she had picked up most of the postincineration remains and conjectured that Kenneth Countie might have been the one that killed her "beloved" rabbit. Kenny did heroin. Kenny had AIDS and had been molested by his mother.

Bailey asked if this note bore more than a little similarity to the letters she had written regarding James Brackett, and the chief admitted that her accusations toward both men were very similar.

"What does that say about her mental state?" Bailey asked.

"Objection," came a chorus of voices at the prosecution table.

"Sustained," Judge Nadeau said. "Calls for a conclusion outside the witness's expertise."

"No further questions, Your Honor," Bailey said.

"Cross-examine," Judge Nadeau said. Jane Young stood.


Requiring yes or no answers, Young had Dodge confirm that the defendant was violent, intelligent, flirtatious, and manipulative. He agreed that she always recognized him when she saw him, that there was never trouble understanding what her complaint was, that he never saw her disoriented or confused, that she never called to complain about a pedophile, that she never referred to herself as an avenging angel, and, yes, he realized that the crucifixes displayed outside the house were a gift from Wilfred and had special meaning to her.

"Did you find it unusual that a woman was burning things out on a farm? Are fires on private property unusual?"

"I found it unusual that she was destroying all this evidence. I think walking in on her with a search warrant, we ruined whatever plan she had in place. She was trying to grasp at straws. It resembled a cover-up."

"And during your subsequent conversation with the defendant, she never admitted to you that she killed Kenneth Countie?"

"No."

"Chief, one last question. How would you characterize your relationship with the defendant?"

"Sheila always knew what she wanted. When she had it in her mind she wanted something, she would stop at nothing to get it. She was always very adamant she would get her way, one way or another."

Lieutenant Michael Wallace testified that he'd been on the Epping police force for almost twenty years. Female jurors perked up because of Wallace's good looks and friendly voice. When Sheila exposed herself to cops, she preferred to flash Lieutenant Wallace. During his career he'd had between fifty and one hundred contacts with Sheila LaBarre, Wallace testified. Yes, he recalled going to Sheila's farm with the search warrant.

"How would you characterize her demeanor during the interview and the search?"

"She was nervous. She was changing what she was saying to me during the conversation. It appeared to me that she was trying to throw the interview off."

"Isn't it true that Sheila requested taking a rabbit with her to be interrogated?"

"Yes."

"Had you ever brought anyone in before who had requested bringing an animal with them?"

"No, it was a first for me."

\* \* \*

On cross-examination Young said that the first time Wallace saw the defendant was—maybe 1988—when she'd called the cops after a fight with Dr. LaBarre. Sheila said he attacked her, but nothing was done. The evidence didn't fit her story. Wilfred's face was all scratched up; Sheila was unmarked. Young took Wallace through his history with the defendant. He was often called to sort out her violent problems with men. She asked if he noticed the suitcase outside the house when they arrived with the search warrant. He said he did, and that it made him suspect she was preparing to leave.

Young's gestures broadened theatrically as she showed the jury other tools that were used: a charred stick, the partially burnt pruning shears, hedge clippers. Carolynn Lodge squirmed in her chair as the cutting implements were displayed; tears welled in her eyes.

Young held up the "sifter" that had been used to separate bone from ash and asked Wallace why the tool was necessary in the process of evidence collection.

"The bone fragments were very small," he said. "They were very brittle. Some would break in your hand."

"Lieutenant Wallace, after the defendant was arrested, did you talk to her sister Lynn Noojin?"

He said he had. He'd traveled to Fort Payne, Alabama, to interview Lynn. He'd asked her about her recent phone conversations with the defendant. At no time did she mention a call during which the defendant claimed to be naked under a table. She never mentioned that the defendant had been sexually assaulted as a child. She didn't mention that the defendant told her the victim Kenneth Countie was looking at her with demonic eyes.

"On April 7, 2006, did you employ the Epping Wastewater Facility as part of your investigation into the murder of Kenneth Countie?"

"Yes."

"And what service did that company perform?"

"They drained and sifted the contents of the defendant's septic tank."

"The contents of the septic tank was predominantly sewage—is that correct?"

"Yes."

"And how was the material sifted?"

"With a screen."

"Was anything found as a result of that process that helped the investigation?"

"Yes, we found bullet casings and a birth certificate."

"And whose birth certificate was found in the septic tank?"

"The certificate said Michael Deloge, born March 29, 1968."

"Did the name mean anything to you when you first saw it?"

"Yes, his name had come up a few times during the investigation. He was a person who had been seen on the farm, and whose whereabouts were unknown."

"What else was found in the septic tank?"

"We found a receipt for a stay at the Ramada Inn on Morrisey Boulevard in Boston, the hotel where she had stayed not long before her arrest," Lieutenant Wallace said.

"Prior to March 25, 2006, that would include between fifty and one hundred contacts with the defendant, did she report anything about pedophiles, complain about pedophiles, mention incest, complain about incest, refer to herself as [an] avenging angel, or mention Michael Deloge?"

"No."

"Did she ever tell you that she murdered Michael

Deloge, that she murdered him because he was a pedophile, or because he hurt her animals?"

"No, she didn't."

"No further questions."

On Wednesday, May 28, 2008, the defense presented their Wal-Mart witnesses. Elaine Sommer had been working in the electronics department of Wal-Mart when the defendant and the victim first made a scene in that store on March 11, 2006. Sommer dealt with the defendant as she claimed her husband, who appeared battered, had been assaulted in the store.

Sommer was asked about the second visit on March 17. The victim's health, she said, had greatly deteriorated during the six days between Wal-Mart visits. He made no eye contact. He only spoke to the defendant, and then only when spoken to. At one point his shirt was lifted and she could see he was all bruised and scabby. She recalled the defendant buying a disposable camera and photographing the store's security system. The last she saw of Sheila was when a manager was escorting Sheila out of the store.

During cross-examination Young drew testimony that as the defendant became frustrated that her scene wasn't going down the way she had planned, she became angrier rather than crazier.

Another Wal-Mart employee, ten-year veteran David Dionne, told the court that during the first visit, Sheila told him her husband had been in an auto accident. Kenneth, he said, looked like a guy who rode a motorcycle without a shirt on. When touched, Kenneth moaned in pain. Sheila herself pulled up his shirt and showed him a fresh scab on Kenny's tricep. "It looked like the skin had been torn," Dionne said.

Sheila told him that she was going to sue Wal-Mart for $100 million, that he was going to lose his job, and that he was to expect a visit from an FBI lie detector operator. He told her that a threat of legal action automatically ends a conversation with a Wal-Mart employee. When she continued to berate him, he asked her to leave. She moved to the front entrance and continued making a scene. Dionne recounted, "I said, 'Okay, time to leave my store.' She told me it wasn't my store, that it was owned by a corporation, and that she didn't have to leave. I told her I had a right, that I was hired by the corporation. She came right up in my face and wanted my name, first and last. Still very loud. I said my last name was Dave and my first name was Assistant Manager. At that point I said I was done asking nicely and now was insisting they leave. Later I received a call from a person with an Oriental accent who told me how awful I was for mistreating that poor couple that evening. I was pretty sure it was her. She ranted at me for six minutes in a fake accent!" Dionne testified that he wasn't working when Sheila and Kenny returned on March 17.

Under cross-examination from Rice, Dionne admitted that the defendant was neither the first nor the last Wal-Mart customer to raise her voice in the store. Although angry and persistent, the defendant made sense, and the conversation with her at no time became illogical.

Janine Levesque testified that she was a salesperson in the Wal-Mart jewelry department in 2006. She heard Sheila before she saw her. Sheila was in the next aisle, the seasonal aisle, and was loudly complaining that a crazy woman had assaulted her husband.

"How did she sound?" Bailey asked.

"Scared," Janine Levesque replied.

Levesque said that Kenneth was walking fine, but he seemed frail, thin, and "battered-looking." Sheila was yelling about wanting security. The last Levesque saw of her that day, Sheila and Kenneth were heading for the customer service desk at the front of the store. On March 17, during the second visit, Levesque saw Sheila pushing Kenneth in the wheelchair with diesel containers stacked on his lap.

Levesque told Young on cross that although Sheila might have sounded frightened calling out for security from the next aisle, the witness had no idea what had actually happened in the seasonal department. And despite seeing Sheila pushing Kenny in the wheelchair, Levesque had no idea that Sheila had created another scene during her second visit.

Wendy Peterson testified that she currently worked at the Wal-Mart in Plattsburgh, New York, but had worked in Epping back in 2006. Wendy first met Sheila on March 17, the second visit, in the cosmetics section. Sheila calmly explained the "incident" that had occurred six days earlier. Sheila said she had friends in law enforcement and she wanted something done about it.

"She told me that she was a lawyer and could afford to shop at many of the high-end stores, but that she chose to shop at Wal-Mart, because if it's good enough for Sam Walton, it's good enough for her." She mentioned Chief Dodge and threatened to sue—which automatically ended the conversation. Sheila kept talking, however, about a $700 polygraph exam, and as she did, Peterson took a closer look at the man in the wheelchair. He looked green in color, beaten, like a fellow who needed medical attention, perhaps hospitalization. When Sheila started taking photos, Peterson called the cops. The police arrived, clearly had a history with the woman, knew how to handle her, and got her outside.

Rice established on cross that if one had a complaint, Peterson *was* the correct person with whom to speak.

"Did you call the police because you were worried about the defendant's mental health?"

"No."

"Why did you call?"

"I was worried because she had threatened a lawsuit and was taking photos."

The defense's case returned to the cops. Epping police officer Gregory Nye took the stand and explained that he had been on the force for six years. During that time he had handled approximately fifteen calls that involved Sheila.

On February 7, 2006, one week before Sheila met Kenny, he had answered a call from Sheila complaining that she was being harassed by Irishmen who had deluged her with unwanted phone calls. Officer Nye advised Sheila to obtain a line trap from the phone company; Sheila did obtain the line trap four days later. Nye had done the research for her and said it was a good first step toward building a possible criminal prosecution. Sheila wasn't happy. She said that it wasn't enough. She was going to complain to the Board of Selectmen. Sheila called Nye repeatedly for updates, so often that Nye had to tell her to stop. Sheila got so upset at the way

Nye was treating her that she claimed heart palpitations and called an ambulance for herself. She changed her mind, however, possibly after realizing that she might have to pay for it, and canceled the ambulance before it arrived.

"Would you call Sheila's behavior bizarre, Officer Nye?" Bailey asked.

"Well, it's true that she could be extremely persistent. She would call six or eight times a night. I guess that's bizarre."

On cross-examination Rice asked Nye if she ever talked about avenging angels, pedophilia, or incest. Nye said she did not.

William Bourque testified that he was a veteran of both the Hampton and Exeter police forces, and, yes, very familiar with Sheila over the years. He had responded to a call of domestic violence on September 30, 1998, and the parties turned out to be Sheila and James Brackett. They'd fought and Sheila had opened a gash in Brackett's forehead with a scissors. Afterward, in court, she made a scene screaming that Officer Bourque refused to help her, even though she was bleeding from the vagina.

During cross-examination Young asked Bourque what things the defendant had told him during and after the 1998 scissors incident. Bourque said that she brought up the topic of injuries. She made the comment that she had totaled her Mercedes a few weeks earlier and that she had internal bleeding, plus on her hand, her neck, and her private parts. She had tried to show him the intimate bruising, but he'd stopped her. He arranged for a female secretary to photograph the defendant's wounds, but she refused to have her injuries photographed. In the booking room the defendant again claimed that she was bleeding from the vagina. She turned down the offer of a sanitary napkin and told Officer Bourque that she would use toilet tissue instead. Her implication was that she was bleeding from the vagina because Brackett had raped her, but she confided to one of the paramedics that she was actually just having her period.

"She was responsive and told you what happened?"

"Yes."

"She listened to your questions and gave a response that seemed logical."

"Yes."

"In the end she admitted to having a lovers' quarrel with Brackett?"

"Yes."

"She admitted to stabbing him with the scissors, opening the gash?"

"She did."

"Did she at any time mention anything having to do with pedophilia?"

"No, she did not."

"No, further questions, Your Honor," Jane Young said. Officer Bourque was allowed to leave.

Officer Joseph Ronchi, a three-year veteran of the Somersworth Police Department, testified that on March 30, 2006, he had answered a call regarding criminal mischief at an address on High Street in Somersworth. Outside, he spoke with a man named David Simpson. His house had been ransacked. Entering the house, Ronchi noticed that things were in disarray. The linoleum on the floor appeared to have been purposefully torn up. There were water marks on the floor. The refrigerator had been pulled away from the wall. On one wall, written in black Magic Marker, were the words *VENGEANCE IS MINE, SAYETH THE LORD*. Who was the landlady? Sheila, of course.

Kevin Kelley took the stand and said he was currently employed as a billing and code enforcement inspector in Hampton Falls, but back in 1998 he had served with the Epping Police Department. He'd encountered Sheila in both of those capacities. As a cop he recalled an incident in 2002 when he had responded to Sheila's residence after she reported a burglary. Her story was that she had left her house for a half hour, locked with dead bolt and padlock, and when she returned, the locks were open. She told Kelley that she had been stalked by "unknown and unseen persons," and she had a history of being terrorized. Kelley recalled that the front door was undamaged, and although the locks were open, they didn't appear damaged either. Sheila said this sort of thing had happened before. She mentioned neighbor Bruce Allen's name more than once.

Although Kevin Kelley didn't recall the incident, even after he looked at the original report to refresh his memory, he conceded that he once responded to a call from Sheila complaining that her Shetland pony was screaming in pain. Since the pony seemed fine, and Sheila admitted to not seeing whatever it was that caused the screams, there wasn't much that could be done. One call from Sheila that Kelley did remember was the time she complained that there were trespassers on her property. Kelley hurried out to the scene after Sheila told him she had a .22 and was willing to take care of the trespassers the old-fashioned way. It turned out the trespassers were friends of Sheila's next-door neighbor who had wandered onto her property without knowing it.

Under Rice's cross-examination, Kevin Kelley said that at no time did he think the defendant was crazy. He thought she enjoyed the attention she got when police came to her house and that she just possibly had forgotten to lock her house the time she thought she'd been burglarized. But crazy? No.

Hampton Police Department patrolman Timothy Galvin testified that he first encountered Sheila in November 1993 at the apartment over Dr. LaBarre's chiropractic office at Winnacunnet Road. He remembered the complaint. An "incident involving a hysterical woman" had been reported. When he got there, Sheila was with a man named Brian Saunders, and she claimed he had assaulted her. She showed no signs of injury. Someone requested an ambulance for Sheila, not because she was hysterical but because she screamed that she'd had a miscarriage a few weeks prior.

"How hysterical was Sheila?" Bailey asked.

"Come on, this was fifteen years ago. I don't remember how hysterical she was."

He did remember that Sheila was known to the HPD before his first encounter with her, and the word was that she needed to be dealt with very gingerly and carefully.

Boffetti asked on cross if that one incident was the sum total of his contact with the defendant and he said that it was.

\* \* \*

Trooper Jill Rockey, already familiar to the jury because she questioned Sheila about Adam on a videotape they had viewed, took the stand in person. She said that when the "be-on-the-lookout" was put out for Sheila, she'd called the Somersworth Police Department and gave them a heads-up, warning them that Sheila was "extremely mentally unstable."

"No further questions," Bailey said.

On cross-examination, Young elicited from Rockey testimony regarding the videotaped interview, the methods the defendant used to distract her questioners from the topic, and how her answers were clear and rational, as long as no one was asking where Adam was. The defendant, however, never admitted to killing anyone and never mentioned anything about being an avenging angel. Once, Rockey had tried to get the defendant to sign a "consent to search" form. The defendant signed only after deleting a few key phrases from the contract. The form she signed said that she consented to being searched, except for a cavity search of her person, but that anything that might be found during the search could not be used against her. Rockey said she'd never seen or heard of a suspect doing that before. It was clever. She could say that she had signed the form, but she'd rendered it useless to the investigation.

Young asked about the warning Rockey had given the Somersworth police, and the phrase she had used: "mentally unstable."

"I was very concerned. Obviously, Miss LaBarre was under a lot of pressure at that point. When people are under that type of pressure, they can become dangerous. She had property in Somersworth. I was afraid that if she were stopped, she had the potential to hurt someone because of this pressure."

"Were you worried about the defendant's mental health overall?"

"Overall? No."

"You were in the car after the defendant's arrest when she was transported back?"

"Yes."

"And you were part of the conversation during which the defendant talked about who you wanted to play you in the movie?"

"Yes. I told her that I wanted Sandra Bullock to play me. She said Sandra Bullock couldn't play me because I had natural beauty, and Sandra Bullock had had a lot of work done."

"Did she seem in need of a mental evaluation during that conversation?"

"Not at all."

"Did the name Michael Deloge ever come up?"

"No."

Bailey asked on redirect, "Do you remember the time during the videotaped interview when the rabbit urinated on Sheila?"

"Very well."

"Did you notice Sheila do anything unusual with the paper towel you supplied her?"

"Yes. She cleaned up the rabbit urine, and she wiped her mouth with the same paper towel."

Rockey also opined that all of the talk about incest and pedophilia during that interview seemed less crazy than like an attempt to divert the interview.

"Isn't it true that Sheila's editing of the consent-to-search form, the edit you called brilliant, had no legal effect?"

"That's true."

"She was still searched, wasn't she? Her home and land were searched?"

"Yes."

"And the evidence gathered is being used against her, correct?"

"Yes."

"Because a judge granted a search warrant rendering the consent-to-search form moot, correct?"

"Correct."

"Brilliant?"

"I thought it was clever."

Some spectators wondered why the defense had bothered to call the police as witnesses. Try as they might, they weren't going to get police officers to say Sheila was crazy. And the standard cross—the one that went: avenging angel, no; pedophile, no; incest, no—had been devastating.

# Those Who Survived

Her lawyers had clearly told Sheila what the day's schedule entailed. She showed up that Thursday morning unusually animated and looking particularly pretty, with her hair French-braided. On May 29, 2008, the defense called another group of expert witnesses, the men who had worked on Sheila's farm, shared Sheila's mattress, and who had lived to tell the tale.

Some of Sheila's exes had emerged whole: others, permanently scarred by the ordeal. First up was James Brackett. Jimmy was a good-looking guy to whom the jury immediately took a liking.

Though he was a defense witness, Sheila's team wanted it clear that Brackett had refused to cooperate in any way with their investigation. He was a hostile witness, and he was appearing that morning only because he had been served with a subpoena.

He was employed at a company and lived in a nearby town. He'd quit school in the ninth grade because he had trouble reading and writing.

"I met her back in 1989, but there was a long period in there that I didn't see her at all. I guess I known her for about six and a half years altogether, or something like that," he said. "I met her through the mechanic who worked on Sheila's cars. I lived with Sheila in an apartment by the clinic." He was referring to Dr. LaBarre's chiropractic clinic on Winnacunnet Road.

He said he didn't know that Sheila and Wilfred had once had a romantic relationship, and he thought the pair was "strictly business" with one another. Bill owned the apartment; Sheila ran the clinic.

But it was different with Jimmy and Sheila. They were boyfriend and girlfriend. They did it in Hampton, in Epping, outdoors, indoors, all over!

"How would you characterize your relationship with Sheila?" Bailey asked.

"It was peaceful in the beginning, but after a while it got violent."

Brackett told of the fight at the apartment during which Sheila used a cuticle scissors to open up his forehead. They both were arrested.

"She was trying to call another guy and I was going after the telephone cord with a knife to cut it, and her reaction was immediate." He wasn't being aggressive toward her, and he hadn't threatened to harm her. "She just lunged at me. She blew it out of proportion. I went to the emergency room at Exeter and got stitches."

Fights with Sheila started when she made a false accusation toward him and refused to budge from her opinion—no matter how much he protested its invalidity. What were some of the things she accused him of? Scratching the walls of the house, damaging her Mercedes, things like that.

"She said that I killed one of her animals. But I couldn't, I couldn't hurt an animal. I love animals. *She was the one who killed the rabbit.*"

"Did she accuse you of being with other women?"

"Yes, those were the worst times of all." Brackett named the local woman that had been the subject of Sheila's accusation. "She'd, like, claw my face, and—I don't know—she'd just claw me and stuff. Flip out." He told of a time that they'd had a fight once at the farm and he'd gone to hide from her in one of the farm's trailer campers, which functioned as a storage shed. Sheila was going to have none of that. She grabbed an ax and took it to the trailer door.

"I could see the blade coming through the door. It was shiny," Brackett testified. "She was telling me to get off her property. I was afraid of her. She was cruel and might try to hurt me, so I climbed out and jumped and ran away. I climbed out of the vent in the roof and ran into the woods. She had a handgun. She shot at me. I could hear the bullets going by me, hitting branches and stuff, so it had to be pretty close. Happened more than once, at least three times. We were arguing and I was calling her names, and she didn't like the name I was calling her."

"Do you remember an incident inside the house?" Bailey asked.

"I kind of forgot about some things, you know, so much stuff happened."

Bailey realized that Brackett had forgotten his lines and so prompted, "Something that occurred in the bathroom?"

"Oh yeah," Brackett said. "She told me I was going to listen to her, to what she had to say. I bolted down the stairs, and that was when I pretty much left and got away from her."

Sheila did nothing to stifle a big yawn as Brackett spoke these words.

"How often did Sheila claw you, Mr. Brackett?" Bailey asked.

"Many times. It was bad. Left scars. She was seeing another guy at this point named Yvon, and we took a trip to New York and she clawed my face up, and I had to stay in the motel room the rest of the weekend. She clawed my face up so bad, I couldn't go outside."

"Why did she do it?"

"I don't know. I don't remember what she was saying."

"Was there an incident involving you sleeping in a car?"

"I was sleeping in my car on the farm road because we got in a fight. She told me not to, she didn't want me sleeping on her road. She came back with her pickup truck and hit me three or four times before I finally got out of the car. It was a GMC truck versus a Toyota Corolla. The Toyota moved into the street. I was frightened. It totaled the car. I got out and ran into the woods and hid."

"Why did she do this?"

"Because she's evil, I guess."

Brackett said she broke a windshield on one of his cars once.

"And she took my driver's license and she scratched the devil signs on it, on my picture. At first, she denied doing it, but later on she admitted it. She also wrecked my Mazda, hit it with a vehicle. There were so many things. I can't remember them all."

She beat him with a metal belt until he was covered with bruises.

"Prob'ly the worst came when Sheila hit me with a brush while we was in the tub."

"What kind of brush?"

"A marinating brush," he said. Bailey didn't ask what the marinating brush was doing in the bathroom.

Brackett said she had gone for his throat, but he ducked and took it in the mouth. He saw stars. His teeth bled.

"We were in the tub together. We weren't even arguing. It came out of the blue. Hit me here." He pointed at his teeth. The front two teeth had come out. "I had it fixed, though."

Sheila smiled as she listened to this testimony. *Good times.*

Once, they'd been fighting in her truck and he jumped out of the moving cab to get away from her, Brackett said. "I went face-first into the asphalt," he said. It was okay, though, because his eyelid grew back. There had been a long time when he'd been hanging outside the truck, still holding the handle on the inside of the opened door. She had screamed, "Let go!"—again and again until he did. The night before Sheila and Jimmy had gone to Hampton to check on her properties, she'd left him there so he had to hitchhike back to the farm. But the next night, with his eyelid torn, she allowed him to ride with her back to the farm, and she even doctored him up when they got there.

"Do you have vanity plates on your current car?"

"Yes, I do."

"Could you tell the court, please, Mr. Brackett, what do the letters on your plate spell out?"

"Spells 'I'm alive,'" he said. "Because I thought I'm lucky to be alive. It could have been me. The way that she was violent to me, always shooting at me and everything. If she ever had to get rid of me, she'd put me in her swamp in the back of the farm. She'd kill me and put me in the swamp. Another time she said she would take another trip to Jamaica and put me in with the crocodiles. She'd hire Alabama people to put me in a snake pit if I ever left her."

As she listened to this, Sheila began to laugh and shake her head and move her mouth.

Brackett testified that sometime in 2002 Sheila had forced him to take a lie detector test. He was asked about whether he'd left the horse stall open at night, or if he was having sexual relations with any other women. Several local women, suspects, were singled out by the guy administering the test.

"Did you ever call Sheila 'nuts' or 'crazy'?" Bailey asked.

"Yes, a lot."

"What was one of the occasions that caused you to call Sheila 'crazy' or 'nuts'?"

He said one of the really weird things she did was turn on her tape recorder whenever they were in a fight.

"What made you think she was crazy?" Bailey asked. He didn't get the answer he wanted.

"I just thought she was evil. I don't know about crazy. I'm not a doctor. 'You're the one with mental problems.' She would tell me I was."

Both his mother and father were alive when he was with Sheila, but his father had since passed away. Brackett said that Sheila had tried to alienate him from his family. Whenever she was really mad at him, she would say that he was acting just like his family. When he returned from a visit with his family, she always said it had a poor effect on his behavior.

"I felt she was trying to keep me away from my parents," he said.

Bailey shifted gears: "Mr. Brackett, did you know a man named Michael Deloge?"

"Yeah, I met him at Cross Roads," he said, referring to the homeless shelter where Sheila recruited men. "When I got away from Sheila, I ran away this time in a blizzard, I went to Cross Roads. I met him there. He was healthy and he talked a lot. Sheila and I went there once to get him, and she asked me to invite him over for supper." The three spent the evening together. Mikey slept on the couch. The next day they took him back to the shelter. Sheila said she wanted to get back together with Brackett, but soon the abuse started again and he was gone.

"You knew that Michael Deloge was Sheila's new boyfriend."

"I figured as much, yeah."

"Did you say anything to warn him about what he could expect?"

"I warned him. I told him. He was telling me everything about the farm and how nice it was, and I told him it don't make no difference how nice the farm is, it ain't worth it. I'd rather be poor than put up with that."

"Put up with what?"

"Her evilness more than anything."

"Did Sheila ever mention Michael Deloge in any of her correspondence to you?"

"I'm sorry . . ."

"Did she write something about him on a card she sent you?"

"Yeah. She wrote on a card, a late birthday card, that it was a big mistake to go out with Michael Deloge because he was only pretending to be straight, and now she knew he was gay."

"Did you believe that Sheila was crazy enough to kill you, Mr. Brackett?" Bailey asked.

"I believe she could have killed me, yeah. It could have been me. The woman is crazy enough." Brackett was starting to look frightened on the witness stand.

"No more questions," Bailey said.


On cross-examination Boffetti established that Brackett had been living at a campground in Deerfield when he met the defendant, that he'd first had sex with her a few days later, that they lived together for six and a half years, that during that time he never cheated on her with another woman.

As Brackett spoke, Sheila began to flirt flamboyantly with one of the lawyers, a younger one, sitting at the defense table. Brackett said that yes, he had signed a document once that threatened a possibly fraudulent worker's comp complaint, but he didn't know what he was signing. He wasn't that good in the reading department. Sheila just told him what to sign and he did it. And, yes, that was his signature on an affidavit stating that he had never been physically abused by Sheila LaBarre in any way. And, yes, that was his signature on another document, in which he said that as far as he was concerned, Sheila and Wilfred LaBarre were a happily married couple until Bill's untimely demise. But he didn't know what any of those documents said.

Boffetti read that last one aloud for the jury's benefit: *"I am James H. Brackett, resident of New Hampshire in Epping. I was both a patient and friend to Dr. LaBarre. From*

*the beginning of my friendship with Dr. LaBarre, I have known
both Dr. and Mrs. LaBarre. I heard him call her Mrs. LaBarre,
where they worked side by side taking care of all the patients. I
took care of their animals when they took trips together. Dr.
LaBarre was like a father to me."*

Boffetti turned to the witness and asked, "Who wrote
this? Did you write that?"

"I know I didn't write it."

"You type?"

"Nope."

"Was the defendant single or married when you first
met?"

"Married, to Wayne Ennis. She was in the process of
getting a divorce."

"And you testified earlier that your relationship
started out well?"

"Yes, we went on a couple of trips together to Jamaica.
She brought me to Alabama."

He had lived with the defendant for a long time. There
had been talk of marriage. It had grown violent over
time. She told him, in case the cops ever came, he was to
keep his mouth shut. With the cuticle scissors incident,
she had gotten the charges against her "annulled" and
she tried to get him to pay some of her legal costs.

"When the two of you were in court, the defendant
made a scene in the courtroom, didn't she?"

The jury already knew that she had accused a cop of
ignoring her, despite the flow of blood from her vagina.

"Did she later explain why she had made such a scene,
so much so that the police officer had to leave the courtroom?"

"She said she was just 'playing the system' so that she
wouldn't get in trouble and go to jail."

Sheila was shaking her head vigorously as she listened to this testimony.

At one point Brackett's family had filed a missing persons report on him, he said, and the police came out to the farm to locate him.

"Did Sheila ever share any unusual sexual fantasies with you, Mr. Brackett?"

"Yes, she wanted me to do something sexual with Yvon and let her watch it."

"You mentioned earlier that you took a polygraph. Do you recall if you passed?"

"Sheila told me I flunked it. She got more violent after the test."

"Were there any other bizarre sexual things she talked to you about?"

"She called sex lines on the phone—and after we'd have sex. Also we watched gay porn together, but it was hers, not mine."

Bailey got tough on redirect. He made Brackett talk about the number of times he'd got together with the prosecutors to practice what he was supposed to say, even though he was under subpoena to testify for the defense. Brackett agreed that there had been some of that. Bailey attacked the "playing the system" quote and wondered aloud if Sheila had really said that at all, or if that was an idea someone had planted in Brackett's head during the two-plus years he had been answering questions posed by the state regarding Sheila. Bailey went, one by one, over all of those interviews. He had the transcription of each, and nowhere could he find the comment supposedly made by Sheila that she was "playing the system" with her odd behavior in a courtroom.

"In fact, the very first time you said 'playing the system' was today, right?"

"Correct," Brackett said.

"Was there violence during the first six months of your relationship with Sheila?"

Brackett looked over at the prosecution table, as if looking for signals, and said, "No. They began soon after that."

"And after that, the violence kept increasing? Could you look at me, please?"

"Yes."

"Was all of the violence her hurting you? Were you violent toward her as well?"

"Yeah, the night I ran away in the blizzard I was going to choke her. I figured I'd better get out of there before I killed her, or she killed me."

Boffetti asked on recross, "We sat down this morning and I talked to you about some of the questions, but the words 'playing the system,' there's no doubt she said those words? Those were her words, correct?"

"Correct," Brackett said, and with that, he was allowed to leave the stand with a visible sigh.

Yvon Blais, a chunky man with long hair pulled into a ponytail, testified that he was not married, had three kids, and met Sheila in 1998 or 1999. Just as Brackett had, Blais met Sheila through her mechanic. He was living at the time with his parents in a nearby town. He and Sheila became romantically involved two months after they met, and they were boyfriend and girlfriend for about eight months, on and off.

"Why did you break up?"

"I just did. We didn't get along. She's, uh, she's controlling," Blais said. "She got a temper she can't control."

"Didn't you characterize her as nuts?"

"When?"

"In your testimony at the suppression hearing, you used the term 'nuts.'"

"'Nuts' can be different things."

Blais testified that he knew Dr. LaBarre and had argued with him, long and loud, about Sheila. He and Dr. LaBarre got along "lousy." The doctor always ragged on Sheila. "'She's a fruitcake,'" he quoted Dr. LaBarre as saying.

"Mr. Blais, did you witness violence between Sheila and James Brackett?"

"I saw her hit him. They were fighting, so I broke them apart. They were pulling each other's hair. I had to hit James to get him away from her and out of there."

"Did you know when you were romantic with Sheila that she was also James Brackett's girlfriend?"

"Yeah. She supposedly broke up with him, but she kept going back and forth."

"When Sheila and Brackett were breaking up, did you hear her call him any names?"

"I heard her call him pedophile," Blais said.

"Did she express her opinion of pedophiles?"

"She said she didn't like 'em."

"Was she ever violent with you?"

"Just yelling."

Blais told a story about one night when he was home,

spending the night with an ex-girlfriend. Sheila got wind of it and started kicking the front door. Blais's mom called 911, and while she was talking to the cops, Sheila took off.

"Did you think she was mentally ill?"

"No, I just knew she had a temper. I didn't know she was mental."

Blais said that he was often scolded for things he didn't do, like breaking a window on her car. She tried to control him. Once she got Brackett to try to talk him into quitting smoking, but Blais was having none of that. He wanted to smoke and didn't appreciate being preached to. She wanted him to move in with her and move out on his mother. If she couldn't find him, she would call his friends to see if he was with them. That bothered him.

"Why did it bother you?"

"It wasn't nice. It's not normal."

"Crazy?"

"Yes."

"You described that particular conduct as being nuts and someone who does that is crazy, correct?'

"Yes."

He recounted the times when she had threatened to sue him for something or other, nothing in particular he could remember, though. Yeah, she tape-recorded their arguments. Yeah, she told him she was a lawyer. Yeah, he knew she really wasn't. He was afraid of her. He didn't remember ever calling her psycho. And after all the stuff about Sheila he'd seen on TV, he considered himself lucky to be alive.

\* \* \*

Rice had Blais confirm on cross that even though
Sheila called Brackett a pedophile, she, nonetheless,
went back to being Brackett's girlfriend. Blais himself
had been emotionally vulnerable because he met Sheila
only three days after his father died. Sheila tried to get
Blais to sign a power of attorney document, in case she
needed to take care of some of his medical issues, but he
refused. She ran a credit check on him; she tried in vain
to get him to move in with her in the clinic apartment.
She took him to Alabama to "get his leg fixed," that he
was very happy to get back to New Hampshire. She
*stalked* him when he tried to break up.

On redirect Bailey said, "You have never used the
word 'controlling,' right?"

"Yes."

"When did the word 'controlling' first pop into your
head?"

"Just recently."

"Did your mother ever deal drugs?"

"No."

"Did you ever deal drugs?"

"Yes."

On recross Rice established that Blais had used the
word "controlling" before the day's testimony. He had,
indeed, used it in the same context during his testimony
at a preliminary hearing. Both sides were out of questions, and Blais was off the hot seat.

Then Philip Sullos was on, looking about as comfortable as a guppy on a waffle iron. He was fifty-two years

old, lived in Epping, was unemployed, had been for four years, and last worked at a wood-processing outfit. When asked how he supported himself, he replied that he lived at home. He knew Sheila for about four years. "She lives at the farm," Sullos said. She owned the farm, in fact, and "Doc LaBarre" owned it before her. Philip had been to the farm, but only to work. Mostly helping her with wood. Sure, she paid him. In beer and cigarettes. Once or twice she paid him in cash. She'd come pick him up, driving a green pickup. Three or four times a week, he did chores, but he wasn't sure what year that was. "That'd be hard to say." He met Sheila through Jimmy Brackett. He didn't know if Sheila and Jimmy were involved. Yes, he'd heard of Michael Deloge. Yes, he'd met him. He'd lived at the farm. He might have been living there already when Philip first worked there. Philip did know that Deloge and Sheila were boyfriend and girlfriend.

"Did you ever witness Sheila getting violent with Michael Deloge?"

"Yes."

"Did you ever witness her using a weapon as she hurt Michael Deloge?"

"Yes."

"And what was that weapon?"

"I saw her beating him with a stick. It was round, maybe fourteen inch. I think it might have been red oak. It was a hardwood. She was using it and beating on 'im. I was in, like, a living area as you walk in the door, and I was in watchin' TV, and I come out and I see her beating him. He wasn't fighting back. He wasn't even trying to defend himself. She mostly hit him in the arms and legs. Not that much in the head. I saw him bleed. He was standing and she beat him until he fell on the floor. I think she stopped beating him when he fell. He had a hard time getting back up. He was still bleeding. He laid on the floor for a little while before he got up. He was kind of curled up, protecting his body, protecting so she wouldn't hit him anymore, probably ten minutes he lay there. I didn't try to help him. Sheila was right there. It wasn't my business to, I don't think," Sullos said. "She didn't say nothing. He started to cry pretty much when he was on the floor. He got up. She helped him. Put bandages on his arm. She didn't apologize, explain, give reason, or talk while she was doing this. She was angry when she beat him, but after about ten minutes, she calmed down."

Sullos had seen Sheila hit Michael other times too. Once, when they were in a vehicle, he saw her hit him backhanded. "She was always saying that he was looking at other women, or little boys and girls," he said.

With Young doing the cross-examining, Sullos said that when he worked at the farm, Sheila sometimes worked right alongside, whether it was using a chain saw to cut wood or an iron wedge to split wood. And she took good care of the animals.

"The rabbits were well cared for?"

"Yes, they was."

He said he only went to the farm to work, never for any other reason, and on those occasions he never talked much with Michael Deloge, because the guy would just mumble, so Sullos didn't bother. He was little, shorter than Sheila. Maybe five-one. The beating made Michael howl and cry.

"As she administered this beating, did she call Michael Deloge a pedophile?"

"No."

"Did she refer to herself as an avenging angel as she beat him with the hardwood stick?"

"No."

"Did she say that she needed to save him from himself, and that was why she was dishing out the abuse?"

"No."

On another occasion Sheila had punished Mikey by locking him in the chicken coop. She'd opened the door a little so Sullos could look in there and see that Mikey was really there. That was what happened to bad boys on the farm. He saw her lock the door again and walk away. Several times Mikey had tried to get away, Sullos said, but Sheila always went and got him and brought him back. One time they went to Manchester to get him and they found him walking alongside the road. Sullos last saw Mikey during the fall of 2005. Sometimes Sullos asked Sheila where Mikey was. She said he was upstairs and he wasn't feeling good. No, she never said she murdered him. After the fall of 2005, he didn't see Sheila for three or four months.

Around February 2006 she showed up on a Sunday and picked Philip up at his home. She needed some wood moved. He filled up her pickup truck and unloaded the wood right in front of the porch. As he unloaded the wood, Sheila said he couldn't go in the house because she had a man in there and he was lying down watching TV. Later on, though, he did have a beer at the counter in the kitchen.

Young pulled out the model of the farmhouse and asked the witness to point things out, but Sullos complained that the model didn't resemble the defendant's house at all, and that the model was way too big.

After the beer the defendant fixed him a mixed drink. Something out of a blue bottle. He never met the man in the living room. He did see him emerge from the house once, and he was all wrapped up, like a mummy, with a hat and scarf so that none of his face was visible. Sheila never said the man's name and the mummy man never spoke to Sullos. It was less than a week later that he saw on the TV news that the defendant was wanted because Kenneth Countie had disappeared.

Sheila spoke sometimes about how she handled it when animals died on the farm. She cremated them. A rabbit once and a horse once. Burned them into ashes.

"She ever call you a pedophile?"

"No."

"Accuse you of having sex with your mother?"

"No."

"She slapped you in the head a few times?"

"Yeah, when I did something she didn't like, and I was within arm's reach."

"Did she ever tell you she was abused as a child?"

"No."

Bailey asked on recross if Sullos had ever been romantic with Sheila. He had not. Bailey's implication was that Sheila accused only her lovers of pedophilia and incest.

Steven Martello testified that he was the guy who had driven Sheila to Boston while she was on the run, and had had sex with her in a motel. But once he realized who she was, he immediately told the cops everything he knew. He was a likeable and chatty fellow, with long hair and some missing teeth up front, a guy whose private business had become public because he felt obligated to do his civic duty. He was a big biker who loved his kids, but he had slept with the Devil, and had been a little bit scared ever since.

Bailey explained that Martello had refused to cooperate with the defense and that he was a hostile witness responding to a subpoena. Bailey led him through his story and began to pick at the discrepancies between his testimony and the written statement he had made at the state police station.

"I got a couple of things out of order, that's all," he said.

"In your written report you said that Sheila called her ex-boyfriend a 'sex offender.' Today, here in court and under oath, you changed that to 'pedophile.' Is that not true?"

"I couldn't spell 'pedophile.' I asked the cop there if writing 'sex offender' was okay and he said sure."

Bailey harped about the point, at the end of the story, when Sheila wrote Martello's phone number backward and said it was in code.

"Did you find that crazy?" he asked.

"No, people are often careful when they write down phone numbers," Martello replied.

Spectators, and perhaps the jury, felt that Bailey—desperate to get someone, anyone, to say that Sheila was nuts—was picking on Martello. By the time Bailey was through questioning, Martello—who felt that he had been candid above and beyond the call of duty about his tryst with the killer—was angry that his credibility had been questioned.

\* \* \*

Under Boffetti's cross-examination Martello reiterated that the discrepancies between his written report and today's testimony were merely the product of nerves, and that he'd had no clue that changing the word "pedophile" to "sex offender" in his written report was going to cause controversy. Boffetti drove home the point that Martello could not have thought Sheila was too crazy if he was comfortable enough to let her in the car when his son was there, and later drive all the way to Massachusetts with her, get a hotel room, and have sex with her. In fact, after he called the cops and they told him they weren't on the lookout for anyone, he assumed that she was a woman with money who was running away from a boyfriend. Nothing insane about that.

And the backward phone number?

"I know in the past when I had an affair, people write down their number in different ways so they won't be caught on," Martello said.

Bailey pointed out on redirect some more discrepancies between Martello's original story and his trial testimony. He hadn't written that Sheila didn't want the hotel TV on, for example.

"I was in a police station late at night and I didn't have my glasses," Martello said.

"Isn't it true that you called the state to find out when you were going to testify?"

"I wanted to make sure I could get off work," Martello replied.

"You were eager to testify, weren't you?"

"No, I just wanted to get it over with."

"You refused to cooperate with the defense in this case in any way, didn't you?"

"That's because your private investigator lied to my son when you were trying to find me. I didn't like that." (The investigator had told his son that Martello had witnessed an accident, and that was the reason he needed to talk to him.)

"In your written report you didn't mention Sheila coming out of the bathroom in a towel. You just said that she took off her clothes."

"I had just walked into my home, sat in front of my TV set. I had just seen this woman I had spent the day with, had slept with, on the TV being accused of murder. I was nervous!" Martello was angered by Bailey's tone.

"When she said her boyfriend was a pedophile, didn't that sound odd to you?"

"I thought she was venting. People have fights, they like to vent."

"Venting? She said she died and came back as an avenging angel!"

"Okay, not that part."

"She said she'd send a sex offender after your son if you told on her."

"I thought that was just a scare tactic. I knew it would never be real."

Sheila barely glanced at Martello the entire time he was on the stand, but one time, when she did glance, he was looking right at her. She quickly looked away and used the tip of her tongue to slowly, perhaps seductively, lick across her upper lip.

On Friday, May 30, 2008, the defense called to the witness stand Amy Marshall, who had once lived in one of the Somersworth properties owned by Wilfred LaBarre, and had had to deal with Sheila, the landlady from Hell. Marshall testified that she and her husband lived in the house from September 2005 to January 2007, and during that time had a dispute with Sheila over a heater.

"The heater in the house failed," she said. "My husband and I tried to get Sheila to fix it for three weeks. We spent five hundred dollars in extra electricity bills on space heaters, and so we withheld the rent. We wanted her to pay the electricity bill. In response she called us five to ten times using abusive and vulgar language. When we were moving out, she entered the house several times and caused damage. We had an aquarium and a smaller fishbowl, and both had living fish in them when we went out. The fish were dead when we got back. Both the aquarium and the fishbowl reeked of bleach."

In addition, they found a mattress, which was scheduled to be moved, smeared with blood, a glass door had been broken, all of the lights were on, the burners on the stove were on, and the oven was running with the door open. *Vengeance is mine* was scrawled on the wall. After they moved, harassment continued. Sheila called Marshall's husband's place of work and a place where the couple rented furniture, looking for their new home phone number.

Kelly Tobin, a teacher who had lived in another LaBarre-owned property on the same block as Marshall, was next to testify. She quoted Sheila as saying, "You need to put curtains on your third-floor windows because pedophiles could look in on your children." Tobin said the comment made her think Sheila was a window-peeker herself.

Like Marshall, Tobin had a dispute with Sheila over heat. Sheila harassed them by showing up at the property frequently and making a lot of noise.

"I moved a bureau in front of the door that led up from the basement," Tobin said. "She would be down there banging things, talking loud. I got the feeling she was trying to intimidate me."

Tobin and her family eventually moved to Maine. Still, the harassment continued. They received phone calls from a woman who would just laugh into the phone. They were convinced it was Sheila.

Clarence Beaudette was a plumber who had been called to Sheila's farm in 2004 to fix a sink. He testified that he immediately noticed something was out of whack at that residence. He had to walk through a breezeway that was so packed with rabbits that he couldn't lift his feet without stepping on one. When he looked at the sink, he could see why it didn't work. There weren't any pipes leading to or from it. Sheila, nonetheless, hovered over him and demanded that he continue looking under the sink. She urged him to get deeper under the sink and look closer. Weirded out, Beaudette told Sheila it would cost $1,200 to fix the sink. He hoped she would think that outrageous and tell him to leave. Instead, she demanded that he fix it for free. He tried to leave, but she twice grabbed his arm and tried to muscle him back into the house.

"I asked her to please not touch me, and she grabbed me again and said, 'You're not going anywhere, you will not go,'" Beaudette recalled. "And I said, 'I will go, and if you touch me again, I will kill you.'" He pulled himself free, went outside and got into his truck.

At that point Beaudette realized there was a man living at the house. Sheila ordered the man to stand between Beaudette's truck and the gate so he wouldn't be able to leave. Beaudette drove his truck right at the man and Sheila eventually ordered him to move. Beaudette was able to escape without further incident. Beaudette reported the incident to the police, who said that was just Sheila being Sheila. Most delivery and utility workers already knew about her and refused to go onto her property.

At the end of the day's testimony, Judge Nadeau explained that everyone was getting a long weekend and court would resume the following Tuesday. The defense announced they planned to call only one more witness.

# Dr. Gray

The following Tuesday, June 3, 2008, that final witness turned out to be psychiatrist Dr. Roger Gray, of Newton, Massachusetts. He had examined Sheila multiple times and made a thorough case for her insanity. After listing his impressive credentials, he testified that there was no criminal law definition of insanity in the state of New Hampshire, but that a common standard used by many people was that an insane person fails to distinguish right from wrong.

And that was why Sheila was insane. When she killed Deloge and Countie, in her own thoroughly ill head, she thought she was doing the right thing. Her external societal aspect knew that murder was against the law, and self-preservation demanded that she cover up her crime. But for her internal aspect—in her own world of causes and effects and morality—murdering those men had been the right thing to do.

His diagnosis? He warned that this was a complex case and diagnoses describe symptoms, not people. In broad strokes Sheila had a schizoaffective disorder and a delusional disorder. She was psychotic. Her thinking had taken a break from reality.

"When committing her murders, she suffered from delusions. Her belief system was quite fixed. She has a profound long-standing delusional system," Dr. Gray said. "I was impressed with the extent of her thought disorder. Her reality rolled around in her head like a drop of mercury on a roulette wheel." The simile sounded as if he'd used it before.

Dr. Gray explained that the themes of Sheila's delusions were under the category of fear. There was no place in her world where she felt safe. People used her, however they wanted, and no one ever protected her. Her real world as a child was "populated with a real threat of death." Her delusions revolved around never being safe, never having anybody that she could genuinely trust. She believed she was the only one ultimately who could protect herself. She had a mission in life. Her inner world had been built around a piece of reality, just as dreams could be built around something real. Her foundations crumbled early in life. "Parents are the architects of their children's memories." Hers were of a father who was a raging alcoholic, who chased her and her mother and sister through cornfields with an ax. And her mother was married to him for life.

At that moment Sheila sobbed loudly. Judge Nadeau ordered a brief recess. When court resumed, Sheila was composed. Dr. Gray discussed the cause of Sheila's mental illness.

"I don't think we understand the extent of Sheila's childhood abuse. My hunch is that it was extensive," Dr. Gray testified. He explained that it wasn't unusual for children who were subjected to extensive abuse to forget details. "They suppress the information, the horrible information."

And Sheila's memories *were* vague. She remembered men lifting her dress with long objects, maybe an umbrella or a stick, and she told of being molested by a man who might have been her father. In a therapeutic manner, one of the good things about Sheila being arrested was that it had forced her to deal with her past, and she was talking to her sister Lynn for the first time about the events they endured. So the foundation of her delusions were fear and insecurity. The themes involved pedophiles, incest, rape, and people taking advantage of her in any way they could.

"She needed someone who loved her and would protect her, and that 'father' was Bill LaBarre. That is why her condition deteriorated after his death. She had lost her anchor in the world, the one who kept her in touch with reality," Dr Gray testified. She projected the elements of her own childhood trauma onto everyone else. "Everyone became a player in her play, in the play that was going on in her mind."

During one of her examinations by Dr. Gray, Sheila had told him the story of being chased into the cornfield by her father. Seconds later she was saying that when she went to Heaven, her father would be there waiting for her and they would reconcile. In order to justify the revenge against her past that she was dishing out toward everyone she encountered, she came to believe that she was on a mission from God. Her anxiety was impossible. She desperately needed someone to love her, to care about her. She kept drawing people in, repeatedly in the same pattern. And yet she couldn't trust anyone. That anxiety created delusions and forced her to take action. Her level of denial was psychotic. She herself experienced sexual pleasure when she thought of child molestation. That was a normal result of being a victim. That was not acceptable to her, so she projected that lust onto her victims. For Kenny she had created a fantastic persona, Adam Olympian LaBarre, who could run like a cheetah! In Wal-Mart she blamed Kenny's visible wounds on a woman who had brushed by. Her belief system kicked in and she became oblivious to how implausible her claims sounded. And yet there were times when she could function.

"She can present herself as being put together. She makes a call to a recording studio in Nashville and has a very coherent conversation about a tape she has made. That's an organizing experience for her. When you scratch the surface, what you find underneath is all of this chaos," Dr. Gray said. An interesting insight into Sheila came when she described slicing Jimmy's forehead with the cuticle scissors. She said that the instant she saw the blood, she calmed down, no longer felt angry, and wanted to take care of him. Another telling moment, he thought, came on the tape of Sheila arguing with Dr. LaBarre. She said she wanted to chop his hands off. The chopping-hands fantasy was one that Dr. Gray heard every once in a while in his practice, and in his experience it always came from a patient who had been the victim of child abuse.

The avenging part of her psyche was always the part that got to be the angel. Another consistency in her delusions was that they were always narcissistic.

"Narcissists are the center of the world. It's all about you. One feature is they can be very difficult to deal with. 'I'm wonderful, praise me.' There is an inability to take in the kind of healthy narcissist gratification that one normally wants. Someone who is narcissist will crave attention, but they can't really accept it for all sorts of reasons—shame, guilt, anger."

Dr. Gray performed a sort of closing argument for the defense as he went, one by one, through the witnesses who had testified and the tapes the jury had listened to, and discussed how each depicted behavior that fit his diagnosis.

He noted that although Sheila smoked weed and took Valium and Demerol, those drugs were all designed to calm her down. Sheila killed when in a frenzy. The drugs did not cause her to kill. They failed to prevent her from killing.

"I think this is why appreciating the depth and breadth of her mental disease is in some ways overwhelming," Dr. Gray testified.

Dr. Gray did not think she was malingering. With malingering, there was a history. In this case there was a convincing history of psychosis, a progression: trauma into personality disorder into psychosis into fixed delusions.

"Did Sheila have any difficulty describing the murder of Michael Deloge?" Denner asked.

"None. She said she wanted to punish him, to frighten him into behaving, and that he had been abusing her rabbits and cut a hole in the wall so her rabbits could escape. She described how she hit him. She was very clear about that," Dr. Gray said.

When she described Kenny's murder, she insisted it was an accident. This was because, in Dr. Gray's opinion, Sheila had genuine affection for Adam.

"I think there was a part of her that didn't want to take responsibility for what she did. I think that information was unacceptable to her," he explained.

Denner handed Dr. Gray a set of photos taken by Sheila of Kenny days before his death. Kenny looked ashen and jaundiced; scars were on his face, his ear, his lip, all over. In the background of each photo was a crucifix. The crucifixes demonstrated that Sheila felt justified in her actions.

"She doesn't just feel justified, she is documenting her action," Dr. Gray said. "Kenneth Countie looks submissive. He looks like a man who has been persuaded that he is as evil as she finds him to be. It says something about the information we get from torture."

When it came to Mikey's murder, she told Dr. Gray she beat him with a chain and she knew she had hurt him. She wanted to take care of him. She sought sutures to bind his wounds, but she couldn't because "the LaBarre Clinic didn't have a DEA number." For four or five days, he lay dying. He told her that he deserved to die, and thanked her for killing him. After his death she performed a ritualistic cremation. She sang for Dr. Gray the beautiful song she had sung at Mikey's "funeral."

Michael Deloge's family got up at this point and left the courtroom. Carolynn Lodge kept her seat, still like a rock.

The defense played one last tape, this one of Sheila forcing Michael Deloge to confess to incest, pedophilia, and stealing alcohol and drugs from his mother. As Dr. Gray had testified, the tape indicated that the same psychotic delusions were in place in Sheila's head as both of her known victims neared their demise.


On Wednesday morning Dr. Gray was cross-examined by Rice. She got him to admit that although he was working on this case pro bono, he had worked on many cases for the law firm defending Sheila, and they usually paid him $350 an hour. He first interviewed Sheila sixteen months after her arrest, and after her team had decided to attempt an insanity defense. He explained that in order to be insane, you had to be psychotic, but in order to be psychotic, you did *not* have to be insane.

Rice said, "I believe that you said in your report that the defendant is capable of being temporarily socially appropriate, but this very thin veneer of normalcy is easily shattered. Spending any time with her then, that veneer would be shattered?"

"That is dependent on what the environment is in which she manages the chaos in her head. The history is that in certain situations, for certain periods of time, she functioned better because there were external constraints, limits, and hope," Dr. Gray said. He explained that with Dr. LaBarre, she had hope there was somebody who would take care of her, and she took on the structure of his life. That disintegrated over time. Now in jail she had a number of things that were contributing to the containment of her psychosis and her behavior. Sheila was comforted by jail because of the safety and structure—and even being able to find out about the sexual abuse in her family.

"You would agree that in jail, she's done quite well? Her psychosis hasn't been bubbling over, has it?" Rice asked.

"I think it's been contained," Dr. Gray replied.

"When you say you believe the defendant to be psychotic, you are hypothesizing, correct?"

"Yes."

"And much of the evidence you use in your hypothesis is tapes recorded by the defendant herself, stuff that was found during the criminal investigation?"

"Yes, the bulk of the evidence is self-reporting," Dr. Gray conceded.

"Isn't it true that you found in the defendant intense anger, paranoia, and antisocial behavior?"

"Yes."

"You didn't include any of those diagnoses in your report, did you? You only talk about this global psychosis?"

Rice noted that other doctors who had examined the defendant since her arrest found her *not* to be psychotic. Dr. Gray said he disagreed and that the point deserved "a little bit of expansion."

"It's interesting, *everything* deserves a little bit of expansion," Rice said with a verbal wink.

"There is a range of opinions about these things, ongoing debate about how to categorize mental illness and symptoms. The bottom line is the primary diagnosis is a psychotic disorder that involves delusions and hallucinations, and to my mind the product of that was these awful crimes," Dr. Gray said.

"Okay, I don't want to get into psychobabble here," Rice said. "You have testified that the defendant has an abnormal interest or excitement around *unusual* sexual practices. She gets sexually excited by child molestation, enjoys sadomasochistic sex, she has intense hypersexuality. Sex is a pretty constant theme in her existence, isn't it?"

"Yes."

"Her sadistic paraphilia, as you put it, was [a] major component in her relationship with Kenneth Countie. Isn't it true that she was getting tremendous sexual satisfaction out [of] it?"

"The nature of her satisfaction is hard to know, whether the sexual relationship . . . so many aspects . . . I don't think we can answer that fairly," Dr. Gray said.

"Is it fair to say in some part that she was getting sexual gratification from Kenneth Countie?"

"Yes."

Dr. Gray further agreed that the defendant's sadistic paraphilia was part of her relationship with Michael Deloge. Sheila gave to Dr. Gray an account of how Michael Deloge died, and she told him she had beat Deloge repeatedly across his head with a four- or six-foot chain.

"She also told you that Michael Deloge *liked* pain. He'd get an *erection* from pain, but she wasn't sure if he got an erection when she was beating him with the chain. In fact, she's putting these murders down to snuff-type sex stuff. Isn't that right?"

"Yes."

"And yet, in your report, despite clear evidence, you did not discuss her hypersexuality or paraphilia in your report, her enjoyment of sadomasochistic sex, her sadism toward animals, or that she gets aroused by pedophilic encounters. You did not."

"There is more data now than when I wrote the report. If I were writing that report today, those aspects would go in certainly," Dr. Gray conceded.

"Why is it that this 'psychotic woman,'" Rice said, making air quotes with her voice, "was never previously given a psychiatric examination and determined to be psychotic? Why are you the first, Dr. Gray? How did she stay free to function in society, largely in a destructive manner, for so long?"

"For reasons I don't understand, the community was not paying attention. The plumber goes to the police and says, 'I was afraid for my well-being,' and the response is 'Eh! You are not the first.' She parades Kenneth Countie through Wal-Mart and it's ignored. They send the couple home. What's wrong with this picture?"

Rice wondered why if the defendant so enjoyed calling the police and writing letters to Chief Dodge, she didn't call the cops and report Kenneth Countie as a pedophile. She never called and said, "He's killing my animals. He is endangering me." Did she ever call the police and say she was scared of Michael Deloge and that he was going to hurt her? Dr. Gray admitted she had not.

"When she allegedly felt in fear of Kenneth Countie, she called her sister rather than the police, correct?"

"Yes."

Was Dr. Gray aware that the defendant had told another shrink that she didn't hate pedophiles, and that she did not want to banish them from the earth? No, but Dr. Gray thought that this was very interesting data. He said that for Sheila, love and hate coexisted.

"Discussing the testimony of Steven Martello, you said her discussion with him about pedophiles was an act calling out for help—the kind of psychotic act that people do when they don't have better ways of going to somebody and saying I'm in trouble. Correct?"

"Her comments about pedophiles were made only after they had sex and he was getting ready to leave her. She threatened him. That's a way to keep him from saying "Boy, I just had sex with that woman who is on the front page of the paper.'"

Rice asked Dr. Gray to consider that when the defendant told Martello to turn off the car radio and not to turn on the hotel TV, she wasn't reacting to a headache at all, but rather she wanted to keep from him that she was wanted by the law.

"I would agree that she was attempting to limit her exposure."

"Is it safe to say that she knew it was wrong to murder someone?" Rice asked.

"I'm not sure I would agree with that. We are trying to see the world through her eyes. Did her eyes and brain say to her, 'This is wrong, but I really want to do it,' or did her brain say to her, 'I'm right'? Her psychotic brain told her nobody else would avenge for the children. It is a product of the fact that she herself was molested and raped."

"What is the evidence that she was raped?"

"Only her own word, granted, but that's not the point. Do I take everything she says as the rock-solid truth? Of course not. But I do believe that everything she says is significant. In her *perception* she has been sexually abused, severely, and that nobody would protect her. So in her world there was justification to retaliate and protect. And in her world there was even the protection of the hereafter."

"When it came to the murders she had committed, did she understand the consequences and seek to avoid those consequences?"

"She *asked* for the consequences. She asked the police to shoot her."

"Isn't it possible that she meant, 'Shoot me. I don't want to go to prison'?"

"Yes."

"In her account to you of Kenneth Countie's death, she told you it was an accident, correct? A slip and a fall?"

"There were a variety of stories. In one she heard the voice of Captain Shaw, the ghost who haunted her house. And was being strangled by Captain Shaw. In another, Kenneth Countie tried to strangle her. She tried to downplay the awfulness and severity by saying they were having sex. In another she said she chased him up the stairs with the belt they used during sex. Pick a story! Obviously, we don't know what actually happened. But it tells us something about how psychotic she is, or was at that time. In one version he slipped and fell in the tub. All of the stories end in the tub. As I've explained, Sheila calms down when the violence has peaked, and becomes a nurturer, tending to the wounds of her dying victim. She poked a hole in his trachea in an attempt to put in a straw."

"Are you aware she told her attorneys she hit him with a sledgehammer?"

"That wasn't her first version. That came after her attorneys asked her questions about the forensic evidence."

Rice noted the moment when Sheila slapped her hand on the table while being interrogated by police and said, "I did not kill Kenneth Countie!" Rice wondered, would a psychotic person react that way?

"She could."

"Burning evidence is a pretty good way to avoid suffering the consequences of murdering a person? Isn't it?"

"It is."

"No further questions."


"Any redirect?" Judge Nadeau asked.

"Yes," Denner said. "Dr. Gray, is Sheila a reliable reporter of her internal reality?"

"Yes," Dr. Gray replied. "In her tapes she is telling us what her internal world is. I think she's giving a phenomenal and horrible window into what it would be like to be totally crazy."

"And you still believe that Sheila LaBarre murdered

Michael Deloge and Kenneth Countie as a direct result
of her mental illness, and that her mental illness stemmed
from real sexual, physical, and—most damaging—
emotional abuse?"

"I do. She is the most profoundly disturbed patient I
have ever examined."

And with that, the defense rested.

# Corpus Delicti

Judge Nadeau said after a break, "Is the state ready to begin its case?"

"We are, Your Honor."

"Call your first witness."

Just like in a normal murder trial, the state began by establishing the corpus delicti, the *body* of the crime. And so they called Dr. Marcella Sorg, the bones expert from Maine who officially determined that the bone fragments found in the defendant's fire were human. Dr. Sorg testified that the bone fragments she examined had been baked at a very high temperature for several hours, and that after the incineration, all of the soft tissue and 70 percent of the bone were completely destroyed. Ash. The fire had been so hot that all DNA had been destroyed.

"How hot?"

"Eleven hundred degrees, and the fire must have been stoked for the bones to burn so thoroughly."

"Considering the heat at which the bones were baked, and the time they were on the fire, did you find about as many teeth as you would have expected?"

"No. Less were found."

"Do you have a theory as to why that is?"

"I have to believe that some of the teeth were removed. In many cases the roots remained, but the crowns, which could have been used to identify the victim, had been removed."

Carolynn Lodge, who had been strong up until this point, sitting through even the most gruesome testimony, was losing it. Her jaw protruded, then began to quiver. She expelled a pent-up sob and ran from the courtroom to suffer her emotions in private.

The testimony continued: "Could you tell what type of person the bones came from? Which bones they were part of?"

"Yes, I could tell that the bones came from a young man—from his hands, feet, spine, and jaw."

"Did you determine whose bones they were?"

"Yes, using an X-ray of Kenneth Countie's hand, we matched bone fragments to his left index, middle, and ring finger."

Following Dr. Sorg's testimony, the state played a taped deposition by William Moriang, an expert in dental forensics who had worked ID'ing victims after plane crashes. He said that he had looked at thousands of remains but had never once encountered a case in which the roots of teeth were present, but the crowns were missing. Crashes at high speed and powerful explosions would not separate teeth in that way. In other words, in this case the killer had broken the victim's teeth and had removed the part that could be used to make an identification.

\* \* \*

The prosecution's second live witness was Kenneth Countie Sr., the victim's father. Carolynn Lodge had regained her composure and had returned to her customary seat behind the prosecutors' table for her ex-husband's testimony. Countie described for the jury the last few days of his son's life, as he remembered them. Two days after young Kenneth first met Sheila, but before he left his apartment to live with her on the farm, he and his dad had gone to a hockey game at Boston University.

"It was the best day that I ever had," the elder Countie said, choking back tears.

"How did Kenneth seem at the hockey game?"

His son seemed normal. Happy. Never once mentioned *her*. That was the last time he ever saw his son. He did talk to him after that—he called his son on his cell phone while Kenny was at the defendant's house. He left messages. He had gone to Epping to bring his son home, but he had returned without him. Finally he did talk to Kenny on the phone, and the young man was furious with his mother. "She called the police on me," he complained.

"I told him that a lot of people were upset, not knowing where he was."

Then Sheila got on the phone and said that she and Kenny were in love and didn't want to be disturbed. After that, she called back one more time. She said she wanted to play a tape for him that proved Kenny's mother was molesting him.

"How did you feel when she said that to you, Mr. Countie?"

"I was shocked."

"Did you believe it?"

"Not for a second. I didn't believe for a second that his mother would do something like that."

"Did you hear your son on the phone?"

"Yes, I could hear him in the background, screaming."

"What kind of screaming?"

"It sounded like screaming in pain."

"Was he saying anything?"

"Yes, he was repeating the allegations she had made."

"And what did you do?"

"Well, she told me I was on a speakerphone, so I tried to yell out a message to him. I said, 'If you get a chance, give me a call. I love you and we will straighten all of this out.'"

Countie described his son as "average in school," but a lad who tended not to get along and was often picked on by bullies. "If he got into a fight, he wouldn't fight back. He would never be the aggressor in a fight."

On Thursday, June 5, there was no court, so Brad Bailey could attend his son's graduation at Harvard. But on Friday everyone was back. Sheila had her hair in a ponytail and smiled her pretty smile for her favorite photographer.

The state called Chief Medical Examiner Thomas A. Andrew, with Rice examining. Originally from New York City, Dr. Andrew had been CME since 1997. His credentials were established and he described his job as investigating sudden, unexpected, or violent death to determine the cause. Dr. Andrew looked at photos of Kenneth Countie from March 11, 2006, not long before his death. He said the wounds on Kenneth's body and face were not consistent with scalding or an exploding aerosol can. From a photo alone he couldn't determine how old the wounds were. He did, however, see signs of healing, which meant the wounds were not too fresh. The wounds, he theorized, appeared far more consistent with a beating.

"With a stick?"

"Not inconceivable."

"A belt?"

"Not inconceivable. There are numerous possibilities, but all of them suggest some sort of force or trauma. I find the evidence troubling. It suggests this man was mistreated, beaten, especially on his left arm and back."


State trooper John Encarnaceo, of the major crimes unit, took the stand and explained that he was a crime scene photographer. During the search of the LaBarre house and property, he used a camcorder to capture the LaBarre farmhouse, inside and out. He had also been involved in the sifting of the septic tank's contents, a process that yielded Michael Deloge's birth certificate.

Encarnaceo's video was shown. It started outside, the house, two burn piles, one with a mattress in it, another over by the wishing well, some rabbits hanging around. In one burn pile there could be seen the screen Sheila had used to do her sifting. He focused on some bonelike material. There was a pile of wood nearby, ready to keep the fire going if need be. In the garage a chain saw sat next to the Mercedes, and a gas can sat between Sheila's Mercedes and her Caddy. Inside, the house was in disarray. The top of the stove was covered with ashes. The inside of the oven was filthy, ash-covered and caked with burnt material. Beds had no mattresses, the couch and chairs had no cushions. A container of bleach sat in the bathroom sink. A sledgehammer rested in a corner of one room. In the kitchen and in one of the bedrooms, Encarnaceo focused on some spatter that might be blood. As the video played, the trooper commented that the blood was not obvious because of the dark wood and dim lighting, but was apparent upon closer examination. He took a complete tour of the house, the little room that contained nothing but rabbits, the cellar, and the attic. He then went to the barn, where the video showed the stalls to be tidy and carefully tended, in clear contrast to the house. Wilfred's old horse buggy was still there.

In addition to the video, Encarnaceo discovered and seized evidence from the house and grounds, including Sheila's bloody jacket, diesel containers found in Sheila's pickup, a Wal-Mart receipt, and two receipts for the purchase of eight gallons of diesel fuel.

Bailey tried to get the trooper to say on cross that Sheila's amending the consent-to-search form to say that nothing found could be used against her was an indication of insanity—but Encarnaceo wouldn't do it.

"Not necessarily," he said.

"Were you appalled by the conditions inside the house?"

"It's all relative."

"How would you characterize the conditions?"

"Unorganized. The first thing I noticed was that there were cushions missing from furniture, chairs, and sofas. And there was a hole behind the tub so deep, you could see clear through to another area of the house."

Bailey had the trooper describe the oven again. Encarnaceo said that the contents of the refrigerator were normal and not spoiled, and that prescription medications were found in Sheila's freezer.

Bailey turned to the blood spatter. Wasn't the fact that Sheila didn't clean up blood that was visible to the naked eye a sign that she was crazy? Not necessarily, the trooper said. She might have just been in a hurry or unorganized.

Encarnaceo admitted that Sheila's jacket was found on a wall along the far outreaches of the LaBarre property because Sheila herself had told police where she'd taken it off. The trooper then discussed the notebook found in the home, the one that made mention of "Daniel 3" and "burned ashes flushed." Bailey introduced a letter supposedly written by Michael Deloge to his father during the summer of 2004 in which Michael "confessed" to incest and pedophilia. Bailey asked Encarnaceo if he was aware that these were the same allegations Sheila had made about Kenneth Countie. The trooper said he was aware.


The prosecution called Pamela Paquin, the woman who befriended Sheila around the time that a warrant for Sheila's arrest was issued. She told her story, how her kids had met Sheila at the PETCO and brought her home, how Pamela had agreed to take care of Sheila's animals, had let her spend the night in their home, and the next day took her to a lawyer and the bank and lastly to a cemetery so Sheila could hide. Sheila had taken the wheel of Pamela's car just before police picked her up.

"Did you have a destination in mind?"

"East, I think."

"Were you going somewhere in particular?"

"I'm not sure. I guess maybe back to my house."

After police picked up Sheila, Pamela never saw her again. The letter Sheila wrote to Pamela while in Burger

King was read aloud, as was a letter written on March 4, 2007, while Sheila was in jail, to Pamela's daughter Becky. This letter read: *Dear Rebecca, I am praying for the health and prosperity of all your family and Marie. I haven't heard from any of you, please keep believing in me, you know I am a good person. Please kiss and hold Snookie for me. Give my best, you are an angel. Wishes to your beautiful mother. Sheila.*

Pamela testified that she never felt threatened or in danger in Sheila's presence. Sheila denied killing anyone and made no mention of being an avenging angel on a mission from God.

Bailey conducted Pamela Paquin's cross-examination. Although the Harvard grad and the woman on disability had difficulty communicating at first, Bailey did induce Paquin to admit that a lot of the things Sheila had told her—comments about Irishmen, her ex-boyfriend's incestuous relationship, that he wanted to set himself on fire, that she'd given a bag of bones to the cops—was pretty crazy stuff.

"She told you this stuff right in your house, correct?"

"Yes."

"You were thinking, 'How do I get rid of this woman?'"

"Yep."

"She seemed like a confused woman, didn't she?"

"At times."

"Didn't you tell Trooper Rockey that you thought something was wrong with Sheila?"

"Yes, yes, I do. I did. Something was wrong with her upstairs. I noticed that."

"You said, 'I think she's delusional,' didn't you?"

"My father was a paranoid schizophrenic."

"Some of the things Sheila did reminded you of your dad?"

"I don't know about that."

"Getting back to the letter she sent you. That was the weirdest letter you've ever received, right?"

"Yes, it was," Pamela Paquin agreed.

# Mikey Speaks
# to the Jury

Over that weekend a heat wave descended upon New Hampshire. By Monday the air had the temperature and texture of fresh sweat. One juror thought court started at 10:00 A.M., and the trial was forty minutes late resuming because of his tardiness. The prosecution called to the stand state police detective Steve Rowland, of the major crimes unit, who had collected evidence at Sheila's house and property.

"Did you notice an odor, upon entering the house?" Rice asked.

"I noticed a mildew smell and a vomit smell in the living room. There was a bad odor coming from the washing machine. I located the source of the vomit smell as a floor vent in the living room, along the east wall. I found vomitous material down inside and around the vent."

"How did you collect the vomitous material, Detective Rowland?"

"We pulled the vent from the floor and took it as evidence—along with the ductwork."

He said he discovered blood in one hundred places throughout the house, on the stove, refrigerator, kitchen cabinets, and on the kitchen, dining-room, and living-room walls.

Rice showed Rowland items to ID: the leopard-patterned comforter discovered half in, half out of the washing machine, the kitchen cabinets that had been removed from the house and held as evidence because of their blood spatter, Sheila's medicine bottles found in her freezer—three meperidine, a morphinelike pain-killer, and two diazepam, which was generic Valium—and a Buck knife from the dining room found with blood on its blade. Rowland testified that he found a note that Sheila had written. It appeared to list her options for excuses why Michael Deloge was gone: *Got a ride to his mother's. Is hiding somewhere. Got in a car with someone.* There were also notes pertaining to Sheila's perception of Bill's children as evil, and about her rights as Bill's wife.

Then the prosecution played a videotape of Michael Deloge. Up until that moment the only publicly available photos of Mikey had been taken when he was a teenager or a young adult. The Mikey on this tape was a middle-aged man with a permanently furrowed brow. Mikey wore a knit cap and spoke directly into the camera. His words were slow and rehearsed. The tape was made in two takes, one inside the barn, and another standing outside in front of the house. His words were directed to his mother, whom he accused of standing by and allowing men—especially a man named Tony—to molest him. "You really messed me up," Mikey said.

Bailey cross-examined Detective Rowland. "When you got to the house, there was blood everywhere, correct? A good amount visible to the naked eye, right?"

"Yes."

Bailey drew Rowland's attention back to the notebook he had earlier identified.

"Let's look at some of the other things Sheila wrote," Bailey said. Among the quotes he wanted to emphasize: *Judgment, one day there will be a bright sun. One day there will be a glory of the Father. One day there will be happiness and joy at my savior's side. One day when the world stops turning, good and evil, right and wrong, honesty and deception, My Lord open the book and read the pages of promise. The words of hope, the narrative of decision. Sheila LaBarre, October 5, 2003.*

"Any comment about that passage, Detective Rowland?" Bailey asked.

"I would certainly say there are some interesting notes in here."

"Unusual notes?"

"Yes."

Bailey then presented to the court another passage from the notebook, this one some sort of list, perhaps of nicknames: *Whiner, bobby do right, mama's boy, yeah man smokin', mickey me, pedophile, ally gay, randy the robber, daddy's lap dancer, cindy sissy (when I first met him), needle nelly, poo poo pat, the anti-government queen, count blood (animal/human), would-be husband, snail chicken, benny the blamer, the evil, e kim.*

Another list might have been methods of committing murder: *Too many to count. Steel, pipe, brick, rocks, strangled, suffocation.*

Then the most pertinent list of all: *Daniel 3: fiery furnace. Hotel furnace? Crematoriums? 4000F. 110 pounds, 5 foot 4. One incinerated, 2. burned, 3. ashes flushed/scattered, 4. water, 5. bury and shovel, 6. private pilot helicopter boat, 7. death. 8. Torch. Incinerated-burned-ashes flushed scattered."*

The word "*Death*" was circled, as it often was, in Sheila's notes.

The next witness was Ken Washington, Sheila's final male lover, the man she was with between parting ways with Steven Martello and her arrest, and the reason she ID'd herself as Cayce Washington when she was arrested. Washington was a large African-American with cornrows and a mustache. He was questioned by Boffetti.

Washington said he'd been convicted of a few things over the years, passing bad checks, and he'd had his share of aliases—Kenny Walsh, Kenny Haynes—and he lived in Roxbury, Massachusetts. He met Sheila on March 29, 2006. They spent three days together at various hotels, smoking weed and having sex, and he split. He saw her on TV at his cousin's and called the cops on Sunday morning, April 2, 2006.

"Did Sheila mention anything about pedophiles during your time together, Mr. Washington?" Boffetti asked.

"No."

"Anything about being an avenging angel, about saving the world from pedophiles?"

"No."

Brad Bailey cross-examined the witness. Appearing to the jury to communicate disrepect, he asked his questions with a droplet of sarcasm in his voice.

"When you first drove around with Sheila in your car, you went to a McDonald's to get something to eat, right?"

"Yes, sir."

"Did you go in?"

"No."

"Did she go in?"

"No."

Bailey, convinced he had found a discrepancy in Washington's testimony, played his trump card: "But you said you got something to eat?"

Washington brushed the attempt to discredit him aside easily, and made Bailey seem out of touch with the real world in the process: "It's called a drive-through, sir," he said.

Bailey got Washington to admit that Sheila did not appear to him to be hiding out or on the run. She wasn't hiding behind potted plants or anything.

"You were going along for the sex, right?"

"Actually, to tell you the truth, I was going along for the money. I didn't have a job. She was pretty loose with it. She was peeling one-hundred-dollar bills off a roll and giving them to me."

"During your time together you went to several public places to eat. She didn't have you pick up takeout so she could stay in the room?"

"No."

"Were you aware that Sheila was using the name Cayce Washington? Had you asked her to marry you, or given her permission to use your name?"

"No, sir. I think it was just because she was in trouble. I'm not proud of it, but I've been in trouble over the course of my life. Gave cops a false name to stay out of trouble. Sometimes it worked, sometimes it didn't." Washington's testimony was complete.


Rice called Kimberly Rumrill, of the New Hampshire State Police Forensic Laboratory, to the stand. After her credentials as a blood spatter expert were established, she began to testify about the use of various chemicals to find blood not apparent to the naked eye. Her testimony was disrupted when a juror complained of not feeling well and Judge Nadeau adjourned court for the day.

Come Tuesday morning, Rumrill was back on the stand, telling the now-healthy jury that she'd found numerous large circular bloodstains in Sheila's house, across the dining-room floor, kitchen cabinets, and stove. "There were hundreds of bloodstains in the living room," Rumrill said. There were more than fifty stains alone on one framed poster on the living-room wall. The poster was for "Discover Chiropractic" and featured two horses running through shallow water, spray licking up at their haunches.

She said, "There were bloodstains in the bathtub and also on the ceiling. With the reacting agent I sprayed in the tub—which stains a nice, deep purple color in presence of blood—the circles on the suction cups of the bath mat that was there became visible." There had been blood on the ceiling of the upstairs bedroom, the one that was empty, and along the stairway. In the downstairs bathroom Rumrill found evidence of blood around the toilet and on the plunger. Blood was also found on Sheila's jacket and in the same vent where vomit was found. Blood was found on the leopard-patterned comforter, but in a greatly diluted state, since the comforter had been through the laundry.

To conclude her direct testimony, Rumrill explained to the jury how she retrieved a DNA sample from a blood swab. DNA taken from dozens of the blood spots, as well as from the Buck knife found in the kitchen, matched that of Kenneth Countie. Blood found in the kitchen and on the second floor was ID'd as that of

Michael Deloge by comparing its DNA with that of Deloge's mother.

Under Bailey's cross-examination, Rumrill explained that one of this job's difficulties was keeping samples from being contaminated by rabbit feces and animal hair—and that there were animal chew marks on some of the wooden cabinets. The heating-vent vomit tested positive for nicotine, as did Kenneth Countie's blood. Since Kenneth did not smoke, this spawned conjecture that Kenneth's greenish coloring during his last days was caused by his being force-fed tobacco.

Jane Young took the helm for the prosecution and called Dr. Marilyn Miller, an associate professor at Virginia Commonwealth University in the forensic science department. Dr. Miller was an expert in the physics of blood spatter. She could use the angle at which a droplet of blood hits a surface, and the size of the splash, to help determine how the blood got there. To make such conclusions, she would compare the shape of a droplet, or the pattern of a spray of blood, to her extensive files of test results—experimentally reproduced beatings, stabbings, and gunshot wounds. Using a squeeze bottle of red ink, Dr. Miller simulated an arterial gush. Seeking an impressive gush, Dr. Miller squeezed too hard, overshot her mark, and got ink on Young. As the women cleaned up, Dr. Miller itemized the spatter she had found in Sheila's living room: seven individual arterial gushes. Some of the blood spots on the walls were diluted. The stains on the dining-room floor came from a moving object from which blood was dripping, although it was impossible to tell if the object was a person or a "moving instrument."

"Did you find any large pools of blood anywhere in the house?" Young asked.

"No. And I found no evidence of flesh or other human tissue," Dr. Miller replied.

Bailey latched onto a portion of Dr. Miller's testimony on cross that interested him. Some of the blood spots had been diluted.

"When you say 'dilute,' you are talking about a mixture of blood and water that is [in] some manner splashed onto these surfaces, correct?" Bailey asked.

"It could be any fluid, not just water," Dr. Miller replied.

"Could it have become diluted during crime scene processing?"

"Unlikely. The spattering indicated that it hit the wall diluted."

"Dr. Miller, do you believe that blood was diluted perhaps by water and then spattered back on the wall?"

"I have no idea." She said that there were two sets of bloodstains, one reddish brown consisting of Kenneth Countie's blood; then there was a darker set of bloodstains, near black, and they could have been anywhere from two-plus years to ten years old. If a bloodstain was older than two years, it was difficult to determine its age with any specificity.

Bailey finished by establishing that Dr. Miller knew this was an insanity trial, and that she had no expertise whatsoever in ailments of the mind.

"The state calls Michelle Bennett to the stand," said Jane Young.

With a weary sigh Bennett took the oath and had a seat. She was employed, worked as a clerk, and had been living in Epping for twenty-one years. In 2006 she and Sheila were acquaintances. She met the defendant through Bennett's son Mark, who was twenty-two years old, meek ("he was a follower"), easily manipulated, and a slow thinker. In retrospect, clearly Sheila's type. Mark did some work for Sheila once at the farm, and he'd spent the night. Sheila would call the Bennett home, looking for Mark, saying she really liked him because he reminded her of one of her nephews. Bennett said once she took her kids to see Sheila's horses, and described, to her way of thinking, an awesome scene in which Sheila stuck her fingers in her mouth and whistled for the horses, who obediently came down from grazing in the field. In an orderly fashion each got into his own stall. Sheila never once used the word "pedophile." This was when Sheila was with James Brackett. Bennett remembered asking at one point where Jimmy was. She said he was "in the cage." When Bennett visited the farm with her seventeen-year-old son Kirk, Sheila took a liking to him as well. She found an excuse to talk about her husband—Jesus rest his soul—who was a chiropractor, and how Bill had taught her everything he knew. Sheila gave Kirk an adjustment. Kirk ended up working twice for Sheila, once in Somersworth, once down at the farm.

On March 20, 2006, Sheila showed up at Bennett's house, "all dolled up," smelling of perfume, wearing a leopard-type coat, and looking really nice. After an hour-long visit, Bennett explained to Sheila that her dog was dying of kidney failure and would only eat pizza. So they went to the Fremont Pizzeria in Sheila's car. Kenneth Countie was in the backseat. Bennett asked why Sheila hadn't brought him inside, and Sheila said she could never bring a stranger into Bennett's home. Bennett testified that she couldn't see his face, he hardly spoke, and she thought he looked "scary."

"Sheila said, 'Kenneth, this is Michelle,' and 'Michelle, this is Kenneth—but we prefer the name Adam, don't we?' And Kenneth said, 'Yes.'"

Bennett went into the pizza parlor and bought two pizzas, one for her family and one for the dog. On the way home Kenneth said nothing. Sheila told Bennett that she wanted to come over the next day and give the dog a chiropractic adjustment. Bennett, desperate to get the dog's health back, said all right. She would have said all right to anything. On March 21 Sheila did come over and adjust the dog. She also brought with her a long table that Bennett needed for a school banquet. She did not have Kenneth with her and she did not mention him. On March 22 Bennett woke up to voices in her kitchen. It was Sheila, who looked fine, and her son Mark and Mark's girlfriend, Jen. Sheila was writing Mark a reference for a trailer park in Dover Park. She wanted one or both of Bennett's boys to come work on the farm that day, probably to cut wood, but the boys said no.

Sheila later called on the phone and said she was a landlord, maybe she should go check out the trailer park. Bennett thought that was a good idea. Trailers went for $5,000, which seemed pretty cheap. Bennett was afraid the place was a dump. Bennett went to Sheila's farm to pick her up in her car and was immediately struck by the smell in the air.

"It was the smell of something burning," Bennett testified.

"Had you ever noticed a smell like that before?"

"No."

"Have you ever smelled an odor like that since?"

"No."

"Did you see Kenneth Countie that day?"

"No."

"Did Sheila make any comment about the smell?"

"Yes, she said, 'Don't mind the smell. I'm burning my garbage.'"

On the way to the trailer park Sheila complained about property taxes, about Wal-Mat, where they thought she was a suspicious person, and about her sister and mother because of comments they'd made about her weight. At the trailer park Sheila advised Bennett to buy the trailer for her son. Afterward, they went to an Olive Garden in Portsmouth to eat; Sheila paid for the meal in cash. Sheila said she had to visit her lawyer and Bennett drove her there, following Sheila's directions. Sheila briefly went in alone. She just had to drop something off, a check or something. They stopped at a liquor store, picked up some lemon liqueur, and returned to Bennett's house. While visiting, Sheila told Bennett that she and Kenneth had mutually broken up, and that she'd woken up and he was gone.

"Did she at any time mention anything about him being a pedophile?"

"No."

After a couple of shots of the lemon liqueur, Sheila said that Kenneth was unstable. She said she sure hoped he hadn't wandered out onto her property and hung himself, because she didn't want to get in trouble for that. Bennett noticed she had scratches on her hands, and Sheila mentioned something about broken glass.

Broken glass became a motif. Sheila noticed that Bennett had a broken window. Bennett said her son broke it during a temper tantrum. Sheila said Bennett's son and Kenneth had something in common. Sheila then put down her shot glass—a souvenir from Cancun—too hard and it broke. She said she felt bad about breaking the souvenir and maybe she would take them all to Cancun so they could get another one. Bennett said she did about five shots, but Sheila had more, both of the lemon stuff and of lime vodka. When Bennett drove Sheila home, she noticed the fire near Sheila's porch was still burning. Sheila said she had called Chief Dodge and complained about Wal-Mart. She told Bennett about the Irish guys who were after her. She told Bennett that if her dog died, she would cremate it for her. Bennett asked how cremation was done, did she put the animal on a spit. Sheila said no, she put the animal down in the ground and piled over him a bunch of wood. They had a discussion about how to kill a person, you know, joking around.

"She said she would take a knife and go like that . . ." Bennett made stabbing motions with her hand. Bennett then made *"eeee, eeee, eeee"* noises, simulating the soundtrack from the movie *Psycho*.

"I did not!" Sheila called out in the courtroom, and her lawyers quickly hushed her.

Bennett said that she didn't notice any blood spatter, saw no rabbits, and that the toilet had a wooden seat. The couch had cushions, but there was a foul smell in the living room.

"Smelled like throw up to me," Bennett said.

During that stretch Bennett saw Sheila every day. It wasn't, to the best of Bennett's recollection, until Friday, March 24, 2006, in the afternoon, when Sheila first mentioned that Kenneth had been a pedophile and had slept with his mother. They ran some errands that day together in Sheila's truck. Sheila's mood was very different. She seemed on the verge of panic. Sheila told her that Dr. LaBarre had married his cousin and that his kids were the product of an incestuous relationship. Bennett had no idea why Sheila was telling her these things. Bennett noticed gas containers in the back of Sheila's truck. They went grocery shopping, and when they returned to Sheila's farm, the police were there. Sheila parked the truck and got out, yelling a cordial hello to the police. Bennett stayed in the vehicle and watched for about a half hour as the cops and Sheila toured Sheila's house.

"They all came out at the same time. The cops backed out and Sheila came out to the truck. She said she didn't know why the cops were there, and that was about it. We go to unload the groceries. She drove the truck up to the front door."

"How were you feeling at this point?"

"I just wanted to go home. We had to get out and move a mattress that was in the way. It was close enough that we couldn't back up to the front door. It looked like it had maybe been charred a little bit. She had said that the police moved it. The mattress was whole. It was a complete mattress. We took the groceries inside. I tried to help her put them away. I had noticed, when we got in there, the police had, um, she had like a piece of wood that went across the door and they had broken the wood prior to us getting there. She fed the dog. I told her, 'I just want to know what's going on,' but I wasn't really getting answers. She told me to hush, that she was trying to think. Then she told me they were there because her boyfriend was missing. I said, 'What boyfriend, the Irish guy?' She said, 'No, Kenneth, the one I introduced you to the other night.' She said she thought the Epping police were trying to set her up. She was pretty stressed. She asked me to take care of her dog if anything happened to her and I said I would."

Sheila drove her home in the truck. During the seven-minute ride Bennett looked in the side mirror and could see there was a police car behind them. Sheila never admitted to killing Kenneth, or anyone else, and she never mentioned that she was an avenging angel trying to protect children.

That concluded the direct examination of the witness, and court, for the day.


Three things were different about Wednesday morning, June 11. First, Sheila was back in her French braids, for the first time since ex-boyfriend day. Second, the spectator section was filled with Russian-speaking students, who all wore earbuds and were plugged into an interpreter. It was a lesson in American justice. And third, Judge Nadeau entered and immediately announced that Juror #15 had been dismissed for undisclosed reasons. She encouraged everyone, in vain, not to ponder the reason why. These things happen for a wide variety of reasons, she explained. "He's not upset. I spoke to him and he's fine," Judge Nadeau said. That morning Juror #15 watched the proceedings from the spectator section for a time, but then left. Outside the courtroom reporters pestered the man for info, but he kept mum.

Michelle Bennett was back on the stand with Bailey cross-examining. Bailey patiently went through Bennett's history with the case, a signed affidavit, her testimony at a preliminary hearing. She wrote a statement for the police and gave the state an interview in preparation for her trial testimony. Bailey pointed out details from later statements that were missing from earlier statements, and asked if her memory grew better with time.

She said it did, because her children reminded her of things that happened and that sparked her memories.

Earlier she said Kenneth Countie was left outside alone in the car in the cold for an hour and a half, and earlier she said approximately an hour. What was up with that?

"I wasn't looking at a clock," she said.

"Isn't it true that Sheila once talked to your dying dog, instructed him on what to do when he got to Heaven?"

"I don't remember the Heaven part." Bennett, however, did not recall specifically on which day Sheila had said this.

"What was the nature of her statement to your dog?"

"I don't remember that. I remember at one point in time she was talking to the dog in German."

She agreed with Bailey's characterization that she hadn't seen Sheila in years, but when Sheila took an interest in her teen sons, there was no getting rid of her. She made inappropriate remarks in front of Bennett's teenage daughters, discussing pedophilia and incest, until Bennett made up an excuse to get Sheila out of her house.

There was another attack on Bennett's credibility, and again the witness held her own.

"You go to the house and you notice a fire burning in a barrel right by the porch entry to the house, correct?"

"I can't remember if it was a fire on the ground or in a barrel. I did not examine the fire."

"Let me read from your affidavit. You may recall that you said, *The fire was burning, I think in a burn barrel but I'm not positive.* You also mentioned that in your recorded interview, didn't you? Your words—"

"I just knew there was a fire there, I could see a fire—"

"But your words—"

"I didn't go near the fire."

"You had to walk right past it."

"I did not go near that fire at all."

"Whose word was 'barrel'?"

"It was my word."

"You actually walk into her house, you walk right past either where the fire was—"

"I did not walk past the fire. I walked into the house through the front door, fire was up there in the back someplace, past the porch."

"You could see a barrel!"

"I did not know if it was burning in a barrel or on the ground."

"When it came to the odor from the fire, you didn't say anything about this very odd smell?"

"I didn't have to, because she came around the corner and mentioned it first."

"My question was, *you* didn't say anything—"

"I didn't have a chance to say anything."

"When Sheila talked about pedophilia, was this the first time you'd heard her use that word?"

"No, she used it back in 2002, when I first knew her. She used it to describe Jimmy Brackett."

"When she mentioned it, you thought, 'Hmmm, she meets a lot of pedophiles.' That is what you told Trooper Rockey, didn't you?"

"Yes." She admitted that she thought it "pretty odd," that she thought of Sheila as pretty eccentric, and, yes, crazy.

"You also told Trooper Rockey that she would tell crazy stories, correct?"

"Yes."

"You thought Sheila was crazy, correct?"

"I think everybody is a little crazy in their own minds. My son used to call her 'Crazy Sheila.'"

"Both your sons made reference to that?"

"Mark also said she was a witch."

"Didn't you tell Trooper Rockey that Sheila told you she spent one night running around her fields, shooting at lights? Did you say you thought she was a little insane? Didn't you refer to her as a 'fruit loop'?"

"Yes."

"She told your son the house had a ghost with a rocking chair that rocked on its own?"

"Yes. That was one of the big reasons he wanted to go back, to see the rocking ghost."

"You told Trooper Rockey that Sheila appeared to have some psychological problems."

"I haven't memorized my statements. If it says I said it, I said it."

"But the statement is accurate, isn't it?"

"She appeared to have psychological problems. Yes."

"No further questions, Your Honor," Bailey said.

On redirect Young established that, in large part, the discrepancies between Bennett's various statements were caused by nerves. "Isn't it true that you gave your first interview to the police on the day your dog died?"

"Yes."

"You were stressed because of what you had learned about the defendant, of course, but what else was causing your stress?"

"I had been working a lot of hours—some days fifteen days in a row." She had also taken in her eldest son, his girlfriend, and their baby.

"Isn't it a fact, Ms. Bennett, that you are nervous right now?"

"Yes, it is," the witness agreed wholeheartedly.

On recross Bailey tried to establish that the many hours of work and full house came months after his client's arrest, and that these conditions did not exist when Bennett called Sheila a "fruit loop."

"I didn't memorize these scripts," Bennett replied.

Bailey leaped at the word. "Let's talk about scripts," he said. "The state police told you if you helped out, cooperated, you wouldn't have to come in here. Did they give you a script?"

"No."

Michelle Bennett's excruciatingly long stint on the stand ended.

Ana Cordero testified that she was a Dorchester beauty parlor manager who ran the shop where Sheila received a haircut and a dye job while on the lam. Cordero was Spanish and spoke English poorly. She was questioned by Young with the help of a translator. The witness ID'd Sheila, and using a color board, she ID'd the red color she had used on Sheila's hair. Sheila's hair had been blond with gray roots when she came in. The dye job came in two parts, a copper-color base, then red highlights. She paid $200 for a $125 service. When the job was done, Cordero gave Sheila her card and told her to come back anytime. And Sheila did come back, three to five days later, for a wash and blow-dry. Cordero said that the color was a little bit unusual but not bizarre.

Bailey established on cross that the most unusual and

memorable thing about the job had been the tip.
Young asked on redirect what kind of tip the defendant
left after her second visit. Cordero said she didn't remember.

Sergeant Jeff Langone, of the Revere, Massachusetts,
police, testified for Boffetti regarding the defendant's
arrest at the Northgate Shopping Center. He told Young
that the defendant made it through the arrest and the
booking process without once seeming irrational in any
way, and without using the word "pedophile." She did
use a pseudonym, Cayce Washington, when first confronted, but she signed her name Sheila LaBarre after
being confronted with her real identity.

Donna Boston, Michael Deloge's mother, was a diminutive woman who had been in court for nearly every day of
the trial, always sitting between Kenneth Countie's parents. She testified that she had contacted Epping police
about Michael's whereabouts at the end of 2004 because
she had been hospitalized for thirty days and was afraid
Michael was looking for her and couldn't find her. After
that call she didn't see him again until Christmas in 2004.
Boston testified that she and her ex-husband and their
friends were musicians and enjoyed singing and playing
Christmas songs during the holiday season. When Sheila
and Michael came over for a Christmas party in 2004,
Sheila took over the musical portion of the proceedings,
much to everyone else's frustration.

The last time she saw Michael was on his birthday in
2005 when he, again, visited her with Sheila.

"How would you characterize that visit?"

"Horrible."

"How so?"

"I kissed him on the cheek and Sheila had a fit. She said, 'I'm not bringing him over here if you don't stop the hugging and kissing.'" In retrospect Boston realized that this was the last time she ever kissed and hugged her son. "Michael was very quiet. I asked him what was the matter. Sheila said, 'Michael, you got something to say to your mother or I'm leaving.' I couldn't imagine what it would be. He tells me he's having a hard time with his life because I assaulted him. I raped him, and stuff like this, when he was little." Her shoulders sagged. She put her face in her hands and cried. Regaining her composure, she said, "And his color was so bad. He was all sandy, sandy color. He'd lost so much weight. I was so shocked by the accusations that I kicked the both of them out."

Boston described Michael as a "gentle" and "loving" man, until he met Sheila and turned on his mother.

On cross-examination Bailey asked, "Are the accusations that you and your son had an incestuous relationship true?"

Boston shook her head and broke down in tears, forcing Judge Nadeau to call a recess. When her testimony was complete, she was greeted at the front of the gallery by members of the Countie family, who gathered around and embraced her.

"That's the hardest thing I've ever done," Boston could be heard saying to her supporters.

Austin Wiggins, a man who had worked on the LaBarre farm for years, testified about the times he had seen Sheila physically abusing her men, including Michael Deloge. Once, Sheila accused Mikey of ruining a horse carriage cover. The cover looked like it had rotted and been chewed by animals, but Sheila continued to accuse Mikey until he said, "All right, all right, have it your way. I did it." With that, she threw him to the ground and mercilessly beat him. He never fought back.

Wiggins told a story of the last time he visited Sheila's farm. It was on Halloween, 2005. Mikey wasn't there. Wiggins asked where he was. She said he went to Connecticut to be with his family. Wiggins asked on his way out, "Where did you say Mikey went?" To that, Sheila replied, "You think I killed him, don't you? Don't you?"

The question was so frightening that Wiggins left and never came back.

# Dr. Drukteinis

From Thursday, June 12, to Monday, June 16, 2008, the jury watched videotapes of Sheila talking to a prosecution psychiatrist, Dr. Albert Drukteinis. The interviews had been taped at the Dover Police Department on January 2, January 10, and March 11, 2008.

On the first video Sheila was chipper and animated, happy to discuss the nooks and crannies of her private life, from her sexual threesomes to her experiences with men who "needed to be flogged to get hard." She itemized the medication she was on—Lasix for edema, trazodone to help her sleep. But what she really needed was a pain pill, for her upper right quadrant, where the pain continued to be terrible, despite the negative X-ray.

"I sustained some injuries prior to incarceration. I think one thing that is a factor is that we have to sleep on steel bunks on a woolen mattress unless you have two, which I don't. I also have scoliosis," she said. "All I take [is] Motrin and Benadryl. Sometimes my feet swell and I have to ask for the shackles to be removed."

She told the doctor about her background. Her dad

died on February 15, 2000. Her mom was still alive, aging but closely monitored.

"My daddy, I just know being his daughter there was certainly something wrong with my daddy. He seemed to be two people. He told me I seemed to be two people. At times he had a problem that made him cruel. A devout alcoholic. He almost killed us, and that is not an exaggeration. It's the truth. One time he literally chased us with an ax in a cornfield. So many times we would hide, in blankets and closets. He was verbal. He could go on for hours and hours and he would never shut up. He'd put us out of a car, if he got drunk. I just found out in the last couple of months that he was molesting my sister Lynn," she said. "I don't want to hate my father. I remember me and Daddy with my mother because my daddy would drink and he would stay gone all night. I was lying in bed with her and suddenly I was aware that he was getting into the bed. That woke me up, to my active knowledge—it wasn't like my parents said, 'Sleep with us, it's a thunderstorm'—and he—he—he reached with his hand between my legs and I said, 'Don't, Daddy, don't.' Mama was asleep. He reached for her private areas and she said, 'Stop!' And then he became very violent and kicked us both out of bed very hard, and yelled and screamed the rest of that particular night. There were so many horrible memories in that house."

"How did your mama deal with you?"

"Mama always sided with the men, the boys. I never felt wanted. I try to reach for memories of her and they'll be good, but they're not really good. She seemed to be distant, but she had her hands full with Daddy—the beatings and the running and the hiding from. I never got love. I didn't feel like I had what other girls had!" She added that her brother Kenny had been cruel to her also. "Kenny would put his hand down the top of Mama's blouse before he would go to sleep. I'm not saying they had sex with each other, but I do know he was her favorite in the family. Kenny made me pee in front of him."

Her job in those days was as a ward clerk in a hospital, working with doctors and nurses filing lab slips. She had her first abortion in high school, pregnant by a boyfriend named Michael. The abortion came, she later claimed, when she was seven months along.

"It was hard on me," she later whined. "You know why? Because I was so far along that it was not supposed to be done." Walking home from the procedure, she was frightened into the woods by a carload of boys screaming at her the things they wanted to do to her.

Sheila said that she knew what people were saying about her, the things they were whispering behind her back: that she got together with Dr. LaBarre because she wanted his money. People who thought that weren't familiar with the facts, she said. He wasn't rich when she found him. He was in debt. It was her expert business management that turned things around.

"Did you and Bill have any kind of kinky sex? I'm talking about an incident about hanging in the doorway. Do you remember that?" Dr. Drukteinis asked.

"That never happened. That's a complete lie. He was a gentle lover, very well-hung. I've had kinky sex with others, but not with Dr. LaBarre."

She understood that her relationship with Bill wasn't normal, but it was normal for them. Bill would go ape shit over the littlest thing, but he didn't care if she marched a plethora of playmates through the farmhouse.

"What about with Wayne? Kinky sex?"

"No. Jamaican men, true Jamaicans, born on the

island and raised there, they have their own cultural beliefs. For instance, they do not perform orally on a woman, which is okay with me, because I don't like that anyway. They avoid the menses. Sex with Wayne was straightlaced. I had anal sex before, with pilots— pilots like that. I don't know why, but anyway . . .

"I'm a very sexual person. I masturbate even at the jail. If I'm saying anything out of line, let me know. Even though I've been through menopause, I've got a very strong sex drive."

She said that after her marriage to Wayne Ennis broke up, she went through a particularly promiscuous phase and had sex with a lot of men she "didn't really know." It was during that period that she started talking on the sex chat lines. While talking about fantasies with strangers, she learned something about herself, that she was turned on by the very things she most abhorred. "Freud said that the things that turn you on as a child continue to turn you on as an adult," she said. "On the phone everyone is there to get off, and I would say things like, 'So tell me, do you still smell your sister's panties?' I had men in New England tell me they had sex with their mothers. I can't say it turned me on. It's repulsive. But at the same time, it intrigues me, because as I figure out what happened to them, it would help me figure out what happened to me." She said that sex chat lines, though they could turn her on if she let them, was "my own private research."

"What else turns you on?" Dr. Drukteinis asked.

"Being a dominatrix," she said. "Where I have control. I grew up feeling so out of control, so helpless, so at the mercy of my parents. Many men are turned on by what we call, in the South, flogging. They can't get hard unless they are flogged. Especially conservative men. With my partners I would do fantasies with them, pretend to be other people. I've pretended to be their mother, although that makes me angry. That's very complex in my mind. When I was a dominatrix, I didn't wear the outfit, like you see in the movies, no garter belts. I just used a belt and they would say, 'Make it hurt!'"

"Dr. LaBarre?"

Sheila must have been under the impression that there had been erroneous reports of she and Bill LaBarre engaging in bondage games, because she reacted to this question strongly: "No! I don't know who told you he was hanging up. That's such stupidity."

"Are you turned on by men who are into other men?"

"Yes! Yes! That still turns me on."

"Did you ever have a threesome?"

"Twice. Once we didn't go all the way, me and the two partners. Once the two men hated each other. I put their hands on each other's penis. There might have been some fellatio. I don't know. I was on pills."

She discussed curing James Brackett of his premature ejaculation. She did this by allowing him to remain inside her after his orgasm, and she continued to move her body until she had hers. "I don't demand an orgasm," she said. "I'm not that type. If some reason my body doesn't want to, I get up, go clean myself, clean the man. For men, it really, really does something to them if they are not able to perform. I can trace that part with James to his mother. It took hours and hours of talking to him. I said, 'Your mother has said something to you. Something has triggered this fear in you. Something has made you feel you can't be with a woman.' He told about a time that he was climbing, fell, straddled a fence, and hurt his testicles. His mother said, 'Let me see them.' She told him he might have trouble the rest of his life."

Sheila said the first incident of violence between the two of them was James hurting her. She claimed he had a recurring sexual nightmare of being chased by a man on a moped, and one night, while having this dream, he dug his fingernails into her. She and James had a fight once at the farm, and Bill ordered Sheila to leave. James was allowed to stay.

The pair's fights were about infidelity, she with a twentysomething pot dealer named Tommy, he with a "traveling tramp" named Nicole. He denied having sex with Nicole, but Sheila had a lie detector test administered and James flunked big-time. Sheila came to believe James was a pedophilic homosexual. She met a "mental-health counselor" named Rubin on a chat line and invited him to the farm to talk to James. Rubin said that James didn't love her at all, that he saw her as a mother figure. "You are wasting your time with him," Rubin said.

"James and I had fantasies. I participated in his fantasies that he wanted to have because he's turned on by young boys. I didn't hate James, I still don't hate James. That's ridiculous, there is nothing to be solved by hating," Sheila told Dr. Drukteinis. She wasn't sure if there was a police report, but she did remember discussing James's pedophilia with an officer at the time.

"Does playing fantasy games involving pedophilia turn you on?"

Sheila explained, "Well, it's not something I would condone, allow, but I'm saying that for someone I already have an emotional connection to, that I have feeling for, that I'm actively about to have sex with, I try to have an open mind. For me to be truly connected to a man, I like to know about his sexuality. If I'm disconnected from that person, I control my sexuality. I might lubricate—what might sicken me one minute, or piss me off, there are times I won't do it. But then, a different mood. It depends on my mood because my mood will change. I don't like the police to portray me as someone who hates pedophiles. I don't hate pedophiles. I don't approve of what they do. I'm not looking for them to be banished from the earth. We all make mistakes. We all have kinks. We all have sexual fetishes. I don't hate pedophiles. I just don't want to date them anymore."

Sheila described her most frightening experience on a chat line: "I was doing one-on-one connections, are you familiar with that? I don't like party rooms. It's boring. One-on-one, you call in. You get into the menu for that type of service, you hit a certain button, one man right after another, as soon as they come, they connect you to another person. I can talk for hours. Six or seven hours. First he was breathing. I thought, 'Okay, this is interesting.' Finally I said, 'I bet you're really kinky, I know you are. Tell me about the last time you had sex.' He started talking in short sentences. kind of clipped. He said, 'She wouldn't stop screaming.' You just have to talk to them, not judge them. And, no, I didn't lubricate for this. And he was breathing. I said, 'I'm not judging you.' He said that he held this young woman down with long hair. It was like a movie, creepy. It gives me chills thinking about it. I said, 'What did you do when she screamed?' He said,"—and she harshly whispered—"'*I lost it.*' I said, 'Tell me. Go on now, tell me.' He said, 'I choked her! I choked her.' I said, 'That's what turns you on, isn't it? It turns you on to stalk them, get them, get them with you, then you start to do things. They cry, they scream, and you silence them.' If he was an actor, he deserves an Academy Award. So that's the only weird creepy phone call I had." Spectators were struck by the notion that Sheila had been describing herself.

Sheila discussed other lovers from her past. There was Brian, a commercial pilot, who slapped her face and spit on her, again and again, when she was pregnant. There was John, an electrician who was obsessed with his mother. Another one of *those*. Then there was . . .

Dr. Drukteinis steered her toward talking about "the gentleman who died." She told the story of meeting Kenneth on the chat line, how he sounded nice, so she agreed to meet him at the Ashworth. She had cut her foot out on the lawn that day, and she should have seen that as a bad omen, but she didn't. She didn't notice that there was anything wrong with him mentally at first, but she later realized he was emotionally off. She wouldn't have rejected him because of that. Handicaps were cool. She couldn't rule out a lover in a wheelchair. She couldn't have a Japanese lover, though. She didn't think she would fit in with his culture.

She admitted to being obsessed with her Adam and his history. Sheila believed that Kenneth had been trained by his mother, trained in the ways of masochistic pleasure. She claimed he asked her to beat him with the belt, and she was only too happy to do that for him because she knew it was what he wanted.

"So he wanted you to hit him with a belt because that is what he was used to with his mother?" Dr. Drukteinis asked.

"I feel, based on what he told me—we had a lot of sex—sometimes, yeah, that's what he wanted," she replied. "The hitting was sexual. It was a kinky sexual game. I didn't take high heels and hit him and say, 'There, take that, you f***ing loser,' like she did."

"Did you play his mother?"

"I didn't role-play. We had a lot of fun. We enjoyed each other's company. He said he felt free." She was crying now. "He made me promise that no matter what, that if he and I got into a car accident or anything, that he never wanted her hands on him again. He asked me to be his attorney. I said I can be your attorney. In fact, you *can* empower me that way if you choose to. We worked together to expose his mother. I felt, I still feel, his mother should not be around children. She abused them. She abused him. Of course, the family would say, this isn't true, this isn't true, because that's the way they are in complete denial. Just the way she's been going around Epping spreading stories about me. She's not a good person. Anyone who would abuse their son, mentally, physically, verbally—"

"Then what happened?"

"What's your point?"

"How did you get arrested?"

"I've been falsely accused of something that did not occur."

"Do you think Adam was evil?"

She nodded her head through her sobs.

"How do you let somebody evil like that live with you?"

"I was thinking, 'This isn't real, this isn't real, it's not really happening.' I was taking a couple of his morphine and what the doctor was prescribing for me. I was not in the right frame of mind. Just like the lights in the field."

"You were taking morphine?"

"I only had two hits of morphine, that's [a] prescription for headache. I'd fallen, I'd fallen in the barn, I'd fallen in the pasture. I had a lot of falls hitting my head. He prescribed it because of the intensity of the pain." Sheila itemized the other meds she was on.

She then moved her narrative ahead to the first Wal-Mart visit. Kenneth was hurt by an exploding can of Easy-Off, and this stupid woman in Wal-Mart put her hands on him and squeezed him until he cried out in pain.

"In the days after that, you bought diesel fuel," Dr. Drukteinis commented.

"Things started missing. The house was completely disheveled at that point. I was not in the mood to clean anything anymore. I felt, I didn't feel right in my mind. I think I was in the middle of some kind of breakdown when I met him. Things were moving around. I was having some memories, my mother scalding me when I was a little girl. I try not to think about these things. I had eaten all this ex-lax because she said it was chocolate candy—a little teakettle, she just poured it. I'm sorry." Sheila wept.

"So, did Adam die at your house?"

"Yes."

"Can you tell me about that?"

"Yes, I don't remember what day it was. I don't remember everything. It's not like I can see it in my head, from one thing to the next. It's just bits and pieces that come into my head right now. Floggings. He had fallen asleep the night before. Had the mattress in the living room. We went to sleep together, watching TV. And I went to sleep. I woke up at one point. I looked over and he wasn't there. That's all I remembered for a long time. That he was gone. I don't know how that happened. I started to . . . I looked around and I felt hands on my throat. And he was choking me. And I was all confused. I didn't know, at first, what was going on because I was at a disadvantage. I guess, I don't know, I was shocked by it. But then I thought, 'Is this Adam or Captain Shaw?' I thought it was the ghost of Captain Shaw. I wrestled out of the grip on my throat and slid down to the floor and stood up and I was very afraid, and he and I started going at each other. I started swinging and I said, 'You've been prowling my house, where are my things?' I scared him. I said, 'I'm a justice of the peace, don't put your hands on me.' I opened my leopard hatbox. There's all kinds of fingerprints in there. I said, 'What are you doing in there?' He said, 'Looking for money.' He said, 'I love you, Sheila, I love you.' He wanted money to go get heroin. We struggled and I don't want to remember it. I don't want to think about it. He kicked me. We fought physically with each other. Then I started saying, 'Where's my three thousand dollars?' He started toward me and I picked up a belt and I hit him with it, across the back. He was naked. I ran, to be sure the gun was not loaded, there were no shells around. I did that real quick. It was a very upsetting moment. He was very strong. I think I had bruises all over me, later from the fight, the struggle. I knew I had hidden cash upstairs. I wanted to go upstairs, I don't remember who went up first, I know we bolted up the stairs. We ended up in the bathroom upstairs, where I had two thousand dollars, but it wasn't there. I said, 'Where is my money? Where is my money?' He said, 'I don't know.' He just grabbed ahold of me. We started pushing and shoving at each other. There was a hole there. I had stepped into the tub to reach into the hole, and I was reaching and he stepped into the tub with me and started hitting me. Then I stood up, he stood up, somehow the water accidentally got turned on. We both got sprayed with water. I don't know if it was conditioner or what, but the tub floor was slick. I pushed him to try to get away from him. I just pushed him. I was in pain. And he fell, he fell. Hit his head on the end of the tub, right there in the tub, and it made the most awful sound." Sheila was wailing with emotion. "It was awful, because I tried everything. His eyes, they were rolling, and he was just staring up. I started CPR and I was screaming his name. I tried for a pulse. Trying and trying and trying. I tried to see if he had an obstruction in his airway. I turned him over on the side. We had unplugged the phone. The wire to it had been unhooked. Somebody kept calling and ringing the phone when we were having sex that night, and we got pissed, and he said I'm going to unplug the phone. I know that if you revive someone, you just have seconds before permanent brain damage. I kept doing CPR on him for over thirty-five minutes. I put cold water on his wrist, everything to try to revive him. He never regained consciousness. I took his shirt off his chest. I was in shock. I didn't know what to do. I felt dead. I felt dead. I can't change anything. He was so heavy. He fell back over. What was I supposed to do? So I opened the airway. I tried to. I didn't know what else to do. I prayed and prayed and prayed. Bring him back. I told God to let me die, just bring him back. I didn't want his mother to have another chance to touch him, so I took fabric from Germany that had been Bill's mother's. I took him into the hallway and I wrapped him in the linen. I pulled him down the stairs. I gathered up firewood from the farm. I went over to the area where I had cremated other animals. I started the fire. I gently pulled him in. He was beautiful. It was humane. A Native American funeral. No coffin. I put gasoline on the wood. If I had it all to do over again, I would not have become involved with him. I wasn't trying to cover anything up. I couldn't just leave him in the house. He would deteriorate."

\* \* \*

That interlude concluded that day's interview with Dr. Drukteinis. After a break the jury watched the psychiatrist's next interview with the defendant, which was videotaped several days later. As before, the subject was Kenneth. She'd heard the accusations that she'd bought the diesel fuel because she was premeditating his murder. *Preposterous!* It was because the furnace was broken. No premeditation whatsoever. "Being charged for that is ludicrous," she said.

"You indicated to me that at some point you had forgotten what happened and only later remembered. At what point did your memory stop, earlier?" Dr. Drukteinis asked.

"It stopped with me waking up and looking over and he was gone. Maybe because all my life, I've had trauma where it's easier to close the door than face the dragon. I didn't want to watch that movie *Saw*. We went to Blockbuster, we should be on security tape there. We rented that movie. We were in bed."

"Did you watch that movie the last night?"

"He did. I don't know if it was the last night. I fell asleep with him watching it, and he had a strange look on his face. Evidently, I'd kind of wake up and look up—"

"How long did you have the memory that he was gone? Days?"

"No, longer than that."

"Weeks?"

"I don't want to say something of which I'm not sure."

"How did your memories start to come back?"

"And I still don't have all the pieces. It was sometime after the arrest. I was just trying to carry on, just like with Michelle Bennett. She asked me to give the dog a chiropractic adjustment, which I did."

"And all this time you just think Adam is gone, because he's gone."

"Right."

Dr. Drukteinis asked what were Sheila's memories of the time between leaving Epping and when she was arrested in Revere.

"I didn't want to rent a car. I knew it was easy to get a ride. Why would I rent a car and make it appear that I was running? I didn't choose to leave, that's the thing. In Boston I needed something to block my pain. I was high just about that whole time. I got some marijuana through Kenneth Washington, who tried to extort me. He told me he had a twenty-two-page rap sheet. The other guy was a white gentleman, kind of strange-looking. He had long, long hair. I believe it was Steve, something like that. He had a child, an itty-bitty child. He took me to Boston, to Dorchester."

"Not trying to embarrass you here, you said something like the two of you had a little fling along the way."

"Here's the thing, we didn't have a fling. I didn't buy hair dye. I did buy condoms, that's true, I did do that. I like a big bed, for me—me—not him, me. I checked in, he did come up with me, and he did make a pass at me and he did get me to lay down in bed with him."

"Sex?"

"No, in his mind there might have been. He might have ejaculated by holding me. Some men do that."

"Why did you buy condoms?"

"I planned to have sex. I just wanted to have sex. I don't how to explain to you. I don't know what it is called when you get the feeling you want to have sex."

After Steve left, she walked to the Rainbow, a little store. Then her story wandered backward in time. She said, "My mind wasn't right. It hadn't been right for quite some time. I didn't have control, felt like two people. I don't believe I was two people, but I definitely know that by the time I met Adam, I started slipping into some kind of darkness in my mind. I believed he was someone who was playing psychological games with me. After Dr. LaBarre died, I could be sitting in the living room alone, and someone would hit the far end of the house. That's not a wind hitting the house, I didn't imagine that. Someone was trying to draw me off. I didn't feel normal, right. I was not able to get decent sleep without nightmares. I felt that I was in some kind of a dreamland, some kind of a different world. I think there was a certain toxicity, I believe, that built up in my bloodstream. My headaches were worse than usual during my time with Adam. I had become an extremely eccentric person. Ingesting those types of drugs—Demerol, Valium, Demerol, Valium—and even though I'm not a drinker, I had some types of shots because I wanted the pain to stop."

"It sounds like during that time with Adam, there were a lot of things going on that made you feel you were not in your right frame of mind. If that is true, can you be sure about what really happened?"

Uncharacteristically, Sheila fell silent. After a long pause she said, "I believe that I'm sure. There may be some gaps—"

"For example, are you certain he actually died in the bathroom after slipping and hitting his head?"

"I'm sure about that."

"Even though you weren't in your right mind?"

"That's a loaded question. I don't know how to answer that to a psychiatrist."

"You told me earlier you didn't feel in control. Could you have not been in control when it came to Adam?"

She evaded the question: "I didn't control Adam. I tried to get free of Adam."

Dr. Drukteinis tried to determine if Kenneth and Sheila hit each other, just because they were angry, in a nonsexual situation.

"Oh, you mean spankings," she said.

The doctor conceded to Sheila's sexualization of everything and said, "Tell me about the flogging."

"He wanted to be flogged. He liked it. He got hard. He didn't have to have it every time to get hard. I said it before, even if it sprayed blood on the wall, he liked it. I will do certain things with sexual partners. I hate anal sex. I've done that twice in my life. I will not penetrate a man in the rectum. That, I will not do. But he was conditioned for flogging by his mother."

Sheila was asked to explain Kenneth's condition in the Wal-Mart. She said he was cut from doing farm chores and looked green because they'd given each other facials and he hadn't thoroughly washed off the mud mask. She explained that he did a lot of dry heaving, probably because he was a heroin addict. He was a pedophile and she was going to turn him in. That's why he turned on her, she was convinced. He was into pain and he hurt himself, so some of his wounds might have been self-administered. His blood could be anywhere in the house. They had S/M sex in the kitchen, bathroom, living room, all over.

Sheila was trying to account for the physical evidence with her "memory," but she had nothing to explain why Kenneth had shot blood across the living room with a spurt that came from a severed artery.

"Have you had many other lovers who wanted to have this S/M aspect?" Dr. Drukteinis asked.

"Yes. I'm not going to sit here and name people and

connect their name into my trial. I don't want to do that. You know, CEOs of some companies. I've had several, you know, a lot of sexual partners. Not necessarily relationships, but sex. I guess I've been promiscuous. Some people like you to light a candle and drip wax on them. They like it on their penis. I don't think I'm the only person in the world who's ever done that."

"Have you taken your anger out on people?"

"I have."

"Who is Michael Deloge?"

"He has nothing to do with this case whatsoever. My instincts tell me not to talk about him, and I won't."

"A number of people saw you being violent to him."

"I have no comment."


Sheila's second interview with Dr. Drukteinis had concluded. A third had been recorded on March 11, 2008, and that tape was played for the jury. Sheila began telling the psychiatrist that she'd had a dream the night before, that she'd encountered Kenneth's father. He forgave her. He knew his son had tried to kill her and she had just defended herself. She woke up sad because she knew her lawyers would never put her on the witness stand and let her tell her story.

"Last time we spoke, I asked you about Michael Deloge—"

"I shouldn't have to talk about it. Why should I talk about it? I've already admitted to doing it in court. I already said I did it."

"From a psychiatric standpoint it becomes an important piece of information—"

"He killed my animals. He was killing all my animals.

He pushed me over the edge. No rhyme or reason, he killed them."

"When did you first meet him? How did that come about?"

"I first saw him in Portsmouth. He was in a truck with James. I didn't know where James was and I wanted to find him. I thought he was on crack or something and I wanted to find him. He was with James in a vehicle and they were smoking dope. I saw them, that's the first time I ever saw him. My first instinct was this is a dark, dangerous person."

"What about him gave you that impression?"

"He wore creepy sunglasses. He was hiding his eyes. I could smell alcohol on him. Instinct. First instinct. I didn't go to Cross Roads and pick him up like the newspapers are reporting. I picked up James at Cross Roads after I had told him to get the hell out of my house. I didn't go to homeless shelters looking for people."

She said that it started when James refused to help her do something, and Michael got mad at James and volunteered that he would help her. And Michael eventually moved in for the same reason, to help out. At first, they slept separately. Actually, they always slept separately, even after they had a sexual relationship. After sex Michael preferred to sleep in the reclining chair. Her brain suddenly shot ahead to the police searching her fire pits, jumping to conclusions.

"Nobody died on that mattress. That never occurred. I never stabbed anybody either. I'm not a serial killer. I can't tell you the stress that caused me. I didn't dismember either man. The bodies were cremated, the flesh, the sinew, the organs, the bones are just there, they dropped. Do you know how that came about?"

Her explanation that no dismemberment took place

ignored the set of cutting tools found in and around Sheila's fires.

"Obviously, there were parts of bodies," Dr. Drukteinis said.

"No, there were no parts of any bodies. I said possibly a rabbit, because I didn't know, and I still don't know. Some of my rabbits were very big, and that is true. I had to tell the truth that I did kill these two men."

She sobbed. The psychiatrist got her story back on track, back to Michael Deloge. "So now the relationship became sexual. How was the sexual relationship? Was it good?"

"No, he wanted me to whip him with a belt. Both men were similar. Both had the perversion regarding their mother. Liked the belt."

"Did you not like doing that?"

"That's an unusual question."

"Did you like doing it to him?"

"I wouldn't say I liked it, but I did it. It's something a woman does for her lover."

"Not because you had sexual satisfaction from being in that role?"

"I didn't have an orgasm from it, if that's what you mean."

"Did the flogging lead to sexual relations with an orgasm?"

"Yes."

"Was it part of the excitement for you?"

"No, it was *his* excitement. Both of them liked a dominant woman, someone to say, 'Unzip your pants, take your cock out.' They liked to be told what to do. Me, no. I won't lie. There were times with Michael when the whippings got harder and harder. I would say, 'Why did the animals die?' And he kept saying, 'James did it.'

What he did to my animals—that is what led up to his death. I took pills then, a lot of marijuana, drinking. I was trying to wipe out all the stress I was under, ever since Bill passed away."

"So you whipped him harder and harder?"

"Correct. Because he would kill my animals. I had two horses that died, not far apart. Nellie was old, but she didn't have any health problems, and she was fine when I put her in the stall. He always came up to me with a horrible, evil dark look and say, 'Sheila, there's another one dead.'"

"Why would he do that?"

"I know why, I know why. He was molested. He was a murderer. He told me he had killed people, some guy named Paul. He had a picture of him. He claimed that they worked together and they beat gay men. The creepiest thing to me, he said, 'You can't get rid of the bones, you can't get rid of the bones.' I don't know what he did. He told me he was a Devil worshipper. I think he hated all women. He told me he thought he was actually gay, and I think he was too. He hated himself for that. I don't know and I don't care, but he did behave like he hated women. I know he liked children. I told the state the truth, if they bothered to investigate. He told me he liked to kill. He and his friends killed cats as part of Devil worship. They held satanic meetings, animal blood."

Dr. Drukteinis asked her to talk about the day with Michael when she couldn't take it anymore, the day she snapped.

"I said, 'It's you! It's you, it's you, it's you, it's you.' He looked at me and he said, 'It *is* me, Sheila, and I want to kill you.' I ran into the house, in the kitchen. I was freaking. I didn't know what to do. He told me he *crushed* the rabbit."

"What did you do then?"

"My mind just, it went sideways, like he warped my mind with what he did to my animals. That's what led to his death. I was out of my body. It felt like something else was directing me. He's gonna kill me next, he's going to kill everything, and then just disappear. I was sitting on the woodstove. It wasn't heated at the time. He was in the corner by the range. I went over to the wall and I picked up a chain about four feet long. He threatened to kill me and I said, 'You're not going to kill me.' That's when I hit him on the side. He didn't try to run. He didn't scream out. I wasn't even sure what was happening. I hit him and hit him. I was just, I don't know. I sat back down. And he sat down on the floor. And I said, 'You have to get out of here.' I don't remember after that. I just remember that he was alive. I remember after a few hours I just kept staring at him, he was staring at me, nobody talking."

She made sure that the surviving rabbits were okay and returned to dress Michael's wounds, she said. She told him he should go to a hospital, but he refused. He told her he knew he deserved the beating she'd given him. He stayed alive for two weeks.

"I just have an amazing track record for picking bad lovers," she said.

Dr. Drukteinis asked Sheila to explain why she covered up her crimes. She threw away the baling knife she used to give Kenneth a postmortem tracheotomy because she "didn't want it with me anymore." The diesel fuel was to keep her wood-burning furnace going.

"I don't care what it looks like to society, to the state, or to Wal-Mart. I didn't premeditate! I just went into my head. I went over the edge," she explained.

She said the man who said she beat Michael senseless

with a stick was a crackhead. She laughed. "Beat him senselessly? That is complete bullshit, that's a lie. I beat him with a small stick one time, but senselessly?" There followed a pattern in which Sheila pointed out the flaws with all of the witnesses against her. Some were on drugs, others had relatives in mental institutions, but they were all off in the head, and that was why they told lies about her. She said the notes about Daniel 3 and incineration in her notebook all had to do with her fascination with Natalee Holloway, the beautiful young woman who disappeared in Aruba.

Dr. Drukteinis wanted to delve further into the reasons why Michael and Kenneth died. "Here we have Michel Deloge, who you suspected of being a pedophile—"

"No, I knew. I knew he was a pedophile."

"And we have Adam. He was a pedophile. And now they are dead. The two are so similar, both pedophiles, both died, both cremated, both injured before they died, but it was not because they were pedophiles."

"Michael didn't just kill the animals. He tortured . . ." She sobbed.

"How come you still feel sad about Michael if he did these awful things?"

"I think it's because I love people."

"Even people who are mean to your family?"

"It is wrong to harbor hate to any person, no matter what they've done. It was like a crescendo that wouldn't end—this rabbit dead, that rabbit dead, this rabbit, my two horses, my cat disappeared, crushing them with rocks. I can only tell you that building up to that point, I lost . . . my reason."

"That's two different situations, Sheila. With Adam, it was not because of the animals."

"No, he did slip. That's true."

"Is there no connection between the two deaths?"

"Connection? Yes, that they both meant harm to me. That's a connection. I don't know what you mean when you say 'connection.' I don't think that with any crime one can say this happened because that happened. In other words, I'm not a serial killer. Something was printed in the paper about that. That was very disturbing to me. I wasn't in my right mind. What happened with Adam was accidental. As I said, I killed Michael Deloge. I couldn't believe that happened either."

"Attorneys are arguing a connection between the two—in fact, they are saying that you are insane. They are saying that somehow you were trying to save society from pedophiles, which is very different from what you told me just now, and, second, it implies that Adam didn't die that way by accident."

"You know, Doctor, sometimes people who are mentally ill don't think they are!"

"That's true, but they know whether they killed someone or whether it was an accident. You know, they say you are delusional because you think you are an angel."

"I do think I'm an angel. God said to me, 'Thou *cannot* remain, thou *must* return.' I was in spirit, I was in Heaven, I was taken up into spirit—that did happen. I think it's real. I think the fact that I have the medical documentation, if the state bothers to subpoena. Have you seen my records? I was not imagining I was in a brain-dead coma."

"There are also insinuations by them that you are delusional because you believe in Captain Shaw."

"Anyone that has been in that house will tell you that is the effin' truth. There is a Captain Shaw. He is in that house. That was told to me by Dr. LaBarre, and he was not someone who went in for ghostly things. And anyone who goes into the house will bear the mark, because that house either accepts or rejects people. Something pushed me down the stairs. I couldn't walk normally for over two weeks. Dr. LaBarre adjusted me. I had X-rays."

"What is this business that your attorney is saying you killed Countie and Deloge by beating them to death?"

"I can't comment on that, because I don't think my attorney said that. Who said my attorney said that? I know one thing, they weren't there and I was. I admitted to them I flogged both of them. If I had beaten—beaten—the story wouldn't be like it turned out. It's true the beating with Deloge led to his death. That is correct. I flogged Adam, I took a belt to him that day." The videotape ended.


After a break Dr. Drukteinis— director of New England Psychodiagnostics, and an adjunct associate professor of psychiatry at Dartmouth Medical School—took the stand. It was Tuesday afternoon, June 17, 2008. Jane Young conducted the direct examination. He testified, "Miss LaBarre suffers from a mood disorder, which may include some psychotic features. She also had signs of a paraphilia, a sexual disorder, and signs of a personality disorder, both paranoid, borderline, and antisocial features. She is not suffering from schizophrenia. She's been too functional throughout her life. Yes, she demonstrates erratic compulsive behavior and odd thinking, but she's pretty intelligent and she can talk in fairly rational ways about many aspects of her life. When she calls people 'pedophiles,' it's not clear to me she is sure of that. She can use that label to be demeaning, to put them down, or to arouse herself or her partner. She needs to see people in this demeaning way in order to justify her controlling and sadistic behaviors. She isn't trying to discover and expose pedophiles, she actually relishes them! If your mission is to get rid of pedophiles, why would you have sex with them and role-play some type of pedophilic behavior? If you were morally outraged, why would you play the mother who tortures the victim and get sexually aroused?"

"She has called herself an avenging angel. How is that not delusional thinking?" Young asked.

"Maybe it is, but I don't think it is. Her belief about this is something that came out of her coma experience. I think there is a spiritual aspect she has incorporated. Many people in a coma do this. Calling herself an angel is another example of her thinking of herself in an inflated way. She has referred to herself in many different inflated ways—doctor, lawyer, silver leopard."

"Other doctors have testified that she is so psychotic that she had no control over herself when she murdered Deloge and Countie," Young said.

"I think she has a lot of control. She is effectively manipulative. I think she was very controlled in her interviews with me. The APA believes that psychiatrists are not good at distinguishing between who *couldn't* control their actions and who *didn't* control their actions. When it comes to homicide, people say, 'I don't know what got over me, it was like my hand was pulling the trigger.' Is that no control, or do they look back on their behavior and explain it somehow to themselves?"

"Do you believe her memory of killing Kenneth Countie came back after she was arrested?"

"I don't put any stock in what she says. Her actions appeared to be a cover-up. How could she cover up what she didn't remember?"

"Is 'bizarre' the same as 'psychotic'?"

"Not at all. Your behavior may be bizarre, yet you still know who you are, who your victim is, what you did, and that it was wrong, and try to cover it up."

"With Michael Deloge and the killing of her animals, does that rise to delusional thinking?"

"It could, but if they were really killed and he didn't do it, the question is, who did it? It would not be unusual for a sadistic person to hurt their own animals and blame someone else. She incorporated him into her world of sadistic sexual activity. She—"

Sheila began to scream in the courtroom: "I didn't kill my animals! I never hurt an animal! I never shot a dog! You're getting paid to say this about me!"

"We're taking a break," Judge Nadeau said with re-markable calm as bailiffs grabbed handsful of Sheila's prison jumpsuit and yanked her out of the courtroom.


After the break Sheila was brought back and calmly watched the rest of the day's testimony in silence. Dr. Drukteinis scoffed at the theory that Dr. LaBarre's death led to Sheila's psychosis. He said it seemed to him as if she was the one in control in that relationship.

Dr. Drukteinis admitted that he did not completely understand what was behind either Sheila's visits to Wal-Mart with the visibly wounded Kenneth Countie or her penchant for recording hundreds of tapes over the years. Despite that, he firmly restated his opinion that Sheila was sane when she murdered Deloge and Countie.


Denner cross-examined Dr. Drukteinis, and started by establishing that, despite the witness's vast experience, he had a less impressive quantity of experience in determining criminal responsibility, and that he had previously worked as a paid expert for the state of New Hampshire. Since Dr. Drukteinis had admitted to not understanding Sheila's motive for the Wal-Mart visits, Denner questioned him about that for a while. Then he moved on to the tapes, forcing Dr. Drukteinis to itemize which of Sheila's self-recorded audiotapes he listened to and what he remembered from them.

"Do you believe that Sheila's inner and outer world were interchangeable and that she was functioning on a delusional belief system?"

"I think that is very theoretical and hard to justify. I don't agree with that," Dr. Drukteinis replied.

Denner then focused on Sheila's functionality after Dr. LaBarre's death. The prosecution had made the point that Sheila continued to function in a way that a psychotic could not, but Denner made Dr. Drukteinis admit that Sheila was not functioning well, that tenants left the rental properties, that she struggled to make money, that things were not repaired once they broke down, etc. Dr. Drukteinis did not disagree.

Regarding child abuse as the source of Sheila's mental problems, Dr. Drukteinis said, "We try to find understanding of the background, but it doesn't mean the background plays into or causes the behavior. With all due respect to the other doctors, I think it's a lot of psychobabble. Their theories don't take into account why she is titillated by the very things she is supposedly against. It's a simple issue, that you don't get aroused by pedophilia if you want to get rid of it. All the focus on all the sexual stuff that excites her, reaction formation is not part of that. She had difficulty with sexual satisfaction in the earlier part of her life, and until she got into this other is when she began getting more aroused. The content of those recordings and conversations are not simply inquiries, they are vulgar and graphic descriptions that have a titillating aspect to them, they are not simply an inquisition to Kenneth Countie and Michael Deloge. Both victims were involved in the process as part of her and their sexual behaviors."

"Do we know what really makes anyone molest anyone else?"

"We know it's the individual that does the molesting. When we talk about psychotic, we are talking about out of contact with reality, not an explosion of anger that is uncontrolled and unbridled. We have not demonstrated she does not understand the things around her. Someone sent from Heaven to protect little children doesn't have sex with their victims. The intensity of her preoccupation with pedophilia almost approaches psychotic behavior, I'll grant you that. Again, it's not as if she is trying to discover pedophiles and that is her task—to get rid of them. It's a whole other process. They excite her. It excites her. Then it gets mixed up with the sadism. She wants to dominate, control people, and torture and kill them."

Denner pointed out that Sheila regularly rejected elements of her story that would have helped her insanity defense.

Dr. Drukteinis opined, "I think she agreed to admit she killed them for the purposes of the plea. She wants to have it both ways. What she really could tell is far more than what can come out here in court and be any kind of favor to her. She has to avoid this whole area, if—as I suspect—there are signs of sadistic torture. She can't begin to talk about that. She doesn't want to admit it. You see that with personality disorders all the time."

Dr. Drukteinis pointed out that what other psychiatrists had referred to as "psychotic denial," he called "lying."

Denner asked if Sheila really wanted to change her appearance and try to get away from police, would she have dyed her hair the shade of red she chose? Dr. Drukteinis said that her wish to change her appearance simply failed to overwhelm her desire to be the center of attention.

Denner had no further questions, and the state rested its case.

# End Game

On Wednesday, June 18, 2008, both sides presented to the jury their closing arguments. After Judge Nadeau warned everyone in the courtroom to "keep their emotions in check out of respect for the process," James Boffetti took the podium and addressed the jury.

"The defense in this case made certain promises at the beginning of this trial, that you would know sanity when you saw it, that it wouldn't even be close, it would be staring right at you. They promised they would meet their considerable burden of proof, by presenting clear and convincing evidence that she was insane when she killed two men at two different times. I ask you to hold them to their promises, because those promises went unfulfilled," Boffetti said. "The defendant comes before you with the presumption of sanity. It was up to them to convince you that she was not sane and should not be held criminally responsible for her crimes. They have not met their burden. The evidence is strong that this woman was and is sane. She knew what she had done was wrong. She made a careful decision to conceal her crimes and

destroy evidence. She made conscious attempts to run
away and conceal herself. As James Brackett told you, she
knows how to 'play the system.' She continues to play the
system. We should hold her criminally responsible. In
the past few weeks, you have seen and heard a great deal
of evidence, seen and heard her in a variety of settings.
You have information about some of the choices she
made, choices in the way she treated other human beings
she brought into her life. Now it is your turn to consider
the decision and apply your collective common sense.
This will guide you to the right judgment. All the defense
has proven is that she had a mood disorder and personality disorder. All three psychiatrists agree on this. No
doubt she can act eccentric, odd, and bizarre. She can be
controlling, threatening, paranoid, litigious, explosive,
violent, and manipulative. Those are characteristics of
her personality, not the basis of finding her insane.

"*She is just plain mean.* Some people are like that in life.
They are manipulative, controlling, jealous. How much
in this case have we seen this? Simple meanness. The
killing of Kenneth Countie and Michael Deloge were the
escalation of her pattern of choices to taunt, torment,
and ultimately torture those people who she chose to en-
snare into her life. The defense tried to get witnesses to
say she was crazy, nuts, fruitcake—a 'fruit loop.' In every-
day terms we use words like that. Here we are dealing
with whether or not she was suffering from a psychotic
delusional disorder, and whether the murders were a
product of that condition. The defense's psychiatrist
would have you believe she suffered from long-standing
psychosis, and that she was delusional when she committed murder, that she believed these men were dangerous
pedophiles, and that she was doing society a favor by
destroying them. But is what she did consistent and

under the control of this delusional psychosis? Many witnesses were reluctant to have these words put in their mouth. They knew she did odd and strange things, bizarre things—none of them insane. Perhaps the one witness who knew the witness best, James Brackett, the defense pressed him to say she was crazy. James Brackett looked you right in the eye and told you she is not crazy. She's evil.

"You can consider any evidence you wish when making your decision—the nature of her acts, whether she was suffering from delusions and hallucinations, whether she knew the difference between right and wrong. Further, you may consider whether she acted impulsively, with cunning and planning in executing the crimes—and in escaping or avoiding detection. You can consider if she could recognize acquaintances, transact business. You heard a lot of evidence to that. It points to sanity."

Boffetti pointed out that both defense psychiatrists admitted that the defendant knew right from wrong when she committed the murders. He listed the items the defendant destroyed in her burning frenzy following Kenny's murder, not just the victim's body, but the mattress, chair and couch cushions, wooden toilet seat. "She spent that entire night burning, and sifting, and pulverizing bone fragments. She used this stick to keep the fire going. Lab reports indicate there was human hair at the end of the stick. She used this sifter, to separate out the human remains. She admitted to Chief Dodge she was sifting out teeth. She admitted cremations take a very long time. She had to keep adding wood and gas to the fire. She made deliberate calculated efforts over a long period designed to obliterate a human body, not once, but twice in six months. She tended to that fire. She stirred it and manipulated the human remains. Then she took off, and when she needed a lawyer, she went to the bank and withdrew $87,000 of her own money to retain one. She wanted to prevent the Countie family from getting that money in a civil judgment. She drafted powers of attorney for her animals. She knew enough to duck in the car with Steve Martello when a police cruiser went by, to keep the radio and TV off. She knew enough to get Steve Martello and Kenny Washington to rent a room, in their names. And then she went to a hairdresser and changed her appearance. She started looking for apartments and women's shelters.

"After she was caught, she repeatedly denied killing Kenneth Countie. And she specifically denied killing him *because* he was a pedophile. She denied he overdosed on her medication, that he asked her to kill him, anything that could possibly implicate her in any way, she adamantly denied.

"She admits to arousal when thinking of pedophilia and incest, that she got these men aroused by flogging them. That is her sexual disorder. Both of these men were the object of her sexual desire. As we now know, it was a perverse sexual desire, involving sadomasochistic sex and torture from which she derived sexual pleasure. It is very likely she lost control of her anger and lust and she killed them.

"The defense takes as an historical fact that the defendant was sexually abused by her father. It is clear that this defendant and her sister compared notes. They talked, a lot, about this. Her sister, in an effort to help her, began to talk about possible sexual abuse, around the time the insanity defense came up—a year and a half after her arrest. She included remarkable details—including that there was a thunderstorm and specific words that were said. But the sister said [Sheila] was four months old at the time. Four months old. Would a four-month-old baby remember these things—or would she and her sister concoct a story to put her in the best possible light?

"This defendant has the capacity to make choices and reveal only what she wants, to make her appear less of a cold-blooded killer. She is a predator. She is a black widow. Doctors Gray and Rogers may have offered you a complex, convoluted theory replete with psychobabble. The truth is, those killings were the result of her perverse sexual desire and uncontrolled violence that went too far. Hold her responsible, because she is responsible.

"It was the defense's job to present *clear and convincing* evidence, that it was *highly probable* she was insane at [the] time of both murders. It just wasn't proven here. The defense didn't keep their promise. Because of that, you should find the defendant guilty of the murder of both Michael Deloge and Kenneth Countie."

Both sides approached the bench after Boffetti finished, and when the sidebar concluded, Judge Nadeau told the jury, "During her first interview with Dr. Druckteinis, the defendant had not been charged with the murder of Michael Deloge, and she was instructed by her attorneys not to discuss Michael Deloge."

After a break the prosecution prepared the court for Jeffrey Denner's closing argument. Easels were set up and on them were placed large photographs, including one of the burn barrel outside the farmhouse. Beside the barrel was the chair with the photo of a Native American on it. Another was a photo of Kenny in a wheelchair with diesel cans on his lap. The defense wanted to set up ten easels, but Judge Nadeau ruled they could only use three for security reasons.

Denner addressed the jury in his usual low tones and disregard for proximity to the microphone. A few times Judge Nadeau asked Denner to speak up and into the mike so everyone could hear. He began by thanking the jury.

"If I inadvertently refer to my own personal opinions, you should disregard it. What I believe is truly irrelevant. The evidence is what is important. My personal beliefs have no place in this trial. Sheila is crazy, utterly crazy, a deeply disturbed woman. She is nuts. With all due respect, you know that. Almost everyone who has met her in the last fifteen years knows that. Dr. Rogers knows that. Dr. Gray knows that—and I suggest to you Dr. Drukteinis knows it. It doesn't matter what you call it—crazy, nuts, fruit loop. She is a deeply troubled human being. Even people who only knew her for an hour, an hour and a half, knew that there was just something wrong with this woman. Whether she is insane or not is something we are talking about today. The police did not do their job in responding to Sheila, stopping her. With the great amount of information and evidence police had over the years, they have a great deal of *civil liability*.

"All doctors agree she is suffering from a psychiatric disorder of psychotic proportion. Psychosis, the blurring of fantasy and reality. The external and internal world at some point become interchangeable." He pointed out that not all psychoses work the same way. Schizophrenics have trouble functioning in society, but delusionals, like Sheila, could function in the world until some outside trigger causes a flare-up, making it very difficult for the person to determine what is real. When a flare-up is not occurring, these people can appear relatively normal. "Remember what Dr. Gray said. Sheila is the most disturbed individual he had ever seen. He said that while Sheila may not always be a reliable reporter of factual events, she is a reliable reporter of the inside of her mind.

"Mr. Boffetti talked to you about Sheila's sister Lynn Noojin. Without any evidence whatsoever he suggested that she and Sheila had concocted a story. You saw her testify. You make your own judgment. I suggest she was a very credible witness."

Denner talked about the trustworthiness of the defense's psychiatrists, then added, "When Dr. Drukteinis didn't agree with one of their opinions, he called it 'psychobabble' or 'spin.' When the others didn't agree with him, they were more respectful. They said they disagreed without calling it 'psychobabble.'

"I believe the defense has successfully shown, through clear and convincing evidence, that Sheila is severely mentally ill and that the murders were the product of that illness." Denner pointed out that while Rogers and Gray listened to all of Sheila's audiotapes, Drukteinis could only specifically remember listening to three or four.

Denner picked at Boffetti's theory that Sheila brought Kenneth to Wal-Mart with her because she was afraid he would run away. "If she were afraid he wanted to get away, wouldn't she want to keep him away from Wal-Mart in case he asked for help. *Help!* It makes more sense, particularly when the police were there. All he had to do was wave and say, 'She's going to kill me.' That didn't happen. That didn't happen. A big piece of Sheila was saying, 'Stop me, stop me, for God's sake. What do I have to do to be stopped?' I think her bringing Kenneth Countie to Wal-Mart was more an expression of that than proactive defense. It is clear to us that Sheila is not rational, despite her capacity to appear so. The state has described her sadism, her unspeakable viciousness. We agree. The murders *were* a product of horrible violence and unspeakable viciousness—but also the product of a woman who has been threatened by almost everyone she's met, and who has no one around her to try to protect her. She is essentially unable to see other human beings for who they really are. She has no insight. She assigns mercurial fluctuating roles to everyone she meets."

Denner then "respectfully suggested" that local law enforcement take courses to learn more about mental illness, so in the future there would be no more "that's just Sheila being Sheila" attitude when people were clearly getting hurt.

He described in detail the cremation process, the length of time it took, the foul odor, the crucifixes, and the photo of the Cherokee chief—all only a few feet from Sheila's front door. Were these the actions of a sane woman?

"The scene was so bizarre, it could have come straight out of the pages of a psychotic Gothic novel," he said. He described her behavior when dealing with the police, the "rabbit or a pedophile" comment, the "he's in that bag" comment, the grand tour of the house—despite the visible blood spatter—and asked, was this how a sane woman would deny her crimes? "This is psychosis!" he exclaimed.

"Ladies and gentlemen of the jury, you know through her phone calls and writings and recordings, Sheila lived in *a haunted house in a haunted land*. Her head, heart, and soul were also haunted. Ultimately she *became* the demons. She became the victim, the abuser, the neglected—she became everything she abhorred. Everything she abhorred.

"When you were chosen to serve on this jury, we made

promises to you, and you made a promise to us. You promised to take a dispassionate look at mental illness, no matter how horrible the circumstances. You promised us. Thank you."

After a break Judge Nadeau thanked the jury for being such a patient panel. The trial had been one of the longest in New Hampshire history. They had been great—but now their real work began. Jury duty was hard. Determining the fate of a human being was heavy stuff, but it was one of the costs of citizenship. The first step was to separate the twelve jurors who would decide Sheila's fate. The remaining alternates were thanked and dismissed. The judge read the jury their instructions and told them that their deliberations would begin the next morning, Thursday, June 19.

Thirteen hours of deliberation followed, and on Friday afternoon, June 20, 2008, the jury returned a verdict of sane. Sheila showed no emotion.

Before sentencing, Carolynn Lodge read an impact statement to the court: *"I cannot sleep. I dare not sleep, for when my eyes close, I see my son's terrified eyes pleading for me to save him. I hear his voice echo through my soul, 'Ma, help me!' Oh, Kenny, my love. I did everything in my power to save you. You were at my fingertips and I could not reach you. I was so close. I am so sorry."*

Judge Nadeau sentenced Sheila to two lives in prison without the possibility of parole. As the jury filed out of the courtroom, their job done, some with tears in their eyes, they received a standing ovation. Carolynn Lodge and Donna Boston embraced.

"We got it," Boston said.

Lodge then hugged her ex-husband, Kenneth Countie Sr., and said, "It's over."

Lodge later said to the press, "This is for my son. For two years my son couldn't rest. Now he can rest. Sheila LaBarre took advantage of my son, who was a kind, caring, gentle young man who could not socially defend himself. She was a master of evil who deliberately tortured him. Sheila LaBarre stripped my son of all his dignity and self-worth, and in the end she murdered him."

A male juror later told WCVB-TV that the panel had used charts and timelines to come to their consensus. He lauded the jury's foreman, who helped them with the difficult challenge of separating facts from emotion.

Another juror discussed the emotional toll with *Seacoast Online*: "Six weeks with Sheila was plenty tough. It was pretty intense in terms of evidence. We were listening and watching hours of videos and audiotapes. The intensity of the evidence is going to stand out in my mind."

A female juror told reporter Elizabeth Dinan that she had felt the full weight of having to judge another human being and was 100 percent sure the verdict was correct. Justice *had* been served. "There wasn't enough evidence to connect her mental illness with the acts of murder," she said. Several jurors noted their need to get home, get back to their jobs, and "decompress."

On the losing side Denner commented, "It continues to be our belief that Sheila is deeply crazy and insane," he said. "We also understand there's a huge amount of emotion in this case that clouds this issue. The craziest part of this was that the jury says she's sane, and she's happy. She looks like a great weight has been lifted off her shoulders after a jury of her peers judges her to be sane. That, to me, is the greatest indicator of the depths of her insanity."

Feeling philosophical in loss, Bailey said, "On a personal level I came away with faith in the system. That unanimous verdict was one we were at peace with. I feel very good about the work we did."

Sheila was transferred to her new—and permanent—home inside the New Hampshire State Prison in Concord.

*And now Sheila sits alone in prison, alone forever, alone even when with people. Humans are like rabbits to her now. They stare at her with tiny red eyes and then bare their teeth. She's alone in her mind, an avenging angel with clipped wings, still convinced that no one gets it—how could they not get it? Her name is Sheeeeeeelaaaaaa. It's Spanish!*

# Afterword

When the trial was over, those closest to the case began to think more philosophically about what happened in Epping. Could the murders have been prevented?

If Kenneth Countie had been a savagely beaten woman in her twenties, and Sheila LaBarre a man in his forties, would Sergeant Sean Gallagher have reacted differently when he encountered the pair at the local Wal-Mart? Many believe he would have—that gender prejudice allowed Kenneth to be murdered. As Jeffrey Denner put it, "If this was a man doing this to a woman, police would have been there in a second."

Sergeant Gallagher was asked about this and said he didn't feel comfortable answering the question while an appeal was under way.

Another question: was Sheila's trial constitutional? In America, where we are presumed innocent until proven guilty, can the burden of proof *ever* be on the defense, even during a sanity trial?

An appeal filed by the defense on July 10, 2008, called for a new trial for Sheila on the grounds that pretrial publicity should have necessitated a change of venue, that a defense expert witness (former FBI criminal profiler Mark E. Safarik) was not allowed to testify, that evidence gathered at Sheila's farm *before* a search warrant was issued was allowed in, and that no juror who was paying attention could have rationally determined that Sheila was sane.

In addition to the appeal, state police sources said that the case was technically still open because one set of remains found at the farm remained unidentified.

Separate lawsuits filed against Sheila by Kenneth Countie's parents and the children of Wilfred LaBarre are still pending.

During March 2009, Countie's family filed suit against the Epping Police claiming breach of duty caused Kenneth harm and contributed to his death. Named in the suit were Chief Dodge, Detective Cote, Lieutenant Wallace, and Sergeant Gallagher. The suit stated that Cote and Gallagher knew of Sheila's penchant for hurting people on March 17, 2006, when they encountered her at Wal-Mart pushing a sickly and wheelchair-bound Countie. Given those circumstances, the suit said, the police "had a duty to provide protection" to Countie "from the domestic violence of Sheila LaBarre when the signs of her abusing him were apparent."

# GREAT BOOKS, GREAT SAVINGS!

When You Visit Our Website:
## www.kensingtonbooks.com
You Can Save Money Off The Retail Price
Of Any Book You Purchase!

- **All Your Favorite Kensington Authors**
- **New Releases & Timeless Classics**
- **Overnight Shipping Available**
- **eBooks Available For Many Titles**
- **All Major Credit Cards Accepted**

Visit Us Today To Start Saving!
## www.kensingtonbooks.com

All Orders Are Subject To Availability.
Shipping and Handling Charges Apply.
Offers and Prices Subject To Change Without Notice.

# MORE MUST-READ TRUE CRIME
# FROM PINNACLE

# MORE SHOCKING TRUE CRIME
# FROM PINNACLE